Felix M. Whitehurst

My Private Diary During the Siege of Paris

Vol. I.

Felix M. Whitehurst

My Private Diary During the Siege of Paris
Vol. I.

ISBN/EAN: 9783337015282

Printed in Europe, USA, Canada, Australia, Japan

Cover: Foto ©ninafisch / pixelio.de

More available books at **www.hansebooks.com**

MY PRIVATE DIARY

DURING

THE SIEGE OF PARIS.

BY THE LATE

FELIX M. WHITEHURST,

AUTHOR OF
"COURT AND SOCIAL LIFE IN FRANCE UNDER NAPOLEON THE THIRD," ETC.

∴

"I can't get out."—*Sterne.*

IN TWO VOLUMES.

VOL. I.

LONDON:
TINSLEY BROTHERS, 8, CATHERINE STREET, STRAND.
1875.

INDEX OF DAYS RECORDED.

―

1870.

MY PRIVATE DIARY

DURING

THE SIEGE OF PARIS.

AUGUST, 1870.

Sunday, 21st.—It is now a fortnight since Paris was declared in a state of siege. True, we are not quite cut off from all outer communication, but that may happen any hour. To-day we have been to the camp of St.-Maur—that is, Vincennes. We went to see M. de Saillard, who commands a battalion. He is in the Foreign Office ; was chef de cabinet to Rouher ; a man of varied experience in Mexico and Africa, and a clever practical soldier. He told us that his own battalion, which consists of the denizens of the Rues de Rivoli, de la Paix, and that quarter of Paris, is to be trusted ; but even they, when on parade he announced a slight success, cried " Vive la France !" and not " Vive l'Empereur !"

There are eighteen thousand Mobiles in camp, and they have just been recalled to Paris by General Trochu, who would perhaps have been wiser if he had sent them in some other direction; for among them are the Villette, or Rochefort division, and they can scarcely be trusted with arms; indeed, they were in open mutiny at Châlons, pulled Marshal Canrobert off his horse, and would have done the same to Colonel de Saillard, only his own men rescued him. The cry of these men is, " We don't want to go to a camp, or to fight. We want to go home." This is not, however, the feeling of M. Gambetta and other leaders of the Left. They will fight " à outrance."

The camp of St.-Maur is a very interesting sight, and you see in a minute what natural campaigners the French are. The eighteen thousand Mobiles have only been under canvas twenty-four hours, and yet they have streets, gardens, restaurants, a theatre, a dancing-booth, and newspapers. All the streets, and most of the tents, have names. On many of the tents the names of all quartered in them are written, and Paris invention has been taxed to coin names for the different residences of the nobility and gentry now, *mal gré bon gré*, living on the barren heath. No one when looking on at the last steeplechase at Vincennes would have believed that in a few weeks preparations for real and serious war would cover the whole course, and a gunner be watering his horse at the brook.

But to come back to my tents. Some of the names were very amusing. The "Prison Mazas," in the Rochefort division, looked very comfortable ; more so, indeed, than the "Hôtel Splendide," which was not outwardly splendid by any means. The " Maison des Cocottes " was surrounded by a small garden ; the " Hôtel des Deux Mondes " and the "Grand Hôtel " were good : and then the "illustrations !" There were the flying Prussians, and hundreds of French on their way to Berlin ; the King of Prussia, uglier if possible than Bismarck ; but, alas! no pictures of the Emperor, Empress, or Prince Imperial : they have, as it were, faded away !

A very strong force of artillery is at present at St.-Maur, of course destined for the fortifications. Sixty very heavy guns came up from Châlons on Sunday last. The idea at the camp is that the enemy will attack the weak point—the gate (Villette) near the Great Northern railway—and pour in mass after mass to keep up a constant assault. As for investing Paris, that is absurd : it would take a million of men. There are thirty-two miles of fortifications. When the King of Prussia came to Paris in 1814 and 1815, he entered by this gate, as he politely mentioned to Baron Haussmann when the Arch-Improver was showing him the beauties of Paris one day when the King and Bismarck were here for that wonderful Exhibition year. What humbugs, in a peace sense, have been all these exhibitions!

We saw to-day that there were great preparations for provisions—the Bois de Boulogne, as well as all the markets, full of cattle. Mr. Wallace, an Irish contractor, being asked what he thought of the animals as food for troops, said, " Well, all I know is that they would not steal them in England." They average eightpence per pound : Ireland and England can sell in Paris at that price. The same gentleman told me that he once bought a hunter for seven-and-sixpence, and won twenty-one steeplechases with him. He also once cleared a brook so wide that a pious man said his prayers before he took off, and had time to repeat the Lord's Prayer in the air. He is here to sell the garrison any quantity of cattle ; " but," said he, looking at some dreadful skeletons, "I fear very much that I can supply nothing like those."

Lord Hertford died here on Wednesday. He has a house full of works of art in the Rue Laffitte—works beyond value. He also owned Bagatelle, a beautiful villa near the race-course in the Bois, which he bought from the Orleans family on the 9th of October, 1835, for 12,524*l.* A few days ago it would have been worth twice as much; but who would buy it now? All his personal property, fifty thousand pounds a year, his Irish estates, and all his works of art in Paris, are left to a Mr. Wallace, a very attentive companion, to whom Lord Hertford had never said "Thank you" for any service. It was remarked at the Embassy, "Well, he has said 'thank you' out loud in his will." Truly, better late than never.

Monday, August 29*th.*—During the past week no great events. French and Prussians seem to be fighting drawn battles, with terrific loss on both sides. Emperor, I am assured, in good health.

To-day it was proposed to send all the British correspondents out of Paris, and suppress their papers; and quite right too, as they have been vicious and unjust, and, as a rule, know nothing but what they read in the "Gaulois" and "Figaro," and that is fiction. Sydney Smith said, that if a pretty woman came to a garrison the sky was clouded with majors. If war comes, there is a plague of contractors : they come, not single partners, but in firms.

The scene during the last few days has been curious. . Every street crowded with furniture waggons —coming from and going to stations—and country carts. Every family that has any family place goes to it, while all the small proprietors and little farmers near Paris are coming in to the shelter of the guns and the city barricades, about which M. Thiers, the grandfather of these forts, is for ever talking and lecturing on their value. A country cart, two old women in great caps, bundles sufficient to drive a traveller mad, three beds complete, half a sheep, five pumpkins, some bedding, a large umbrella, like a tent—that is the baggage of the entering foe ; for they will all be enemies when they begin to eat. Food is already twenty-five per cent. dearer. As for the leaving division, much more furniture and luxury—large vans going up to railways, which will take them somewhere, not at a given, but a taken time.

We tried to get to the Porte Maillot yesterday, but found the whole road blocked up with carriages, carts, omnibuses, waggons, &c., and no chance, even if you got into the swim (which was difficult), of getting through the gates ; so we walked off to the Avenue de l'Impératrice, and having private permission, passed the gate. As we went in a poor Prussian spy, taken red-handed, was being escorted out. I confess to feeling horribly distressed when I saw that small procession. There must during a war be spies, and if caught those spies must be shot; yet you feel that a war spy is not like any other spy. Take Whyte Melville's grand episode in that best of modern novels, "The Interpreters," for instance. When I saw that evident gentleman in the dress of a workman, watched his pale but not frightened face, saw his firm step and unflinching composure—well, I could simply have cried; and the *gamins* about the Bois were pointing at him the finger of scorn, to the chorus of "à Berlin!" "Bismarck!" "Bismarck!" "à Berlin!"

Tuesday, August 30*th*.—There was quite a camp to-day in the Champ de Mars — six or seven regiments of infantry, and a large contingent of artillery.

Butchers refuse credit.

The whole of Paris filled by carts full of arriving peasants and their beds and chairs. Where are they all to stay?

No morning mail left Paris to-day.

It is said that a big battle is being fought now; but then we have no news.

I am writing at 6 P.M. There is great evident

depression all over Paris, but still no official news, good or bad.

Free-shooters leave to-night.

Wednesday, August 31st.—I should say that we shall have a great fight to-morrow; but day follows day and brings disappointment.   If there is a French defeat, the dynasty is lost, and the war will rage stronger than ever under the Orleanists if they get their innings, and still fiercer under the Republic if that system holds and we have even the fainting Rochefort as our ruler.   It is a war of hatred and vengeance.

Yesterday and last night were the very dullest hours I have ever passed in Paris: there was a perfectly awful depression.   "Except officials I cannot find a soul to speak to," said a weeping ex-diplomate who strolled into the Grand Hôtel, "and they know nothing."

This morning you might fire a mitrailleuse down the boulevard and wound nobody.

Last effect of war!   The Grand Hôtel is "concentrating" its visitors, and reducing the staff.   The "lift" ceased to lift last night, and the legs of the few remaining Americans are crying aloud in consequence—that is, if legs can cry.   Saw a fat lady in a fix. . But other effects of the war are dreadful, such as we even, who have carried on this weary business of life since the Prince Consort established peace in one of those glass-houses against which the world has been throwing stones ever since, have never seen. As I write an ambulance goes by with wounded Zouaves. A long line of Marines passes by at the same time, going to the front.

A gentleman comes to buy a thoroughbred horse, brougham, and harness, and kindly offers twenty-eight pounds for the lot. War prices with a vengeance.

Malortie, Baron of that ilk, and Bismarck's nephew (though he has not seen him for four years), was arrested on Saturday for being a Prussian! He is a Hanoverian, and is now sent off.

No English post to-day. Troops are now sent viâ Amiens to the front, and therefore all communications are cut off.

SEPTEMBER, 1870.

Thursday, 1st.—I have passed many very pleasant Firsts of September; but days return, and differ, in spite of the French saying.

Well, the 1st of September in France in 1870 dawned very nicely, only there was no shooting—except, of course, such " big game " as Frenchmen and Prussians.   Birds are spared this year by Act of Parliament.   But actually, as you know, " the First " is not the first in France.   I believe the chief policeman settles the day on which birds are fit for the spit. But, in spite of the law, we ate partridges the other day at a private party to which they came, though probably they had not been invited.

One hundred thousand country Gardes Mobiles are to come into Paris as quickly as possible.   Where the dickens are they to find food for them?

At present food can be bought at a price, but it is reported that we shall not be able to obtain it at any price in a few days.

Friday, September 2nd.—Accounts are very fishy.

" Beaten everywhere," seems the news. Paris like a desert.

Saturday, September 3rd.—The English papers are frightening Paris to death. Anything so disgraceful as their tone cannot be imagined. No doubt things are bad enough in Paris, but why make them worse? The one fault is, that *we have no news;* and no news is bad news.

The Prussians seem to have been terribly punished, and to have gained no victory; but then, what have the French gained? "After so and so, General X. Y. Z. fell back on his former position." Winning generals don't do that.

Where is the Emperor? Nobody knows, and apparently nobody cares ! Horrible accounts of his health are sent from England; luckily they are not true, for he bears reverses like a hero. I have just written to Conti to ask for the actual truth. Shall we get it? Conti writes that he is "just going to dine with her Majesty, and will write in the evening."

Sunday, September 4th.—He did not; and then the shell burst. The Emperor a prisoner! Eighty thousand prisoners, and two hundred guns lost !

MacMahon badly wounded in the thigh. An utter collapse for want of preparation !

MacMahon had forty thousand, not one hundred thousand men ! The Prussians first overlapped, and then surrounded the French. They were caught in a trap, and escape was impossible. The Emperor has since said that he was deceived from the first ; found his army without provisions, arms, or organization, and so sent his sword to the King of Prussia. "Make peace," he telegraphed, "on any terms. I am out of the way, thus doing the duty which all in one way or another should do to France." He yielded as a private officer without any command, his ruling power being vested in the Empress Regent.

So this great and kind man, to whom France has behaved so ungratefully, is a prisoner in the hands of the King of Prussia ! What did the King do ? Does he read history ? Probably not, or he might have remembered the cup of wine offered on his knee by the Black Prince. We have altered all that chivalry. King William of Prussia ordered a march past of the disarmed captured troops of France, and caused the Emperor to "assist" at it. If it be true that Count Solms, so long attached to Paris, and who must have known half the officers in that crack "corps d'armée," stood by and grinned, with his eyeglass to his eye, he has more diplomacy than politeness—a man whom one met every night in Paris society!

Well, I did not think when in that Exhibition year we witnessed the friendly reception by the Emperor of the King of Prussia and Bismarck, that the Kaiser would now be in the hands of the King.

And the poor Empress and Prince!—the latter said to be looking very ill. The Empress drove quietly out of Paris, and was not noticed. The last lady to leave Paris was Princess Clothilde. Her retreat reminds me of that of her gallant ancestor after Novara.

The evil news soon leaked out yesterday! It was known that "something was very wrong indeed." Later in the evening the truth was known, and the fate of the dynasty was sealed.

About 10 P.M. there were some disturbances on the boulevards. All the cafés near the Montmartre district were closed by the Sergents de Ville. In the scrimmage one of the National Guard was shot by one of the Sergents de Ville, and this was the last act of that useful, respectable, but detested body, who have since been confined to their quarters. It is said that the body of the deceased was carried to General

Trochu by his comrades. Picture to yourself the scene—the dim light, the closed shops, the dark-looking corps of the Sergents de Ville, the body of the citizen soldier hardly yet cold, the excited crowd, and the midnight procession! Quite a pathetic picture, is it not?

Only it is not true. By-the-way, the very last act of Piétri and his police was to arrest Mr. George Augustus Sala. Night was calm after that, but as soon as day of Sunday, the 4th of September, dawned, Paris, or at least a large section of it, arose mad with republican excitement. Any one used to the study of the features of Paris could read in a minute that affairs were serious. We were awakened by the cries of " Armes !" " Armes !" " Down with the tyrants !" " à Berlin !" as thousand after thousand of National Guards poured by on their way to ask for the destruction of the Empire, and for arms to save Paris.

At twelve o'clock you could not thrust your way down the Rue de Rivoli. Indeed, I met that most polite of individuals, M. Bellenger of " Voisins," in full retreat, and he advised me also to retire; but " the Guards die, never retire," so we proceeded. I say " we " because two English ladies were with me, and they were quite like " the Guards."

It was a striking spectacle. Of course every shop closed, and the shopkeeper with his wife (if he was too old for active service) sitting on chairs out on the pavement; every window crowded, and a few flags drooping in the hot still air; the imperial standard still hanging listlessly over the Court of Honour of the Tuileries, as if it guessed that its last wave was at hand.

When the Chamber opened it was guarded by a strong force of horse and foot National Guards, whose consign was to "keep off the people." We were still under the rule of the Regent. Shouts of "Republic!" "Abdicate!" "Vive la Ligne!" "Vive la Garde Nationale!" were heard on all sides. Several false reports were in circulation, and every one asked every one, "Is it proclaimed?" "Yes. Vive la République!" The President, poor old Schneider, whom later they denounced as the "Assassin of France," and whose venerable head one free and enlightened citizen punched, tried to speak, but all to no effect. Gambetta followed with no better fate.

Outside, the scene was ominous. The crowd advanced to the cry of "Vive la Garde Nationale!" and that corps opened their ranks and let the mob through; then the Garde à Cheval filed off two by two, and then once again the Corps Législatif was in the hands of the people. They took possession with a rush, and filled the house and courtyard. Women seemed to me to be in the majority in this House, in which, for once, there was no division, for the sovereign people ousted the deputies, Right, Left, and Centre.

The "great majority," which has been the delight of imperialists for so long, melted into thin air, and some fifteen of the very extreme Left drove off in cabs to the Hôtel de Ville, adjourned the "Commons," dissolved the "Lords," and formed a Provisional Government, by what right nobody can conceive; but no doubt it was by that Divine right of impudence which will tell everywhere, from a battle to a ball-room. The names of these very arch-impudents were General Trochu, Emmanuel Arago, Crémieux, Jules Favre, Jules Ferry, Gambetta, Garnier-Pagès, Glaisbizoin, Pelletan, E. Picard, Rochefort, and Jules Simon.

You will observe that the name of Vicomte Henri de Rochefort is in the list of those who to-day saved the country to rather a noisy chorus of "Vive Rochefort!" "Vive la Ligne!" "Vive la Nation!" "Vive," &c.

Then it was known that the Republic was proclaimed, and the real revel of liberty commenced.

It was a mad world, my masters, till four next morning.

"Let us go and plant a tree of liberty," said a youth of eighteen to a brother politician in his third lustre; and off they went to the Square Montholon, and, thank Heaven, there were two less in the crowd. The first act of the Government rather reminds me of the speech : " —— is coming to see us ; lock up the spoons"—they let out Rochefort and all the political prisoners : that of course was to be expected, but they also opened the prison doors to all the assassins, robbers, and ruffians, including those who murdered the fireman at Villette !

Then suddenly the flag which flaunted over the Tuileries was hauled down, and the crowd knew that the Empress had gone. She went unseen and almost unattended. This being established as a fact, there arose another yell, and the crowd broke open the gates of the Tuileries and danced a patriotic dance over the innocent flowers which so much adorned that "national property !" The Rue de Rivoli was now so full that even another baby would have been *de trop.* "Vive la République !" "Vive la France !" "Vive la Ligne !" An eager crowd thronged the footways ; the middle of the street was taken up by a series of processions of volunteers singing, waving flags;

and bearing green branches. These processions were flanked by two rows of rowdies. In no city that I have ever been in have I seen such villanous countenances as appear suddenly in Paris on such occasions as these! The real red-cap ruffian type is reproduced from the workshops of Belleville and Villette.

But hark! The noise grows louder, and the rush more rapid. Hats and caps in the air! Not cheers, but shrieks. Three men, one with a red scarf, and two younger men in decent mourning, approach in a cab— a dense mob surrounds it, for it bears the fortunes of Young France,* just out of St.-Pélagie. The three are Rochefort, with De Fonvielle and his brother. Now Rochefort is bad enough, God knows; but the others! De Fonvielle is the good youth who would have shot Prince Pierre Bonaparte if he had known how to cock his pistol, and was the bosom friend and second of Victor Noir, to whom, by-the-way, one of the finest streets in Paris is to be dedicated!

For some hours all went well, and we hoped literally that all was over but the shouting; but the

---

* *A propos* of this, during the Tours trial the judge was quite angry with De Fonvielle for not having cocked his pistol! "It is very easy," said his lordship; "you have only to do so!" Fancy an English judge making that remark—and the newspapers!

demon of destruction was abroad, and soon "found some mischief still for idle hands to do."

"Behold the vile tyrant's bees," said one ruffian.

"A bas les aigles!" said another; and in a few minutes the imperial bird was unperched and trampled in the street! Even the little medals of the Great Exhibition were not spared. The great eagles at the new Grand Opéra were threatened, but some one covered them up in bags! Since then one has got his right wing out! I, for one, will not say "Absit omen!" In a few minutes there was not an imperial emblem in Paris. At the Hôtel de Ville they destroyed Horace Vernet's splendid portrait of the Emperor Napoleon!

Can any one conceive anything so degrading to human nature as this desire to avenge oneself on an enemy by destroying works of art! The sovereign people also picked the "N"s off the splendid new wing which the Emperor added to the Tuileries. As they were imbedded in the building, the whole river-front looks as if it had had the prevailing epidemic. Miserable iconoclasts!

No other great mischief was done, and the Provisional Government was able to save the Tuileries, of which "Banquet hall deserted" "Le Figaro" says —"The Palace was absolutely empty; the people of the kitchen had alone not deserted. A gentleman, who said he was Sub-Conservator of the Palace of St.-Cloud, and secretary to General Lepic, also remained. He handed a key to M. Ravenez, wherewith the latter penetrated into the reserved apartments, going by himself. The General's secretary was deeply moved. 'Ah! sir,' said he to M. Ravenez, 'it is frightful! The poor Empress! how basely they abandoned her! All those persons whom she pampered left her.' The reception rooms on the first storey preserved their usual aspect, but from the Place de Carrousel one could see that the curtains had been removed from the windows. On the ground-floor the disorder was inexpressible. M. Ravenez's impression was that the Empress had just left; everything bore witness to that precipitate departure. Let us return to the imperial apartments, encumbered with empty trunks, work-boxes, and open bonnet-cases; in the Empress's chamber a bed was still unmade. M. Ravenez, when traversing the suite of apartments which had been occupied by the Emperor and his son, found:—On a sofa there was a child's sword, half unsheathed; on the floor, in the midst of a heap of copies of Paris newspapers, lay a revolver case; here and there slippers on chairs, gentlemen's hats. In all the cupboards, empty cigar-boxes, and, strange enough, a great number of phials of phosphate of iron. In the Prince Imperial's study, little leaden soldiers, put in motion by turning a handle, were lying on the carpet. An exercise-book for writing historical themes was open on the table. One leaf was entirely covered with a small and correct handwriting. It begins thus :—

"'Louis XV. Bourbon, Fleury (1723–1741). Regency resumed. Bourbon. 1723–1726. Bourbon. —Madame de Prie, Paris-*Duvernois* (*Duvernay* was intended). At home, corruption, stock-jobbing, frivolity, intolerance. Abroad, marriage of the King with Marie Lecziuska. Rupture with Spain, which country displays Austrian tendencies,' etc. etc.

" In one of the Empress's rooms the book for the Palace service was found. In the passages, generally lit even in the daytime, there was a vague odour of burning oil proceeding from the lamps but shortly before extinguished. In another room, a breakfast had been interrupted. It was of a most simple character, consisting of a boiled egg, a little cheese, and some bread. In the Emperor's apartment several maps of Prussia—busts and statuettes of the Imperial Prince, a great number of little painted figures, representing Prussian soldiers and officers in uniform ; also volumes with annotations. Let us also mention, along with other objects abandoned to their fate, a Greek cap with a peacock's feather, and inside the letters C. L. N. embroidered in gold. No damage whatever has been done in the interior of the Tuileries. Besides, Gardes Mobiles as well as National Guards were posted within to prevent entrance. A repast was ordered in the kitchen for the irregulars. What its worth might be we do not know, but the wine served was execrable."

I witnessed two good scenes. A man rushed close up to a lady who was one of our party, thrust his face nearly into hers, and said, "Cry Vive la République!" The lady, who is a granddaughter of General Rapp, and who inherits much of his courage, replied coolly, in her perfect French, "Nonsense! you don't know what you are saying! You mean Vive la France!" Another man showed her an "Eagle." "Yes," she said, "they led France to her greatest glories!" As with true "equality" any man in the street joined in these little disputes, I thought it was getting hot, and suggested dinner. Man must dine, even in revolutions, and so must woman.

The Baron de —— amused me at dinner. "I can stand," said he, "a fair allowance of Liberty and Fraternity, but, *merci!* no Equality! If after all these years of education, study, and diplomacy, I am not better than that apple-seller in the street, then old age is indeed a mistake."

Again into the streets to see our brother citizens, and cry "Vive la République," or vive anything. It is better to shout—no, I mean float—with the stream.

There were the same crowds, the same noise, but I thought that the faces of the shouters looked a thought more wild and wicked. This went on till we went to bed, at by no manner of means an early hour. Just before daybreak the mob made a rather serious attack on the main guard of the Palais du Louvre, in the Court of Honour of which were the Imperial Guards. The people wished to play an old Paris game—to break open the gates and fraternize with the soldiers. It was "no go" at the gates, so they tried a little storming; stole a ladder, got up to the window of the guard-room, and tried to force the bars of the window. It happened that two of my friends of the French Foreign Office were on duty as privates, and they rushed up to the window. One tried to seize the ladder. The gentleman citizen on the topmost round then slipped his hand through the bars, and delivered a vicious stab, which luckily struck my friend on the epaulette, and so only inflicted a slight wound.   Now it happens that he is singularly cunning of fence, and so he turned round to the citizen and " let him have it."   The wound might not have been " as deep as a well, nor as wide as a church door," but it was enough ; for down went the man off the ladder, knocking over two others in his fall.   Finding all the guard awake, the mob retired. It chances that the sword used by my friend was once mine.   I picked it up on the field of Voltùrno, where its owner, the Garibaldian General Puppi, dropped it when he was killed.   It is a bayonet-made sword, and so I fear the 4th of September was a bad day for that one man of the people.   I think it was the only blood shed.   Then all was quiet.

So ended the first day of this self-generated Republic, and a more melancholy day I have seldom passed.   There was no rejoicing except in the mob of the streets, nor indeed was the behaviour of the crowd generally worthy of such a nation.   With a routed army, an imprisoned Emperor, to whom all but a small section of Parisians have professed allegiance for eighteen years, and with a change of constitution which would take ten years to obtain in England, they went about gesticulating and singing ; the middle, or respectable, class looking on and grinning as if it was a farce !

Poor Emperor! poor Empress! poor Prince!—poor, fickle, frivolous French people!   As for the destroyers of initials, &c., I hope they may live till they again can say with the royalists—

> " Nous avons encore une fois
> Des N-mis (ennemis) partout."

Monday, September 5th.—It was difficult to believe, when we got up this morning, that within twenty-four hours an Empire had fallen, and that we were living under a republic — that a generation had passed away, and a new era opened!

Yet I can say that I have once before witnessed such a scene.   On the 6th of September, 1860, I was dining on board H.M.S. " Renown" at Naples, and at 7 P.M. the King of Naples steamed past us, and at 10 A.M. on the 7th he had ceased to reign, and there was a republic!

To-day was quite a day of reaction.   This always happens to the Parisians either after a feast or a fray. Headache and hoarseness were rampant at Montmartre, and fatigued voices whispered in the Belleville quarter.   Thousands of volunteers went in bands to get their arms at the Mairies.   That was nearly the only life of to-day.   But if not a day of action, rumour at least was at work.

Reports, more or less true, abounded.   The Empress

had got out of France safely. The Princess Mathilde had fled from St.-Gratien; then it was said that she had been arrested for taking "national property" away with her.

A propos, I hope that the house in the Rue de Courcelles, and St.-Gratien, by the Lake of Enghien, are the private property of the Princess. In the former, which is one of the most charming hôtels in Paris, are perfect mines of artistic wealth. This was one of the most hospitable and charming houses in Paris, and happen what may as to society, the Sunday evening of the Princess Mathilde must be regretted by every one who loves art, music, flowers, and fair faces. Happily for her she is Princess Demidoff, with a large fortune.

The next *on dit!* Baron Nieuwerkerke, Surintendant des Beaux Arts, the pleasantest and politest of barons, is suspected of malpractices, and is watched by two National Guards (he was so truly, but he got off). Again Kératry, the new Prefect of Police, issued orders to arrest his own predecessor, Piétri, wherever he was found; but he was not found. Why this step was taken nobody knows. The new Government is counting its spoons with a vengeance!

The Ducs de Bassano and Persigny went off to

the Emperor like men. Among the prisoners of our acquaintance at Sedan are Prince Achille Murat, Marquis de Gallifet (who made. a splendid charge, and when taken utterly refused to give his parole not to fight again), the Duc de Massa, Lauriston, &c.

The first act of the Government was to get rid of Palikao, who, in fact, fled for his life. For tyranny, commend me to a republic!

In the evening the Jockey Club was hissed. "In there," said the crowd, "are a thousand useless mouths!" Poor dear Club, which never hurt any one but its members!

"Cercle Impériale" is to be "Cercle des Champs-Elysées!" Are the "Impériales"—carriages—to be "Nationales?"

Tuesday, September 6th.—Very wet day. My servant said, "I am so glad of this time of dogs, as the Prussians cannot come out in such weather!" She spoke as if before a siege the enemy sent and said, "If it's fine I'll give you a look up to-morrow."

Vinoy got back with thirty thousand fresh soldiers. Within ten miles of MacMahon, the Prussians cut him off from the action. Finding that he was no use, by a very clever manœuvre he passed through two "corps d'armée" and got back safe. He covered his retreat with his mitrailleuses. N.B. Thirty thousand regulars are very useful here. "As handy as a gimlet," as poor Robert Clifton used to say.

Vinoy's men got more drunk when they arrived than any soldiers I ever saw. One of them walked up the Rue de Rivoli with me, and told me his family history ten times—a man with a grievance. "Sir," he added, "I love the English. I have been to England, and have crossed 'le pont de Vestminster.'" He spoke as if it was Lodi.

Wednesday, September 7th.—The Prefect of Police has issued the following decree :—

"Art. 1. The corps of Sergents de Ville is dissolved.

"Art. 2. It is replaced by a body of police whose exclusive mission is to protect persons and properties.

"Art. 3. The men composing it shall be chosen from amongst old soldiers, and be called ' Gardiens de la Paix Publique.'

"Art. 4. They shall not be armed.

"Art. 5. They will have to contribute, if circumstances require, to the national defence. In that case, they shall receive the arms of soldiers."

They are to march in threes.

So far, so good; but, unluckily, not only all the political exiles, but also the French ruffians of every class of French crime have left London for Paris, for the season of pillage and plunder which is inevitable. Put this and that together!

Tremendous exodus from "Grand" and other hôtels; also most of the waiters are German, and so have been sent off at twenty-four hours' notice. Hoffman of the Grand Hôtel, who knows everybody, is also gone *nolens* to the Fatherland! The streets under a republic of only a few days' standing are simply detestable! Among the Germans sent away are all the curious army of female sweeps, they hailing entirely from the Vaterland, and so since Sunday the streets have neither been swept nor watered, neither have the gutters been cleaned.

I never really missed Haussmann till to-day, when walking on his own boulevard. He was a great man, and a tidy. About five o'clock two batteries of mitrailleuses came in. At a distance they look like brass nine-pounders. Their defect, I hear, is that they do not "spread" enough. The balls are half as big again as the chassepot cartridges, and at chassepot range very deadly.

Never shall I forget the oppressive look of "dear, delightful" Paris to-day. It rained. Many of the shops were closed very early. To keep up our spirits a long line of wounded chargers limped by us—one such a splendid chestnut! I would almost as soon see an ambulance full of wounded men. One of the horses had the green Imperial clothing. The last man but one was almost weeping in the Grand Hôtel, round the door of which caravanserai lounged a lot of evident roughs—I beg their pardon, "Reds." My friend took that opportunity of abusing the Republic. 1 said to him—

"Curious fool, be still !"

but he would not, and I hope later he may have been taken up for a spy—and serve him right ! Fellow countrymen, you talk too much, and too loud.

Thursday, September 8th.—Drums, trumpets, waggons ! accompaniment "adagio." I slept badly, for troops of every description were pouring in all night, and at 6 A.M. I was awakened from a pleasing dream that I was a drum-major, and told that three soldiers had come to see me ! First I thought of arrest, but conscious of innocence only said, "Tell them that I am engaged, and that I see so many soldiers all day that I don't wish to see more." "But, monsieur," said Pierre le Concierge, "they are come to stay !" "The deuce they are !" said I. But knowing that where there is ceremony there is no friendship, and saying to myself, " Au siége comme à la guerre," I got up and received my guests. Alone I did it— alone, tubless, and cross. I found two very gentlemanly non-commissioned officers of the Havre Garde Mobile, who were just arrived, and whom the Maire had kindly invited to stay with me. This was the form of invitation, to which " no answer " was expected :—

34.

Ville ou Commune. } ——————————

BILLET DE LOGEMENT.

Rue Fieschi, No. 1005.

M. X—— will, in conformity with the law of 10 July, 1791, art. 9, clause V., lodge, or cause to be lodged, two soldiers for eight days, without wife or children (thank God for this little mercy), and give them a "seat by the fire" (*i.e.*, shelter), and a candle.

(*Signed*)   Le Maire.

Mairie.

M. X—— says that " he is a stranger, and will see them further first, and then he won't." Then M.

X—— is informed that he will be reported to the military authorities. This suggests drum-heads and chassepots, so M. X—— said, "But I am going away." " So good of monsieur! then there will be space for ten!" You will observe that M. X—— is my funny fashion of speaking of myself. So I gave the two "a place by my fire, and a light," and they are now sleeping the sleep of the brave on the floor of the dining-room. The brave snore; I wish they didn't!

Well, Mrs. Hope has asked for and got twelve, and gives them wine and meat; and Mr. Louis Merton feeds six so like cocks which do battle, that they will never go away if they can help it. He has also put up a shower-bath for them, but of that they are sparing. There is an odd story of Mrs. B——, who would "stay here by her good man." She got up in the dead of the night to get *tisane* out of the dining-room for her husband, and walking into the room without thinking, as she always does, suddenly awakened to the reality of the scene—two soldiers on the floor, and two smoking on the table. She was not full dressed.

The city is a queer sight; nine people out of ten are in uniform of some kind. Squads are at drill in every street; they begin at 6 A.M., and the first noises that reach the irritated ear are the equivalents to " 'Tenshun," " As you were," and " Eyes right." If you walk out, all is military—a waggon full of spades, a flock of sheep, a lot of stores, and orderlies riding (rapidly and very badly) with despatches; the officer of the day and his orderly, Zouaves, Turcos, National Guards from the provinces, Moblots, a regiment of cavalry two thousand strong, provincial Municipal Guards, and a very fine string of waggons.

I saw two melancholy sights to-day. One, the return of a large quantity of stores, forage, ammunition (all of which will come in here like Clifton's gimlet). Would that it ·had ended there. Then came waggons full of that curious medley which is often left on the battle-field—swords, rifles, uniforms, knapsacks, &c., and one was filled with artillery harness! Then a long line of ambulances and open waggons crowded with the sick, wounded, and dying. The sad procession closed with a long train of artillery horses, some without harness—all without guns! I pitied the officer in charge as he rode through Paris.

The other sight was as sad. A young man, a spy, and evidently a gentleman, whose grave has closed over him ere this. Then we met a funny man from London, who made a joke about it.

Victor Hugo has come back, and has commenced speaking.   Louis Blanc is here.

Friday, September 9th.—An awful storm of rain and hurricane in the night, which must have been a deadly enemy to the advancing foe. Orders for all strangers who wish to leave Paris to go at once. To-day arrived three thousand more very fine " Gardes Municipaux à Cheval" from the provinces.

The last free Englishman is supposed to have taken his ticket !   Thorpe's is closed, but a cunning American has opened another " Bar."   It must be for pleasure, not profit, for fear is not thirsty, if sorrow is.

Saturday, September 10th.—Fine day, but blowing hard. Called at several embassies ; not heard any news. Also ventured to the Home Office, and was not pelted with stones ! Faint idea of armistice, and Russia said to be trying for it. I think it will turn out nonsense. France will not give up territory. Prussia (which can swallow France up) will have it ! As dead a lock as that in the " Critic."

The prefect is said to have found thirty thousand needle-guns in Paris to-day; if so—but I do not believe it—this means thirty thousand traitors in the camp, and would account for the " King of Blood and Iron" saying, "I don't want to besiege Paris; I can get aid in the city, and so get in without firing a shot."

Preparations go on, certainly. I saw to-day three hundred and seventy as fine Mobiles as I ever wish to behold march past the house to join their regiment. "Very fine men," said a friend of mine; "if you could expel the clod-hopper, they would make good soldiers."

There is a panic at Boulogne-sur-Mer, and the enemy is said to· be marching towards Havre. The extreme Socialists have left the present Government, which they think childishly mild; so one Cluseret, a Garibaldian general in the "division of Fonvielle," wrote a seditious letter in the "Marseillaise." The actual Government suppressed that inflammable organ, and M. Rochefort, by one of his first acts, kills his own paper! So does even-handed Justice act sometimes. Other signs of the war:—the "Mémorial Diplomatique" is not dead, but sleepeth till the war is over; and on Friday, September 9th, "Galignani" came out in a single sheet.

Among the prisoners at Sedan is Robert Mitchell, the well-known writer in the "Constitutionnel," and M. Cassagnac *fils*. To-day they are sent off to the other extreme of Germany. They are of course only " privates," and I trust on the way they will be better treated than " private" the Duc de Fitzjames, who has just performed the same journey, and was nearly starved before he arrived at his destination.

Had the Empress remained, Prussia would have made peace ; but she was deserted. Trochu a day or two before swore too much about "devotion," &c. "Don't you think," said Prince de la Tour d'Auvergne to Rouher, "he had better put it down on paper, and sign it? He is *too* devoted." By-the-way, a man followed Rouher to the steamer, and wished to shoot him for making war.

Trochu is to-day said to be more Orleanist than Orleans. The Princes of that House were here last week, and saw Gambetta and (I believe) Jules Favre. They were told that the pear was not ripe, and advised to get out of France at once. Gambetta is very Orleanist (that I have long heard), and unluckily General Cluseret found it out.

To-day we have orders not to wash much (the self-sacrifice of the natives in this respect is patriotic to an unpleasant degree). We get water from 8 till 11 A.M. The gas to be cut off next week, which, as the convicts at Toulon are let loose, and we have no police, is not narcotic.

I must not forget my other story. When the Prussians advanced into France, Baron Lohndorf (the Fleury of Prussia) sent a " parlementaire" to Montgéroult, the seat of Baron de Bray, to demand where "Hospodar " was—Hospodar is the well-known horse by Monarque out of Constance—worth thousands. Baron de Bray had got well away, set Hospodar going, and as he can stay, the " Vicar" (you remember our old Vicar?) won so easy that Lohndorf found Hospodar was nowhere.

I walked up to the Porte St.-Martin to-day. Eugh! such a crowd, every third man armed, and such dust, dirt, and stench !

All the theatres closed by order. This in Paris ! Count Braniski has given sixteen thousand pounds for an ambulance, and Mr. Wallace (Lord Hertford's legatee) twelve thousand pounds for another. The ambulance flag floats over the Tuileries, now a hospital, and the gardens are an artillery camp.

Rothschilds to-day charged sixteen pounds for remitting four hundred pounds to London. Rentes, 8 per cent., were to-night (Sept. 10) 55; on Aug. 26, they were 60,80. We have a small Anglo-French coterie which meets every evening in the court of the Grand Hôtel, and where somehow all the news gets. To-night we were dull. Somebody said, " Let us pick lint to keep up our spirits."   Most people look very glum, but our clique keeps up its spirits and laughs.   "Cadde vino allegria," says the Italian.

Sunday, September 11*th.*—Four hundred thousand troops in Paris !

Is there not a proverb about a parched pea and a drum-head ? Yes !   Then if any one will send me a peck of parched peas, I am sure I could find a drum-head for each.   Though what affinity exists between a pea and a drum I cannot conceive, nor why they should jump, unless, indeed, they are *pois sautés.* I have often thought that the *déjeuner* is the ruin of commercial Paris—it is a sort of reversed dinner, which occupies the best part of the day of a Paris professional or mercantile man.   You walk to the Rue de Turbigo, which is any distance from any where, and hot and tired reach the Bureau.   "Monsieur is to his breakfast," and then you know that "all is lost now ;" and it is a fact that during the war, General de Failly has been several times surprised while his men were at *déjeuner.*

Three of our best *petits crevés,* pets of the Little Club, are killed, and died fighting like lions—George de Hœckeren, Bellyme, and Feuillant.   There are some

French Mobiles here who cannot speak French, only Gaelic. They are Armoricans. Four different regiments going to drill crossed one another under my window at 1·30 P.M., most of them fine, well set up young men; but I confess that I should decline to be sent to Coventry with the rest.

An important telegram appeared in the "Daily Telegraph" just arrived here. It is from the special correspondent at Berlin (if he be Mr. Kingston, he is "the best man out" for German news), and is to the effect that the King of Prussia has given orders that the Emperor is to be treated as Sovereign of France. Rather a startler this for some here, and no bad rebuke for the indecent and foolish haste in which the Empress was deserted and sent away. I wonder if his Majesty remembers a remark he made not long ago. "Ah! that dear England, where I was so happy and so free—much freer than I am here."

I was talking yesterday to a French official who has *kept his place.* "After all," said he, "the Emperor was very old and infirm." I could not help replying, "Indeed! but you did not think so last week." But it was and will be ever so.

> "Such was of old the Jewish rabbis' cry—
> Hosannah! first, and after, Crucify!"

Orders are given to burn the Bois at the approach of the Prussians.

The evening was dull, and the only thing which amused one was being consulted as to how best to get carrier pigeons. It is so truly going back to the early ages! Sword canes are a great article of street commerce to-day, life not being safe.

So ends the first week of a republic, and perhaps the last before great carnage. We have had as yet the exciting and amusing scenes, but sad spectacles remain behind.

Monday, September 12th.—It seems as if the weather was to mock this wretched year. It has been summer since April, and to-day dawned like July.

It is said that General Garibaldi is on his way to Paris with a large following. Now, I have had some experience of the General, for whom I have the highest respect, and I wish for his own sake that he had confined his sailing to his little yacht at Caprera, and not stepped into this galley. But he himself will do little harm; it is his *entourage*, of which I entertain a holy horror; *experto crede*, it is a terrible cohort.

The troops here are said to be in excellent condition,

very devoted and enthusiastic. I hope it is the case, but it was not so at the front, where the "International" had infected the Line with its socialistic doctrines to a dangerous degree. This I know from officers.

The state of Paris to-day is a jumble of opposed parties, cemented together for the moment by fierce hatred of Prussia.

The Pope seems "gone!" Is 1870 to be another 1848? As to his Holiness, "There was mair tint at Flodden Field." Byng Hall has just been, and says that the Pope left yesterday in an English vessel. There may be six English "useless mouths" in Paris—not more. The last I have seen was Lord Campbell, armed with a brown silk umbrella, and looking as unconcerned at the row and riot as Ajax defying the lightning. The Duke of Manchester just arrived, fresh from the horrors of Sedan, and praying that he may never see another battle. He has had his little "galley" too, you see.

Fancy! many of the ambulance surgical instruments were blunt! Doctors Marion Sims and Evans are at the front.

The following are the facts of the escape of the poor deserted Empress. She fled with Madame Le

Breton, got into a cab, and drove to three houses and found nobody at home. At last an English doctor gave her shelter and food; and at night she escaped to Trouville. From there they telegraphed for the yacht of Sir John Burgoyne, in which her Majesty sailed for the Isle of Wight.

Jules Favre and the Corps Diplomatique were to have left for Tours to-day, but at the last moment the journey was postponed, from which people argue an armistice. There may be something in it. It is certainly ominous, the eager way in which the " Great Powers," including Russia, recognized a government which has no *raison d'étre!* In 1848 the Great Powers were less pliable.

The French at Verdun have captured Harold de Moltke, brother of the Danish Minister here, and have detained him till further orders. It must be confessed that just now " Moltke" is a bad name to travel under in France. This gentleman is all right, however, and a very good fellow. I wonder if he swaggered as much as he does here. He is a good-looking man, and wears the handsomest Hussar dress in any army list; but Lord! how he does swagger!

We took a melancholy walk to-day. The Champs-Elysées were in their now ordinary state of dust and desertion ; the latter broken by processions of country carts and furniture waggons containing everything above the earth or under the earth ; and indeed above the water, for one family brought in a four-oared cutter in a cart, with a dog-kennel, a quantity of what I believe are called kitchen utensils, a cradle, a truss of straw, and a string of onions. Country carts brought everything, from the baby to the kitchen boiler ; stores high and dry, flour and flowers, with the pet sheep following like the spotted carriage-dog of our grandfathers' time ; and a regiment of Garde Nationale, officered by a man so fat that he could not walk, and whom the authorities had made a " mounted officer" under compulsion.

It is not cheering to see these country carts coming in laden with the poor *penates* of many a ruined cottager, and even small farmer. The scene is laughable at times, perhaps ; yet I fancy we laugh that we may not cry. In war it is not the battle that is frightful and requires courage ; it is the destruction, the carnage, and the hospital.

The Avenue du Roi de Rome is one long encampment, but that we did not visit. We went down the Avenue de la Grande Armée. There are encamped Vinoy's artillery, fresh from the front, and showing all the usual signs of a campaign. The men, however, look well, and if they often get as good rations and as well cooked as to-day, no wonder. The horses are very good, but have evidently been short of forage. All this will be set right again in a few days however. They are encamped, or rather sleep, on straw on both sides of the Avenue, and I regret to say that two out of three of the men off duty were drunk. We passed by those way-worn warriors, and I confess that I thought, with a sigh, of the last time I had seen them, in all the pomp and circumstance of parade, march past the Emperor, who, sitting on his favourite chestnut, with the faithful Gamble close behind him, looked wonderfully satisfied.

But I might have reserved my sighs. I wanted them soon after. In due time, through clouds of dust raised by the incessant strings of country carts, in which weeping women and terrified children were sitting, their household gods shattered around them, we reached the fortifications of the Porte Maillot. They consist of a strong stone fort and a drawbridge, which connects the line of fortifications where they were broken by the road to Courbevoie. The masonry is forty inches thick, and pierced at frequent intervals for rifle practice. After passing the drawbridge (I should say that the fosse is very deep, abrupt, and a strong defence), the road is diverted to the right, and winds—a serpentine lane—back into the road. The bridge is further strengthened by a strong earthwork, the face of which is defended by sharp stakes attached by wires, and by a rather feeble *cheval de frise.* The idea is good, but, alas! the "thief of time" has been at his tricks here too. In three weeks little has been done. Two guns alone are in position, and it will take three weeks to put Porte Maillot in a condition to receive the enemy. Sigh No. 2.

Then what an awful scene of desolation and destruction meets the eye ! The first exclamation was, " Where are we ?" We left there a splendid wide " Place," surrounded by fine houses and good shops : here L'Amour cut and dressed hair ; there La Blanche offered wine to the weary ; on the left the manufactory of soap so necessary, and candles so pleasant, with its elegant shaft ; next to that " Le Berceau de l'Amour—on fait les Noces ;" the little Fortnum and Mason's ; the carriage builders ; the " tea gardens," which were wont to be the delight of Sunday-Paris ; " Là Ville au Bois—diners 3·50, ou à la carte." Where are they ? In utter ruin, as desolate as Tadmor in the Wilderness. Gillet's great restaurant alone is spared, and he had orders to turn out, bag and baggage, to-day. Yes ! there is one other building which they are trying to save. It is the chapel erected to the memory of a prince who, had he lived, would perhaps have spared France this great ignominy and trial. Though it was vilely said by the Rochefortists of that day, " that he owed his elevation to the street, and there he found his fall," yet Louis-Philippe, Duc d'Orléans, was a clever man and a popular prince. When he was killed by a fall from his carriage on the 14th of July, 1842, he was taken to a wine shop at Sablonville, opposite " the Yorkshire Stingo" (the house was bought by the King for four thousand four hundred pounds, and erected in the park of Neuilly), and on the spot was built the chapel which they are trying now to barricade (awful words for the Orleans family, cannot they escape it in the tomb?) and preserve from Prussian shells or French stray shots. It is doomed though, and already, saving two cedars preserved by order of the Commander of Engineers, every tree around it is cut down, and the

> " Only constant mourner o'er the dead"

is inconstant for once.

But I have reserved the horror of horrors to the last. We went to the entrance of the Bois. Many of our set will remember the jolly drive from the races through it, and its great beauties. The gates are closed, the beautiful Swiss châlets (the lodges) were piles of brick, dust, and the *débris* of decoration. The trees are cleared all along the military zone, and even the avenue,

> " Where the acacia waved its yellow hair,"

is not spared.

It was indeed a lamentable sight, and brought war home even to the thoughtless Parisians more than any reports from the front, or even " killed and wounded, List No. 3." Sighs No. 3 and upwards !— deep sighs.

M. Thiers has gone on a mission of alliance, and will fail. The Grand Hôtel closed half its great room, and dullness prevails.

Tuesday, September 13th.—Since 8 A.M. till now, 1 P.M., one stream of National Guards and Mobiles has poured past to be reviewed. The review, however, was not a review, but an inspection. The truth is, that every space where a large number of troops could be handled is occupied with troops, or batteries, or baggage and forage waggons, and so the only arrangement possible was this :—One hundred and forty thousand National Guards were ranged in single file along the pavement on each side facing towards the street, down which General Trochu, who was fairly, but not enthusiastically, received, rode by with a brilliant staff and inspected them. When he had ridden by a regiment, it fell out and marched to quarters, so the mass of troops was easily dispersed, and the review was over in a short time—a great fact in these busy days. All the time the Garde Mobile was marching and countermarching, and I am sure that at least two hundred and fifty thousand men marched down the Rue Auber. I believe it was a demonstration to give confidence to Paris. If so intended, it should have been a success, for finer men as a rule I never wish to see, and if there was but time to make soldiers of them they might yet stand against the Prussians. As it is, they may do an enormous damage to the enemy, and perhaps retard the fall of Paris some few days. As for the other defences, they go on well, and M. Ruggieri, a great gunpowder manufacturer, told M. Treitt (the advocate), who used to command a battalion of the National Guard of the Empire, that the preparation of explosives is extraordinary. Also, there is an engine called the "porte mobile," which is six times as deadly as the mitrailleuse. The Government has appointed a chemical committee to watch over the question of poisonous and deadly explosives. There is also a barricade committee, presidents De Rochefort and Flourens.

Thirty thousand regular troops are in skirmishing order in the roads between Meudon and Paris. But are we to be attacked? I do not doubt it, though some still do. The answer of the United States, that it was no use offering to mediate, as Bismarck had utterly refused (by telegram last night), seems conclusive. Thiers, too, went off in very low spirits. He said he went to England out of etiquette only, expecting nothing. In a month he may do something with Russia and Austria, but what may not happen in a month?

I went to see the camp in the Avenue du Roi de Rome, and found it only a large body of MacMahon's artillery without guns. The scene in that part of Paris was very curious. Standing in the Place François Premier, you command several streets. At 6 P.M. there was not a soul in sight, and a silence as if midnight reigned and was almost oppressive. There was not more than one private carriage out, and that was a " pill-box," or doctor's brougham. It is curious how these revolutionary times resuscitate almost forgotten people. Truly " Il n'y a que les morts qui ne reviennent pas."

Here is Louis Blanc. He is young, though only fifty-six, of whom all men say all good things; come back to France to help to steer her vessel. He has been talked of for Albert Gate, perhaps on the strength of his Pozzo di Borgo diplomatic blood; but this post is to be offered to M. de Choiseul, cousin of the present Duc de Praslins. Certainly when, on the 18th of June, 1856, I saw a *pronunciamento* at Lisbon, and embarked on board the same steamer with M. Louis Blanc, I never expected to be living in Paris when he came into influence, if not office.

Then there is Amantine, Lucile, Aurore, Dupin, Madame de Dudevant, that is, "George Sand," aged, I regret to say, sixty-six, and she has reappeared, and writes as follows :—

"It is still living then, the Republic, since it rises again from its ashes, summoned by a universal cry, by a noble will, without effusion of blood, without fratricidal contest!

"This is the third awakening; and it is beautiful beyond fancy. Even the fourth it might be called; for we must not forget that 1830 was republican at the outset. There have been fights—always feebler and more feeble—for this noble prize; it is gained to-day by one single shout, 'Vive la France!'

"This is, then, the normal state—the state insisted

on by human consciences. It is the inevitable result of humanity's prodigious labour. It is destiny—more, it is law! Man's intelligence, man's strength, can only reach their full powers in an atmosphere of freedom.

"See him, your Lord of Hosts! He is called Native Land and Liberty!

"Hail to thee, Republic! Thou art in worthy hands, and a great people will march under thy banner after a bloody expiation. The struggle will be hard, but if thou shouldst fail yet once, once, thou wilt spring up again always, always!

"The rights of man are never to be destroyed!

"GEORGE SAND.

"Nohant, Sept. 6th, 1870."

Last, but not least, the great exile of Jersey, Victor Hugo, aged sixty-eight, who, said a friend of mine, will be sure to begin to speak when his foot touches French soil. He did so at the very station, and was in consequence followed to his home by a rabble. "There goes Victor Hugo, with a new edition of the Misérables," said one of the lookers-on. He has now favoured the Germans with a large quantity of his mind.   He writes as if he were King of France, or President, at least :—

"Germans—He who speaks to you is a friend. Three years ago, at the time of the Exposition of 1867, from the retreat of my exile, I welcomed you into your city.

" What city ?

" Paris.   For Paris belongs not to us alone ; Paris is yours as much as ours.   Berlin, Vienna, Dresden, Stuttgart, are your capitals ; Paris is your centre. It is in Paris that the beating of Europe's heart is felt.   Paris is the city of cities.   Paris is the city of men.   There has been an Athens, there has been a Rome, and there is a Paris.

" Paris is nothing else but one immense hospitality. To-day you come back to it.

" How ?   Like brothers, as three years ago ?

" No ; as enemies.

" Why ?   What is this sinister misunderstanding ?

" Two nations have made Europe.   These two nations are France and Germany.   Germany is for the West what India is for the East—a sort of great ancestor.   We venerate her.   But what is the matter, and what does this mean?   To-day this Europe, which Germany has constructed by her expansion, and France by her enlightenment, Germany wishes to undo.

"Is it possible? Can Germany wish to undo Europe by mutilating France? Can Germany wish to undo Europe by destroying Paris?

"Reflect. Why this invasion? Why this savage effort against a brother people? What have we done to you?

"This war, does it come from us?

"It is the Empire which desired it; it is the Empire which made it.

"The Empire is dead. It is well. We have nothing in common with this corpse. It is the past; we are the future. It is hatred; we are sympathy. It is treason; we are loyalty. It is Capua and Gomorrah; we are France.

"We are the French Republic. Our motto is 'Liberty, Equality, Fraternity.' We inscribe on our flag 'United States of Europe.' We are the same people as you. We have had Vercingetorix as you have had Arminius. The same fraternal ray, mark of sublime union, pierces through the German heart and the French soul.

"This is so true that we speak to you thus :—If by mischance your fatal error drive you to the extremest violence, if you come to attack us in this august city, confided in some sort by Europe to France, if you besiege Paris, we shall defend ourselves to the last extremity; we shall strive against you with all our strength; but we declare to you that we shall continue to be your brothers. And your wounded—do you know where we shall put them? In the palace of the nation. We have already assigned the Tuileries as the hospital for wounded Prussians. *There* will be the ambulance of your brave Prussian soldiers—it is there our women will be to succour and take care of them. Your wounded shall be our guests. We will treat them loyally, and Paris will receive them in her Louvre.

"It is with this feeling of fraternity in our hearts that we shall accept your war.

" But this war, Germans, what sense is there in it? It is finished, for the Empire is finished. You have killed your enemy, who is also ours; what more do you want?

"You come to take Paris by force. But we have always offered her to you with love. Let not the gates be closed against you by the people who, in all ages, have held out to you their arms. Deceive not yourselves about Paris—Paris loves you, but Paris will fight you; Paris will fight you with all the formidable majesty of her glory and of her. mourning. Paris, threatened with this brutal violation, may become terrible.

"Jules Favre has told you eloquently, and we all repeat to you—expect an indignant resistance.

"You will take the fortress—you will find the fortification ; you will take the fortification—you will find the barricade ; you will take the barricade, and then, perhaps, who knows what patriotism in distress may commit ?—you will find the mined sewers that will blow entire streets into the air. You will have to accept this terrible decree : to take Paris stone by stone, to murder Europe there, to kill France in detail, in each house ; and this great light, you will have to extinguish it soul by soul. Stop !

"Germans, Paris is formidable. In presence of Paris take thought. To her all transformations are possible. Her softness gives you the measure of her energy. We seem to sleep—we awake. We draw from the scabbard an idea no less than a sword, and this city, which yesterday was Sybaris, may to-morrow be Saragossa.

"Do we say this to frighten you ? No, i' faith. You Germans are not frightened. You have had Galgacus against Rome, and Körner against Napoleon. We are the people of the Marseillaise, but you are the people of the *sonnets cuirassés* and of the *cri de l'épée*. You are a nation of thinkers who become at need a legion of heroes. Your soldiers are worthy of ours ; ours are impassable bravery, yours are intrepid calmness.

"But listen! You have cunning and skilful generals : we had incompetent chiefs. You have made a clever rather than a brilliant war. Your generals have preferred the useful to the great : they were right. You have taken us by surprise ; you have been ten to one. Our soldiers have stoically suffered themselves to be massacred by you who had cleverly secured all the chances on your side ; so that up till now in this terrible war, Prussia has gained the victory, France has gained the glory.

"Now think of it. You fancy you have a last *coup* to make ; to precipitate yourselves upon Paris ; to take advantage of our admirable army, deceived and betrayed, being at this moment stretched dead upon the field of battle ; to throw yourselves with your seven hundred thousand soldiers, with all your machines of war, your mitrailleuses, your steel cannon, your Krupp bullets, your Dreyse guns, your innumerable cavalry, your awful artillery, on three hundred thousand citizens standing erect upon their ramparts, on fathers defending their homes, on a city full of trembling families, where there are women, and sisters and mothers, and where at this moment I who speak to you, I have two little children, of whom one is at the breast. It is on this city, innocent of this war—on this city, which has done nothing to you but give you its light—it is on Paris, isolated, proud, and despairing, that you would precipitate yourselves, an immense flood of murder and of battle! This is to be your part, valiant men, great soldiers, illustrious army of noble Germany.   Oh, reflect!

"Is the nineteenth century to witness this frightful prodigy? A nation fallen from polity to barbarism, abolishing the city of nations; Germany extinguishing Paris; Germania lifting the axe against Gaul!   You, the descendants of Teutonic knights, can you make a disloyal war; exterminate the group of men and of ideas needed by the world; destroy the *cité organique*; emulate Attila and Alaric; renew, after Omar, the burning of the human library; raze the Hôtel de Ville, as the Huns razed the Capitol; bombard Notre Dame, as the Turks bombarded the Parthenon?   Can you give this spectacle to the world?   Can you, Germans, become Vandals again; personify barbarism decapitating civilization?

"No, no, no! Do you know what this victory would be for you? It would be dishonour.

" Nobody, i' faith, can think of frightening you Germans, glorious army, courageous people, but one may inform you. It certainly is not opprobrium that you seek ; well, it is opprobrium that you will find, and I, a European—that is to say, a friend of Paris— I, a Parisian—that is to say, a friend of the people— I warn you of your peril, my brothers of Germany, because I admire and honour you, and because I know well that if anything can make you withdraw it is not fear, it is shame.

" Noble soldiers, what would be your return to your hearths and homes ? You would be conquerors ashamed. And what would your wives exclaim ? The death of Paris—what mourning ! The assassination of Paris—what a crime ! The world would have the mourning ; yours would be the crime.

" Do not accept this terrible responsibility. Stop !

" And now a last word. Paris, pushed to extremities ; Paris, supported by all France aroused, can conquer and would conquer ; and you would have tried in vain this course of action, which already revolts the world. In any case, efface from the lines written in haste the words Destruction, Abolition, Death. No, you could not destroy Paris. You may succeed in demolishing it materially, and even that is not easy ; you would make it greater morally. In reducing Paris to ruins, you would sanctify it. The dispersion of the stones will cause the dispersion of ideas. Cast Paris to the four winds, you will only conduce to make from every grain of its ashes the seed of the future. This sepulchre will cry out, 'Liberty, Equality, Fraternity!' Paris is a city, but Paris is also a soul. ·

"Burn our edifices—these are only our bones; their smoke will assume shape, will become great and living, and will rise even to heaven; and there it will be seen for ever on the horizon of nations, above us, above you, above everything, and above all attesting our glory and your shame, this great spectre formed of shadow and light—Paris.

"Now I have spoken. Germans, if you persist, let it be so: you are warned, come! and attack the walls of Paris. Under your bombs and your mitrailleuses she will defend herself. As for me—an old man now—I shall be there unarmed. It behoves me to be with the people who die. I pity you for being with the kings who kill.

"Victor Hugo.

"Paris, September 9th, 1870."

As for the cluster of "minora sidera," it is impossible to detect them with the naked eye.

An odd effect of the war was to be seen and heard

to-day. To prevent the Prussians getting the game in the Imperial preserves, a public *battue* was proclaimed to-day. Imagine the sight—figure to yourself all the population of the neighbourhood turning out to revenge themselves on the Empire by shooting its game.

By-the-way, I have never, even in Windsor Park, where the Prince Consort some twenty years ago had several pheasants, seen such a head of game as there was at Compiègne, and to reflect that I was once asked to shoot there, and could not go because it was Rossini's funeral !

I remember that in Naples the first thing the republicans did was to make an onslaught on the game at Capo di Monte, and Mr. Edwin James, Q.C., invited a select party to kill Bombicello's pheasants —poor man ! They thought that he was that mysterious being—" an agent of Palmerston."

The treatment of Queen's messengers is horrid, and they will not allow a shilling extra for expenses. Major Byng Hall arrived at 5 P.M., and leaves for Calais at 10 P.M. He is on the " station," and goes to Calais every night. The line to Italy is closed, and the English mails go by way of Rouen, and are in consequence twelve hours late.

Wednesday, September 14th.—At 1 A.M. a big gun fired! What was it? How it must have alarmed thousands of Parisians if, happily, they were not sleeping the sleep of the weary and dusty! It did "fright a many and all, I believe," as they say in Northamptonshire; but I found it was the blowing up of a bridge—I believe the bridge of Asnières. How it must have startled the gudgeons!

We have had dozens of reports about the departure of the Empress: all were untrue or exaggerated. Last evening I saw Baron Ferdinand de Lesseps, a relative of her Majesty, and partly left in charge of her, and he told me that as far back as the 20th of August he had told the Empress that all was over—that the Emperor would lose everything and could never return; the dynasty was exhausted; monarchy had no chance, and that she had better prepare to leave France. Her Majesty flatly refused. When things got worse—and, as I suspected, the collapse was known at the Tuileries hours before it was made public—M. de Lesseps advised her to proclaim a republic, "the only form of government now possible." Prince de la Tour d'Auvergne gave the same advice. This her Majesty refused. So things went on till the catastrophe came on Sunday. M. de Lesseps rushed into the Tuileries, and said, " Your Majesty must go!" At length she consented. Prince de Metternich and Madame Le Breton Bourbaki conducted her Majesty through the galleries of the Louvre. She forbade the Prince to follow her farther, for fear of detection, and so escaped by way of Trouville to England. "Whether her Majesty was recognized or not we cannot say, but nobody noticed her. Her Majesty's conduct has endeared her to everybody by its patient suffering, and her courage has gained her the reverence of all gentlemen." It is not a bad epitaph; and it was pronounced by that great gentleman, Ferdinand de Lesseps.

Then M. de Lesseps, who was left in charge of the Tuileries, returned and faced the mob. Climbing the iron fence he went straight into the crowd, and said, "You know me—what do you want?" "The Empress!" "Her Majesty! She has gone." Then there was a pause. "We desire that the flag be hauled down!" "A la bonheur," said M. de Lesseps, and he gave the order. The seneschal, however, hesitated. "Imbécile!" said M. de Lesseps, "don't you see that if you do not do so, they will climb up, pull it down, and the palace with it!" The imperial flag was struck. Then he turned to the mob, and said, "No robbery! You know me;" and five thousand people passed through the Tuileries without touching a thing. " They flowed by us like water into a canal,".said Baron Ferdinand just now.

I fear I shall have little more to say of the Empress in this diary, which, like my life in France, will, I hope, cease with this siege. There is still a Paris; but it is not our Paris, and I hope to go to a more genial climate; and so I will say, that having had the honour of knowing her Majesty for seven years, and having seen her often quietly alone with the Emperor, and perhaps the same night gorgeous at some great reception, I have found her ever the same; kind and un-affected in private; stately and dignified, but courteous, in public—in a word, a lady. Her withdrawal from Paris, according to M. de Lesseps, must much advance her in the rank of women. And the French and English press print " Billingsgate" against her!

Major Hicks called. He has been sixteen days getting here from Strasbourg. Requisition of the Prussians at Nancy—four *plats*, bread, wine *à discrétion*, and cigars. Of course that is a soldier's, not an official, requisition. Query, what is *discrétion* in wine in a Uhlan?

To-day they have commenced burning some of the woods near Montmorency, and Paris will soon be—

" girt by fire,
In circle narrowing as it glows."

To add to our difficulties we have a socialistic government. Lyons has gone beyond Paris, and is red and rabid—arresting the rich and insulting the Tricolour by parading the "Red" flag. The following letter from Nice in the "Liberté" is not reassuring:—

"The proclamation of the Republic has produced here some terrible disturbances. On Monday morning a band of ruffians broke open the doors of the prison, and set at liberty a hundred and fifty thieves or murderers who were waiting to be transferred to Toulon. This mob, followed soon after by many more vagabonds, then proceeded to the barracks of the Mobiles, broke through the gates, tore off the epaulettes and cross of the commanding officer, M. de St.-Quentin, and being then joined by the Gardes, spread devastation through Nice. The principal acts committed on Monday were as follows : a gendarme and an agent of police killed ; three lodgings of commissaries plundered, and their furniture and papers burnt. At Menton the money-chest of the receiver of taxes and the custom-house pillaged ; the commissary killed. At Cannes, some bankers robbed. The National Guard, immediately organized, has not yet been able to retake all the prisoners escaped."

Are we going back to the reign of terror ? I saw an ambassador to-day whose views were most gloomy.

Bourse, very firm. Rentes, 54,05—a rise of seventy centimes on Tuesday's market.

Thursday, September 15*th.*—Things look very black. I have just been to the Embassy and the Ministère de l'Intérieure, and have not come out smiling. Ernest Picard's paper—now an authority—refers to the probable immediate movement of Russia with eight hundred thousand men. I wrote this to England weeks ago, and the wiseacres would not believe it. De. Grammont received a telegram from Fleury to that effect, the cipher of which was translated for me.

" Galignani," which has lasted since 1814, making a very large fortune for its very worthy and popular proprietor, and about the delivery of which we find Byron in frequent fits of passion in his letters from Italy, has to-day the following melancholy announcement :—

" NOTICE.—We announce with deep regret to our subscribers that, in consequence of the present interruption of several of the French railways and the impending cessation of communications with the provinces, we are likely to be compelled to suspend, almost immediately, the publication of the " Messenger" until the siege of Paris shall have terminated. The paper will, however, continue to be forwarded to the last possible moment.

"We shall of course take fully into account such periods of subscription as have not expired, and allow for the same when the journal reappears."

All the *employés* of the "Soir" have bolted, not because they wanted to fight the Prussians, but because they did not.

Spies are being taken up on all sides, but as yet I have heard for certain of no one being shot. To be sure, it would not be done "au grand jour." Anybody resembling a Prussian is seized by a Garde Mobile, who thinks he has got Bismarck, on the principle that

> "Perhaps a recruit might chance to shoot
> The General Bonaparte."

It is dangerous walking about, and now, if ever, is the time to publish the declaration of Mr. Vincent Crummles :—"Mr. Crummles is not a Prussian, having been born at Chelsea."

But where are the Prussians? and, above all, where are the *two* Uhlans? The latter are everywhere—here to-day and gone yesterday. The French have left Creil, and the Prussians are forty-six English miles from the capital. They are in force. The following is a fair description of our situation. I quote the dying "Messenger," the true "Traveller's Joy" of exiled English :—

" The Prussians appear to have adopted three routes to advance from Rheims to Paris. One of them passes by Laon, La Fère, Chauny, Compiègne, and Creil. The catastrophe produced by their arrival at the first-named place is well known. La Fère, a strong little town on that line, which may be avoided by taking the direct road from Laon to Chauny, has made preparations for resistance. The scouts seen at Noisy-sur-Oise were those of the ' corps d'armée ' which was following this course. Another road, by Champagne, goes from Rheims to Epernay, and runs along the Marne by Château-Thierry, La Ferté-sous-Jouarre, and Meaux. Lastly, the central route, by the Soissonnais, was the first traversed by the Prussian reconnoitrers. They were seen at Fismes and at Braisne, and then they suddenly disappeared.

" The programme of Count de Moltke, communicated some time back by the official journal of Berlin, is thus being executed punctually. The columns which are advancing by Nanteuil, in turning Soissons, which has refused to surrender, showed themselves yesterday in the neighbourhood of Meaux. Immediately the prefects and the Guard Mobile fell back on Lagny. But the enemy, without stopping, continued his march, and occupied during the night that small place, very near the capital, where several journals written in Paris are printed, and where many notabilities possess villas. The service has entirely ceased on the Eastern railway line, and a notice from the ministry has been posted up, announcing that the advanced guard had appeared at Noisy-le-Sec. (This cannot be the fort so called near Paris, but another place of the same name not far from Fontainebleau.)

" The capital is now one vast camp, as to whatever side one turns he can only see armed men. Everywhere military drilling has replaced the commercial and manufacturing animation which formerly distinguished the French capital. At the approach of the enemy, Paris does not occupy herself solely with the defence of her walls. General Vinoy, at the head of his army, now thoroughly re-established, well equipped and provisioned, has entered on a campaign to commence exterior operations. He is to manœuvre in such a way as to prevent the invasion of the departments in which the enemy might be tempted to enter in order to extend his occupation, in order to obtain provisions and requisitions from the inhabitants. The object is to retain him as much as possible under the fire of the forts, in order that the weight of the invasion may fall on the smallest possible portion of the territory. Two other 'corps d'armée' are ready to receive a destination analogous to that of the above. The provinces of the West and Centre are those which more especially require protection."

There is a popular delusion that ambassadors have nothing to do, and that they have a large staff of attachés to assist them in performing that difficult task. If any one will visit the British Embassy now, and ask MM. Wodehouse and Saumerez, they will possibly hear another tale. They are worked like horses. Elderly females—prancers—are their worst foes. I will say, that during seven years I have experienced every sort of kindness, hospitality, and good-fellowship from the embassies of Lord Cowley and Lord Lyons. If embassies don't give information it is for two reasons. First, they never know anything; second, they must not tell it if they did.

We went yesterday to see the fort of the Buttes de Montmartre. I dare say that there are not six English who know "Le Moulin de Montmartre—à la Renom-mée de Galettes," in the Rue Girardin.   It is a perfectly unknown quarter, not far from the cemetery, and is not the least like Paris.   It is very like Fiesole. The *moulin* itself is a mouldy and rickety mill, but it has a beautiful terrace, and the finest possible view of this poor beleaguered city.   It also joins a restaurant "renowned for tarts," where there is a ball-room, and a garden which is a cross between Green-wich Fair and Rosherville.   It is a spot where the Paris of that *quartier* goes "to spend a happy day."   There are all sorts of games, at which, even at this crisis, grave, elderly National Guards and Pro-fessors of Lycées were to be seen seriously trying to throw a ring over a pointed stick, or place a ball in a hole.   The Prussians were almost within sight, and devastation was visible to the naked eye.

On the terrace below there is a very strong battery —seven guns, the range of which is six miles ; and rifle-pits are prepared to receive the Prussians when they get under the big guns.   All crack shots are requested to apply for a pit.

This battery is manned by sailors, who look work-manlike all over, and were in those excited spirits which seem the normal state of sailors in difficulty and danger.   The guns command all the plain between St.-Denis and Paris, and can do fearful execution.

It was a terrible sight to see all those beautiful environs of Paris with no sign of life, and a great column of smoke showing the advance on the capital of the desolation of devastation. The wood of St.-Antoine was burning beneath us, and the people giggled and ate *galettes!* Never more shall I respect a Frenchman—or at least a citizen of Paris.

Coming back we saw an advance to the front, which looked like business. The 9th, 11th, 20th, and 25th regiments of the Line complete, and not having yet been in action, with three batteries of artillery and one battery of six mitrailleuses, marching to Charenton, where to-day or to-morrow there will probably be a fight. The men were in the wildest spirits. The mitrailleuses are like nine-pounder brass guns, with an organ handle attached to the breech. The muzzles are carefully covered up. I spoke to my next neighbour in the crowd, of course a National Guard, and to my surprise he began talking English. He had been a French professor at Sandhurst, and seemed to.be a good fellow.

We dined at Vachette's, and as we came back there was an *alerte*. The drums beat to arms, and the trumpets were " calling" in every street. The mob, which was as dense as the opera pit on a Jenny Lind night, from Vachette's to the Grand Hôtel, was terribly excited, and cried, " La Générale! La Générale!" The women were furious, and attacked all civilians with the cry, "Shame, shame! Get arms, get arms!"

It was a false alarm, but it proved to me that a republican army is most difficult to handle. Nobody dare confine "brother citizens" to barracks, and so when the " Générale" sounded to-night, the defending force was scattered all over Paris, and there was a perfect panic.

The alarm was false last night ; it may be true to-night.   The fright of the people intense.

Rentes closed 55,20.

The Thiers mission is thought to be " blague." He requires a month, and the Prussians may appear before Paris in twenty-four hours.

Five spies and their horses were captured yesterday. When they were taken to the Etat Major, in the Place Vendôme, I thought the mob would have seized them and lynched them on the spot.

Friday, September 16*th.*—Wrote to Baron Ferdinand de Lesseps, with enclosure. "Freedom of the press" is a great blessing, but, like other good things, it is apt to be abused. " Licence of the Press" can be good neither for individuals nor nations. But you cannot interfere with " brother citizens," and so we read the following in " Le Courrier Français":—

" A remarkable passage in the address of the German Section of the ' International' to the German working classes, is that which demands, in the name of justice, that Bonaparte, the criminal author of the war, be delivered up to the French Republic, which shall send him to the hulks, and so cause him to expiate his crimes."

But the following article is a still better sample of the effects of unrestricted freedom on a republican press :—

"To the Tyrant William.

" Tyrant, you are threatening a great people ; you are approaching a capital where the revolution will swallow you up, and you know it. You can triumph over the armies of Bonaparte, but not over the legions of the Republic. On your path you scatter mourning and desolation, misery and carnage. You fulfil your mission as Tyrant. We will appeal against you at the tribunal of humanity. We also follow out the work of destruction commenced in 1792. It is the destruction of kings. What can the five or six tyrants left in Europe do against a coalition of the armed people? You know this, and tremble under your mantle, red with human blood. You know this, and so, if we would give you millions of money, you would return to your palace and unchain the slaves which you lead to slaughter. We will tell you where to get this money. Those with whom you have concocted this war—that is to say, the Bonapartes and their accomplices—have palaces and possessions throughout Europe—money invested in England, Russia, and Italy. They have ruined France, and stowed the plunder in a safe place. Their wives and their mistresses have jewels, the value of which we well know. You also know of what a great and generous nation can be robbed when seized by the throat and strangled for nineteen years.

"Hunt, then, the Bonapartes and their accomplices like wild beasts; it is your right and your duty. They wished for war; let them pay for it. Seize upon them wherever you can find them. Force them to give up to Germany their plunder of France. We will not complain, and later the two nations will divide the spoil between them. You have got the chief Corsican, the Bonaparte of Strasbourg and Boulogne, the escaped prisoner of Ham, the assassin of the 2nd of December. Hold him fast,

and if his accomplices escape, threaten his life, and you
will find that they will rather consider their fortunes
than his life. Do this, but do not ask millions of a
freed people, who will finally defeat you, and chain
you living to some of the dead victims of your
carnage, so that you shall be food for ravens and birds
of prey."

This is a nice article to appear in a recognized paper
in a civilized city in the nineteenth century, and yet it
fairly represents the feelings of one district of Paris,
some of the army, and the whole city of Lyons ! We
live in strange times, and he who lives longest will see
most.

We went to-day to the Buttes de Chaumont, which
is in fact a public park, originated by the Emperor for
the benefit of the inhabitants of that squalid, over-
crowded quarter, Belleville. The park is now closed,
and a strong detachment of engineers is busy erecting
a fort, the guns for which are ready. Only the fort is
not, and the Prussians are at Vincennes ! Walking
to the Butte de Chaumont, which is in a direct line
with that Grand Opéra which will not be finished now,
we passed as it were out of the military zone. About
one mile of the Rue Lafayette is simply a great
bivouac—soldiers encamped on the pavement, and

being drilled in the street. Then, as you go on, they get more rare.

M. Jules Favre is a brave man: he has armed Belleville! Such ragamuffins and ruffians I have never seen, and if fighting does not take place directly, the lately served-out tabatières and chassepots will be used against any one with decent clothes and a means of living in the city.

There has been an actual affair of skirmishers and Uhlans beyond Vincennes to-day. The French lost a sergeant-major and his horse prisoner, and the Uhlans had one or two killed.

A French colonel, on his way from St.-Germain, said in the train that the Emperor had been betrayed, and that there was no French army except on paper. "Don't believe that we have an army 'là bas,' for we have not," said he. Among the few acquaintances remaining in Paris is M. Auber, who, at the age of eighty-eight, is the only cheerful person here. He must have seen so many revolutions that he is used to them.

Favre and Picard have no faith in Trochu as a general; they would like peace, but the people will not have it, and Bismarck says that there is not a responsible French government with which to make a treaty; nor does he know if the army and

France adhere to the self-made ministry of Paris. Another dead lock!

Saturday, September 17th.—My wife's birthday we have kept in odd places—in quiet English shooting-boxes, in Scotch lodges, on the dreamy shores of the Lago di Como, in full revolt at Naples; at Pisa, on our way from Aspromonte to the prison of Garibaldi, at Spezzia; for many years in the "Vanity Fair" of Baden, which we shall never see again, and now the day dawns on us in Paris, with an enemy without and an incipient counter-revolution within! "Les jours se passent et ne se ressemblent de tout," except in as far as they tell off another milestone on the road of life.

Yesterday the mob arrested Marshal Vaillant, Ministre de la Maison to the Emperor, and although he had a pass as Member of the Government of Defence from General Trochu, he was nearly torn to pieces as a Prussian spy.

I spoke to a man of Belleville yesterday: he looked at me as if he would have liked to lynch me, and then turned away. Lyons manners are spreading to Paris, and some of our acquaintances who are so fond of republics will be able to test their delight when they come here. However, I have always found the reddest of republicans and most supreme socialists more desirous of seeing their pet theories tested in any other country than their own.

Yesterday the fine equestrian statue of Napoleon III., which decorated the river face of the new Louvre, was removed. I wish I could think it was all patriotism, and not spite and hatred against the Emperor and Haussmann, which caused the present occupiers of power in Paris to destroy every vestige of ornament. But " Sic semper tyrannis"—they must be petty.

While I am writing, two thousand more Mobiles have just arrived from the provinces. I suppose they will fight. Vincennes is full of them, and the " regulars" hold Charenton, a fort which has especially attracted the attention of Moltke. I wish, in the interest of public safety, General Trochu, or some of his subalterns, would cure the Mobiles of the trick of pointing their chassepots, and then pretending to fire point blank on one another and on passing strangers. If they do it when they have cartridges, they may—quite by mistake, of course—"kill more than they can carry home," as poor Charlie —— said when he missed a partridge and killed a donkey on the other side of the hedge.

By the time we get a little picrate of potash and a

few bombs and shells, Paris will be, as Moore said of Ireland, " a charming place to live out of." It is now mined all round, and within it is one dépôt of petroleum.

Another republican alteration which I think all must regret—the Place Royale, the site of the old Palais des Tournelles—is again to change its name. An order in the "Journal Officiel de la République Française" restores to it the title of " Place des Vosges," which was bestowed on it in the year 8 of the Republic. It is the most historical monument in Paris. Here Charles VI. was nearly murdered at a masquerade, and Henri II. was killed in a tournay by De Montgomery, whose descendant kept race-horses, and ran in the Flying Dutchman's colours, when there was a "turf" in France. It was in the Place Royale too that Porthos, Athos, Aramis, and d'Artagnan fought, and so the title should have been kept up in honour of the great (literary) author of " Vingt Ans après." By-the-by, I have just heard that Dumas *père* is dying.

The Parisians will laugh, you know, even under the most trying circumstances. For the moment they have pounced upon King William's telegrams to his wife. (One who knows a little of the domestic history of that royal *ménage*, can hardly refrain from smiling at the ardent affection which is caused by distance and separation.) They are curious, certainly. Thackeray said that Byron used to swear by post: King William' telegraphs his thanksgivings to Heaven—

"Killedalloff. Friday.

"Heaven is merciful! I have killed forty thousand human beings—many of ours. What a blessing it is that neither I nor Fritz are hurt! Praise be to God, the French suffer terribly!

"WILHELM."

I have already told you that the Emperor was forced into the war. By the very important and historical document which I now copy, you will see that his Majesty made the same statement to Bismarck, who, be it said, seems to be "plus Grand Seigneur" than his royal master with fallen enemies, and where delicate feeling and expressions should be the order of the day.

This is the Count Bismarck's report on the capitulation of Sedan :—

"Donchery, Sept. 2.

"After I had repaired hither last evening by your Majesty's command, in order to take part in the negotiations as to the capitulation, they were interrupted till about 1 A.M. by the granting of time for consideration. This General Wimpffen begged for, after General Moltke had firmly declared that no condition other than a laying down of arms would be approved, and that the bombardment would be resumed at 9 A.M. if the capitulation were not previously concluded. Early this morning, towards ten o'clock, General Reille was announced to me, and he informed me that the Emperor wished to see me, and was already on his way from Sedan. The General immediately turned back in order to tell his Majesty that I was following him, and shortly afterwards, half-way between here and Sedan, in the vicinity of Frénois, I found myself opposite the Emperor. His Majesty was in an open carriage with three superior officers, and with a like number on horseback close by. Among the latter, Generals Castelnau, Reille, Moskowa—who appeared wounded in the foot, and Vaubert were personally known to me.

"Arrived at the carriage, I dismounted, stepped up immediately to the Emperor's side, and asked his Majesty's commands. The Emperor expressed a wish to see your Majesty, apparently thinking that your Majesty was at Donchery. After I had replied that your Majesty's head-quarters were at the moment three (German) miles distant, at Vendresse, the Emperor asked whether any place had been fixed in the locality whither he might repair, and, in fine, what my opinion was on the matter. I replied that I had come here when it was quite dark, the country being unknown to me, and placed at his disposal the house occupied by me at Donchery, which I would at once vacate. The Emperor accepted this, and proceeded towards Donchery, but halted about one hundred paces from the Meuse-bridge leading into the town, before a working man's house standing by itself, and asked whether he could not dismount there. I sent Count Bismarck Bohlen, who in the interim had followed me, to inspect the house, and after he had announced that its internal accommodation was very poor and narrow, but that it was free from wounded, the Emperor dismounted and directed me to follow him inside. Here, in a very small room, containing one table and two chairs, I had about an hour's conversation with the Emperor. His Majesty was extremely anxious to obtain more favourable terms of capitulation for the army. I declined to discuss this matter with his Majesty, when so purely military a question was pending between General Moltke and General Wimpffen. On the other hand, I asked the

Emperor whether his Majesty was inclined to nego-
tiate for peace. The Emperor replied that, as a prisoner, he was not now in a position to do so, and on
my further question, by whom, in his view, the
executive authority of France was at present represented, his Majesty referred me to the Government at
Paris.

"After the clearing up of this point, which from
the Emperor's letter of yesterday to your Majesty
could not be certainly judged of, I perceived, and did
not conceal this from the Emperor, that the situation,
to-day as yesterday, offered no other practical question
than the military one; and I signified the necessity
which therefore rested on us of obtaining before all
things, through the capitulation of Sedan, a material
pledge for the stability of the military results already
achieved. I had already, yesterday evening, considered the question on all sides with General Moltke,
whether it would be possible, without prejudice to
German interests, to offer more favourable conditions
than those laid down in deference to the military
feeling of honour of an army which had fought well.
After due consideration we had felt ourselves obliged
to settle this question in the negative. When, therefore, General Moltke, who meanwhile had come from
the town, went to your Majesty for the purpose of

laying before you the Emperor's wishes, this was not, as your Majesty knows, with the intention of supporting them.

"The Emperor then went out into the open air, and invited me to sit by him before the door of the house. His Majesty submitted to me the question whether it was not practicable to allow the French army to cross the Belgian frontier, in order that they might be disarmed and interned. I had already, the previous evening, conversed on this eventuality with General Moltke. As regarded the political situation, I on my side did not take the initiative, nor did the Emperor, except that he deplored the misfortune of war, and affirmed that he himself had not desired war, but had been forced into it by the pressure of public opinion in France.

"Through inquiries in the place, and especially through a search by officers of the general staff, it had meantime, between nine and ten o'clock, been ascertained that the Château of Bellevue, near Frénois, was suited to the reception of the Emperor, and, moreover, was not occupied by wounded. I mentioned this to his Majesty, fixing Frénois as the place which I should propose to your Majesty for the interview, and accordingly put it to the Emperor whether his Majesty would wish to proceed thither at once, as to remain within the small working man's cottage was inconvenient, and the Emperor would possibly require some rest. His Majesty gladly acquiesced, and I accompanied the Emperor—a guard of honour of your Majesty's body-cuirassier regiment preceding him—to the Château of Bellevue, where in the interim the Emperor's additional suite and equipages, the arrival of which out of the town had till then appeared uncertain, had come from Sedan. General Wimpffen also arrived, with whom, in expectation of the return of General Moltke, the discussion of the capitulation negotiations, broken off yesterday, was renewed by General Podbielsky, in the presence of Lieutenant-Colonel Verdy and General Wimpffen's chief of the staff, both which officers drew up the protocol. I only took part in them by sketching the political and legal situation according to the explanations given me by the Emperor himself.

" From Count Nostiz, commissioned by General Moltke, I received the announcement that your Majesty would see the Emperor only after the conclusion of the capitulation—an intimation on which the hope on the other side of obtaining other conditions than those laid down was given up. Upon this I rode off towards Donchery, with the intention

of informing your Majesty of the position of affairs,
but on the way I met General Moltke with the text of
the capitulation approved by your Majesty ; and this,
after we went with him to Frénois, was then accepted
and signed without dispute.   The conduct of General
Wimpffen, as also that of the other French generals
the previous night, was very becoming.   That brave
officer could not refrain from expressing to me his
great pain at being called on, forty-eight hours after
his arrival from Africa, and half a day after taking
the command, to subscribe his name to a capitulation
so deplorable for the French nation.   Want of provisions and munitions, however, and the absolute im-
possibility of any further defence, imposed on him as
a general the duty of restraining his personal feelings,
as further bloodshed could not alter the situation.
The concession of the release of the officers on their
word of honour was accepted with warm thanks, as
an expression of your Majesty's intention not to over-
step the limits which our political and military
interests made necessary with regard to the feelings
of an army which had fought bravely.   To this sentiment General Wimpffen afterwards gave expression in
a letter, in which he thanked General Moltke for the
very considerate manner in which the negotiations
were on his side conducted."

The saying here is, that Bismarck has thought of this campaign for years, but that it has been the waking and sleeping dream of the whole life of Moltke.

But where are the Prussians? At last I can answer the question. They are in force at Meaux, in the department of the Seine and Marne, twelve leagues north-west of Paris. Mallet of the Embassy has just come from there, where he has seen the King and Bismarck. Of course all was confidential; but I drew this conclusion, that nothing will stop the Prussian advance. Mallet says the troops look well, and like fighting. Bismarck offered Mallet his only horse, but he added, " In spite of the flag of truce, the French are apt to fire on our horses." Bismarck said, " If there is fighting in the streets, it will be all in favour of Prussia."

Colonel Claremont, also of the Embassy—a good judge—thinks they will summon Paris, and then fall to. On the first defeat of the French, Colonel Claremont said to me, " With generals like Failly you will have a series of defeats."

Had we had our way, Colonel Claremont, the Honourable Francis Lawley, and myself would have been on the Imperial Etat Major, and I suppose now prisoners. I was the first applicant—the day before war was actually proclaimed, and his Majesty said that if he took the military attachés he would take me. I wish he had; I should have liked to have paid what respect was possible to the fallen friend of England and the English, and shamed the yelping curs who hunt down an unsuccessful man. All ·the middle classes of Paris and London are not of the opinion of those English and French who are enjoying themselves in trampling on a fallen friend. Three days before Sedan I published a long defence of the Emperor in " Le Pays," and later a letter in the " Morning Post," and I have received scores of letters from England and here, expressing the sympathy of the writers with my views. The caricatures of the Emperor disgrace even a shop in a low street in the Quartier de Belleville.

Latest news is, that the Crown Prince is at La Ferrière—the château of Baron Alphonse de Rothschild.

I have just returned from the Tower of Solferino, a monument erected close to the Place de St.-Pierre, from which there is a splendid view of Aubervilliers, St.-Denis, and Pierrefitte. It was a lovely cloudless day, and the whole city—nasty enough in that quarter when near, but borrowing enchantment from distance —glittered in the sun. The sailors worked gaily at a fort; a long line of white tents glistened on the heights to our right; bugles were sounding, drums beating, and soldiers parading everywhere, while a large idle crowd formed a hedge round M. Nadar and his captive balloon. And yet the scene was depressing to an extreme degree. In whichever direction you turned your glass, you saw signs of the rapid advance of war—villages deserted, houses pulled down; the wretched inhabitants pouring into Paris, and last, not least, wood after wood from Paris to Pierrefitte smouldering away in deep smoke or burning briskly in the keen north wind.

The French themselves have done this in defence; but we hear that the Prussians have made a clean sweep of every province through which they have marched.

> " In crackling flames a thousand harvests burn—
>   A thousand villages to ashes turn !"

We fondly flattered ourselves that that kind of warfare had ceased with Anne and Marlborough.

Nadar could not perceive troops with a telescope from the balloon. Perhaps they are already in the woods !

Major Byng Hall, Queen's messenger, called to-day, and says that the route by Havre is dreadful—one hour lost at Rouen, two at Amiens, and then an "omnibus" train. He passes nearly all his life between Calais and Paris, and nobody pays him or thanks him. Our post goes by Havre, and is always twenty-four hours late.

There are more soldiers—no men—here to-day than ever. Some very fine fellows, well dressed, and evidently drilled ; others in rags and tatters, and with a very vague idea even of " shoulder arms." Some have a cap and a pair of gaiters ; others a bayonet, a blouse, and red braid epaulettes. Some have smart regimental trousers and a great-coat; some have chassepots, some tabatières, and some the oldest muzzle-loader. They *will* walk about with fixed bayonets, on which they put their bread, their shoes, their cummerbunds, and even their shirts. A strong body has gone off to Vincennes. A section of Francs-Tireurs have been put on guard at the British Embassy. The Americans are all displaying their flag. If we did so we should have our windows broken. The English are not popular.

Colonel Scipon Nickolai, escaped from Sedan, arrived at the Club last night. He says that whenever the French could get to close quarters with the Prussians they were more than a match for them, but that the Prussian artillery, which is magnificent, cut them to pieces. Twenty thousand men have escaped on their march from Sedan into Germany, and have reported themselves at French head-quarters at Paris, Lyons, &c. They will fight if they get a chance.

Bazaine is not in Metz, but surrounded by Prussians some distance from the city, which is defended by forts just like Paris. To-night they say Canrobert— he is quite capable of it—has cut his way out with six thousand men. I am very fond of the dear old marshal, and will salute him profoundly if I see him here.

Dr. Worms has been to London to pave the way for Thiers. He reports that the English—Lord Granville, Mr. Gladstone, &c.—spoke of France as a nation which existed no more. "They were polite, but seemed to think we were blotted out of the map of Europe."

Terribly dull evening; the ladies did not even pick oakum—I beg their pardon—make "Gitter charpie," that is, trellis lint (one of the best ideas I have come across), so we sat still and predicted immediate shells.

The Grand Hôtel has closed its billiard-room and bar, and so the last of the loafers must seek shelter elsewhere. They were very civil to our party, begging

us always to use the *salon*, but the Club of the Peri-
style is, I fear, dissolved.

Sunday, September 18*th.*—For a wonder it is a
gloomy day, but it is still very warm, and though we
have had one or two cool nights, the weather has not
been bad for soldiering; indeed, I have heard of no
illness among the three hundred thousand or three
hundred and fifty thousand regulars and irregulars in
and round Paris. The Prussians have, on the other
hand, suffered severely from heavy rains, which have
not reached here. What is much more serious for
them is, that the rinderpest has come up with some
cattle from Podolia, and one hundred and fifty oxen
had to be killed the day they arrived at head-quarters.
This, and sickness in the ranks, would be more deadly
than any mitrailleuse.

We have plenty of food here, though it is awfully
dear, as is everything else. In the people's districts
I see a large supply of horse-flesh in the butchers'
shops. It does not, I confess, look very tempting, but
many of the Garde Mobile look as if they could really
" eat a horse behind the saddle." Not only horse,
however, but mule is, I hear, good eating; the
"Alderman's walk" in a mule being the soft part
under the jaw. We have plenty to eat, and a deal

too much to drink, but we want discipline. Imagine, when a wild regiment of MacMahon's Zouaves arrived on Thursday at the Malesherbes barracks it was *consigné*. After an hour or two the men desired to be let out, as " they were dull, and had no drink." The officer, afraid, as a republican, to offend these very useful brother citizens, let them free to wander over Paris. French people tell me that under the late Republic all discipline ceased. Trochu has, however, now ordered all men to be in quarters at 10 P.M.

Their Excellencies the Prince de Metternich and Lord Lyons, with their staffs, went yesterday to Tours. This, especially after Mallet's mission, looks like an attack at once.

We have no news of the enemy to-day, but a very large body of troops have gone to the ramparts and to the outlying forts. Good news has been received from Bazaine's army : it came in a toy balloon, which was found by chance in a wood near Neufchateau. There were five hundred soldiers' letters in the case : they report no illness, good spirits, and plenty of food. As I have said, they are not in Metz. " Nous sommes toujours bloqués sous Metz," is the expression in one of these letters.

I heard a curious fact the other day. Between the forts of Issy (Sèvres) and Vanves (Meudon) there is a large empty house, which commands both. Asking to whom it belonged, we were told that some months ago a Prussian banker had examined it very carefully, and then bought it for a fancy price. He has never been there since; perhaps the banker is coming now!

When a Scotchman or a Prussian makes a joke it is the duty of all to laugh—it is so rare an event; more scarce than that eclipse which the lady at Brighton described as "annular, you know; once every year." So I beg you will all laugh at this specimen of "l'esprit Prussien," which appears in the "Gazette de la Croix":—

The Fall of the Empire.

The Empire *respire* (breathes)—May 8.
The Empire *aspire* (aspires)—July 14.
The Empire *tire* (fires)—Aug. 2.
The Empire *se retire* (retires)—Aug. 6.
The Empire *empire* (grows worse)—Aug. 14—31.
The Empire *expire* (expires)—Sept. 2.

People are very fond of asking, "How is history written?" and, "What is truth?" It is no wonder they put such questions. Look at the different accounts given of the Emperor by "eye-witnesses," who

saw him at the same moment. First we have the
" Times ":—

"Berlin, Sept. 8.—On the 5th of September, at
9·50 P.M., a special train stopped at the small station
of Wilhelmshöhe, near Cassel. It consisted of two
carriages, and contained about a dozen passengers.
After a few servants and inferior attendants had left
the train, a short, stout gentleman alighted. Slowly
walking to an equipage that had been waiting for
him, he seated himself in it with another gentleman,
and drove off. He wore the red trousers of a French
general, and a dark overcoat. His features were
placid, and as he looked about him, from calm, intelligent eyes, it was evident that he was an observer and a thinker to boot. His was one of those
faces which, while indicating habits of reticence, are
yet eloquent in the lines marking the inner work-
ings of the mind."

Then comes Herr Paul Lindau, with an awful pen-
and-ink sketch, which I copy from the " Daily Telegraph ":—

" Herr Paul Lindau, an eye-witness of Napoleon's
arrival at Wilhelmshöhe, describes his personal
appearance in an account from which I extract
the following: 'I drove along in my carriage

so close to that which took Napoleon and his two
aides-de-camp to Wilhelmshöhe, that, had I desired it,
I could have heard every word that was spoken; but
not one sentence broke the stillness of that sad group.
I have seen the Emperor hundreds of times in Paris.
I was in the Opera, and watched him closely, on the
evening of Orsini's attempt on his life. Every line of
his features is as familiar to me as those of my nearest
friend; yet I declare, with the greatest sincerity, that
when he arrived here I did not recognize him. Could
it be possible that the old shrunken man, who raised
his *képi* to acknowledge the salutations that greeted
him, was the same man who, as the Emperor of the
French, has responded to the 'Vive l'Empereurs' of
the Parisians? I am not sentimental, and my nerves
are of normal strength; but the shock that the con-
trast presented sent a shiver to my very heart. All
are familiar with the mode in which Napoleon's hair
was arranged: the crisp curl so carefully trained, and
the historical moustache with its waxed ends, that
gave to his countenance its distinguishing expression—
all that trim, soldierly air was gone. A few straggling
locks of grey hair were scattered in confusion over his
forehead, and his untended moustache drooped heavily
over his closed lips, betokening the despair that must
have reigned in his mind. Napoleon's physiognomy

is either no longer capable of expressing feeling—
which I believe—or it is capable of hiding its every
trace. He moved no muscle—not a line in his face
was stirred as he responded to the military salute.
As he turned from right to left no gleam of expression
passed across his features. His eyes had lost every
vestige of meaning; and he gazed on all, yet evidently
saw nothing. Such a full personification of total
apathy I have never seen: it was not a living
human face I beheld; it was a lifeless, vacant mask.
I could not withdraw my gaze from him; I could not
realize the possibility of the fact that the wreck before
me was the man whose voice was, but a few weeks
since, so potent throughout the world; that this—
this—was the wise and mighty Emperor!"

Then we have the following "special" account from
the "Daily Telegraph." If it be correct, then indeed
must his Majesty be much outwardly and visibly
changed since Friday, the 15th of July:—

"The Emperor . . . was dressed in full uniform of
a French general, with all his orders, though without
his sword, and with a military cap in lieu of the
cocked hat. His look was that of a man much worn,
but not in broken health. His increased corpulence,
his grey hair, his dark face and penetrating eyes, did
not escape the notice of those who were around him,

and with some of whom he conversed, principally in German."

Finally, a German correspondent sends the following to the "Globe":—

"When the train stopped the Emperor alighted, and passed in the front of the officers lining the station, while he uncovered his head and went to General Plonski's carriage, which conveyed him to Wilhelmshöhe, ten minutes' drive off. The Emperor looked earnest, but not broken down; and, as far as I may judge—I was standing five paces from his carriage—his countenance was quite different from that given by 'Kladderadatsch.' There were no signs of an extravagant 'embonpoint,' nor of that illness which he is said to be suffering from."

What is the truth? One gentleman who passed the night of September 3–4 with his Majesty, said he was "wonderfully well and very calm;" and this was confirmed by the Duc de Massa, who was taken at Sedan and is now in Paris; but he thought him shaken.

I must give you one more extract:—"In reply to certain statements which have appeared in the 'Patrie,' reflecting upon the conduct of the Emperor at Sedan, the following letter has been sent to the 'Indépendance Belge' by some of the officers of his Majesty's staff:—'The letter which appeared in the "Patric" of the 11th of September, attributed to an officer of General de Wimpffen's staff, implies with such great seriousness and injustice that the responsibility of the catastrophe at Sedan lies upon the Emperor, that those officers who have the honour to remain near his Majesty must be permitted to place the facts fairly before the public. When the different commanders of " corps d'armée " had informed the Emperor that their troops had been repulsed, dispersed, and in part hurled back in confusion into the town, the Emperor sent them to the commander-in-chief, that he might be made acquainted with the situation; at the same time the General sent to the Emperor two officers of his staff with a note, in which he proposed to his Majesty, not to save the army, but to save his person by placing him in the centre of a column, with which they said they would try to reach Carignan. 'The Emperor refused to sacrifice a further large number of soldiers to save himself; "and besides," he said, "Carignan is occupied by the Prussians; but if the General thinks he can save some part of the army, let him try it." At the same time as the answer of the Emperor reached the commander-in-chief, the latter was explaining to General Lebrun, commanding the 12th Corps, his project of collecting two or three thousand men and putting himself at their head to make an opening through the Prussian lines. General Lebrun replied, " You will lead three thousand men more to death, and you will not succeed; but if you wish to try it, I will go with you." They set out, in fact, and less than half an hour later General de Wimpffen was convinced that his attempt was not feasible, and that no other course remained save to lay down his arms. General de Wimpffen returned into Sedan, and, considering that it was a hardship for him, who had only taken the command *ad interim*, to sign a capitulation, he sent his resignation to the Emperor in the following words :—

" SIRE,—I shall never forget the proofs of kindness with which you have favoured me, and I should have been happy for your sake, as well as that of France, to have concluded this day with a glorious success. I have not been able to attain this result, and I think it well to leave to others the task of leading our armies. I believe in this state of things I should give in my resignation of the post of commander-in-chief, and ask for my discharge.

" I am, &c.,

" DE WIMPFFEN."

" ' The Emperor refused to accept it ; in fact, it was necessary that he who had had the honour of the command during the battle should secure, as far as possible, the safety of what remained of the army. The General comprehended these reasons, and withdrew his resignation ; it was then nine in the evening, and the fire had ceased at the fall of day. It is altogether false to say that the General was opposed by the Emperor in his plans and in his orders which he may have given, for his Majesty only met him for an instant on the field of battle, between nine and ten o'clock. The General was coming from Balan, and the Emperor asked how the battle was going at that side. The General replied, " Sire, things are going as well as possible, and we are gaining ground." To an observation made by his Majesty, that an officer had just warned him that a considerable body of the enemy was outflanking our left, the General replied, " Well ! so much the better ; we must let them do so ; we will throw them into the Meuse, and we shall gain the victory." These were the only words that the Emperor had with General de Wimpffen during the action, and it is equally false to say that there was the smallest altercation between the Emperor and the General, and when they parted the Emperor embraced the General with the greatest affection.

" ' The generals aides-de-camp to the Emperor—

> Prince DE LA MOSKOWA.
> CASTELNAU.
> DE WAUBERT.
> Count REILLE—Viscount PAJOL.' "

Do you know that there is a daily increasing idea that the Emperor may come back?   I do not believe it.   It would be odd if a prophecy which his imperial Highness Prince Napoleon made to me in 1868 should come true.   I don't say it will.   " We shall have a republic, then a socialist movement, which will upset it; then the Orleans, and finally France will come back to us."   The Prince has four children.

We hear nothing of the poor little Prince Imperial. What will be his career?   Do you remember the Duc de Reichstadt, and the epitaph he wrote for himself?   " Ci-gît le fils de Napoléon, né Roi de Rome, mort Colonel Autrichien."   The careers of the parents have many points of similarity—*absit omen!*   Poor boy! they say he was wonderfully intelligent, and used to ask such puzzling questions that he often " shut up " his pastors and masters, and once posed the Emperor on a question of Roman history.

Among the deaths reported are Vicomte de Beaumont, whose duel with the Prince de Metternich created such a sensation at Paris and Baden last year, and Fouqueville (of the Marines).

I have just heard of another short-coming in the French army. The Line aides-de-camp rode so badly that they never got safe with their orders. Masters of Fox Hounds will smile at this, and will talk at "Boodle's" of the saying of the Great Duke: "No aide-de-camp like a fox-hunter and a dandy." If a brave man struggling with difficulties is a sight for the gods, they must have enjoyed seeing a Liner on a bad hack in a hurry.

This is the twenty-first day that furniture and families have poured into Paris from the neighbourhood. Every family, if they have only a chair and a table, have several beds; indeed, in each household I should say there were at least "seven sleepers." The movers of furniture have made fortunes. They charge fifteen francs where they used to charge five. The wine-shop keepers, cheap restaurants, and proprietors of fiacres (in which the soldiers spend great sums) are the exceptions to the general ruin and stagnation of trade. Many shops are closing. No private carriages are to be seen, and the shooting season is postponed till 1871.

I have just seen Vicomte Paul Daru, who, Orleanist to the tips of his fingers, and so hating Jules

Favre and Co., yet firmly believes in the defence of Paris. Mr. Corbin, an American gentleman, and one of the oldest members of the Jockey Club, is still here, and I think dreams of peace. The line is cut between Paris and Havre.

More signs of the times. The mob caught M. Chevaudrier de Valdôme on his way to his country house, and nearly tore him to pieces. They stopped and wished to sack his luggage, and the party had to be rescued and escorted by twenty soldiers. This is freedom indeed! The ex-minister, whose brief career of office was perfectly harmless, has protested loudly against "a state of things which is a disgrace to any government of any shade of politics."

M. Blanqui seriously suggests that some forty thousand men who have been employed under the Empire should be shot!

Oh! sancta libertas! what a pity it is that you may have too much of a good thing.

Paris looks more like war than ever to-day. Here were men receiving uniforms, there marched a regiment in half marching order, and with spare shoes and bread. At one corner was a Cheap-Jack selling socks, and at the next cooking-cans were being served out. There were leave-takings on every side. Soldiers in the streets, soldiers on the pavement playing *écarté*.

Soldiers in the houses, soldiers by sixes in cabs, soldiers everywhere. Artillery in the Palais de l'Industrie; the horses and a large ambulance tent flanking the building on the left, and hundreds of men at drill on the right. All along the Boulevard de l'Alma and the ex-Avenue de l'Empereur, the whole 2nd of the Line and a strong force of artillery; add to that thousands of bullocks, and a mile or two of forage, and you may have some idea of Paris in that new and beautiful quarter at 6 P.M. this tranquil Sunday evening. All the chairs, for which so many *deux sous* were "perceived" by that industrious female, are removed from the Champs-Elysées, and the class of people lounging in little groups there to-day made you fancy you were at Villette or Montmartre.

The crowds in the Place de la Concorde round the highly adorned statue of Strasbourg (the nose of which a workman chipped off not many months ago because it was so like his wife) is denser every day. It is the head-quarters of drill and socialistic sub-scription.

I expect to be awakened to-night or to-morrow night by a real cry of "wolf," and to see the animal very near the gates.

M. Jules Favre has written a circular to the foreign representatives of the Republic, in which he admits that the " Government of Defence " is no government. He has therefore appointed the 2nd of October for the elections for the Constituant Assembly—which will later elect the Government. They would like an eight days' amnesty for the elections, but they will not get it ; and I think that they forget that during an amnesty they could not go on with the military works, while four hundred thousand idle soldiers would be drawing daily on their supplies. The number of representatives to be elected on the 2nd of October are—for eighty-nine departments, seven hundred and fifty-three ; for the colonies, eleven. Total, seven hundred and sixty-four; and they will all vote one way at first. It will be a worse majority than than that of the first Reform parliament in England. This election is a mistake, as it must be incomplete ; some of the provinces being in a state of siege, and others actually in the hands of the enemy.

Here is another decree, which is all fair in war time :—" The Government of the National Defence, considering that many of the inhabitants of Paris have left the capital, and been in that way exonerated from the charges incident to the siege, has imposed the following graduated tax, to commence from September 10, on the apartments so vacated. Those paying less than 600 fr. are exempt ; from 600 fr. to

1000 fr., 20 fr. per month ; 2000 fr., 60 fr. ; 3500 fr., 120 fr.; 6000 fr., 180 fr.; 10,000 fr., 240 fr.; 20,000 fr., 300 fr. ; and over, 500 fr." This tax is to cease on the day on which the siege shall be raised.

Monday, September 19th.—One day at the beginning of August there was in this room, where I am writing, a kind of consultation of English amateurs, who were desirous of getting to the front. I was regretting the refusal which I had met with, when one of the party said, " If you stay in Paris, I believe you will be at the front before any of us." Really it looked like it this morning. No noise of drums or trumpets awoke us, and when I got up at 8·30, and looked out on the Boulevard Haussmann, which for days has been a bivouac by night and a drill ground by day, there was not a soldier visible. All were in the forts or fortifications, and a few regiments, weary and dusty, got back about 10 A.M.

Our state to-day is this : the enemy is close to Paris—at Joinville (Vincennes) on the east, at Vitry on the south-south-east, and at Meudon and Bièvre on the south-south-west; skirmishing going on every-where, and a heavy firing (and a reported serious fight) in the rear of Mont Valérien. These are the facts ; we shall have plenty of *canards*.

To-day the Mobiles were to have elected their officers. Imagine it! and the enemy at the gates! Yesterday a regiment of National Guards insisted on their commanding officer crying out "Vive la République!" but General Ambert declined to do so, or to recognize this Government. Then one of his officers arrested him and his aide-de-camp, and handed them over to the authorities, who have to-day dismissed the General from the service : thus the army of Paris loses another old soldier. It could better have spared a National Guard whom I saw yesterday: he was a dwarf, exactly the height of my umbrella (one yard—this is a fact), and fearfully deformed. He was in full uniform. War makes us acquainted with strange spectacles, and this was one of them.

A prisoner just gone by; the people furious. I was reminded of Macaulay's description of the capture of Judge Jeffreys. The scowl on the face of a Paris mob is demoniacal. Two French soldiers, deserters, were also brought in. Heard the first heavy guns at 12·30 P.M.

At the "Meeting" Blanqui requires that all property of Bonapartists and absentees shall be confiscated. As he and his will soon be in power, I dare say that that idea will become law.

This is the tenth anniversary of the battle of the

Volturno, when Charteris, St.-Maur, Stuart Wortley, parson (naval) Alexander Allen (colonel of Marines), F. Hewetts, and ourselves spent the day in the amphi-theatre of Santa Maria, near Caserta. By-the-way, I hear from good authority (republican) that the republicans in Rome are determined to resist the King and oppose "a bastard union like that of Naples." This from Professor Ranzi of the Historical Institute of France—a Roman, a Mazzinian, and now employed in the French Home Office.

At 6·30 P.M., another prisoner, a Prussian field-officer, was brought in amidst roars of opprobrium. Semaphores are erected on all the highest buildings in Paris. Wire communication is *nil*.

The Defence Government has done a sensible thing in voting twenty-four thousand pounds for the con-struction of improved mitrailleuses; but it is, I fear, too late, unless indeed they do really intend to burn Paris and fight at Lyons. They are behindhand with everything. I was to-day again at the Avenue de l'Impératrice and the Porte Maillot fortifications, and found little advancement in the works and no more guns in position. Strings of furniture, forage, and a long line of carts full of old muskets found in some forts were pouring in, but the actual works are unfinished, and the enemy at Meudon. A long string of gunners with their horses, but no guns, passed us at a gallop shouting " A bas les Prussiens !" and that was the most warlike sight we saw.

Barricades are to be erected at once : this is done to keep Belleville quiet. The " Bellevillageois" are in a wonderfully excited state ; evidently arming and plotting to upset the existing Republic, and what is to happen then Heaven only knows ! A row is predicted to-night, but then predicted rows never come off. However, nothing can be more grave than the situation. The arrival of Prince Czartoryski and of Dr. Campbell (the Dr. Locock of Paris) is reported : the latter is said to be the bearer of despatches to the Government. Can he be happily going to safely deliver Paris ?

The English Embassy is left in charge of Colonel Claremont and the Hon. Henry Wodehouse. The British flag is hoisted, and " Ambassade d'Angleterre" is placarded so that those who run may read and respect.

Two Americans tried to get away to-day. They hired a carriage and drove to Suresnes. Just as they had passed it the bridge was blown up. A few miles further they were eating their breakfast, when a dish which they had not ordered was served up hot. It was " pont sauté à la poudre de canon." Then the driver put to his horses, bolted for Paris, and left "our cousins" somewhere in the Seine et Oise.

Mr. Blount, the well-known banker of the Rue de la Paix, a resident of forty years, has sent the following letter to a friend:—

"My dear Sir—If I have not written to you before, the reason has been that I feel it totally impossible to convey to anybody the state we are in here. The past seems like a frightful dream; the present is, without personal observation, impossible to describe. To-day we have a grand review of at least a hundred and fifty thousand men, if not two hundred thousand, the greatest portion Garde Nationale of Paris and Garde Mobile of the provinces. The former are well clothed, well armed, and look in famous order and spirits. The latter are admirable. Exercised in ten days, they have learnt their trade, and are far superior in appearance to the regular troops that left to meet the Prussians. They are well behaved, quiet, no drunkenness. The churches were full of them on Sunday; and I had twelve of them in my house for the last eight days, and I never saw a more respectable corps. They are now all armed and disciplined. They have the spirit of obedience, which the army lacked completely. Can they defend Paris? I believe they can for some time to come—and that the Prussians will find them tougher to deal with than what they have met with as yet.

" Negotiations are going on for peace, but, remember what I say, the French will not accept dishonourable conditions. I mean by 'dishonourable,' cession of territory or ships. They would rather fight to the end, and when Paris is lost, retreat to the last fortress left in France. They would pay money, as public opinion acknowledges the last Government began an unjust war, but more than this neither the Government now constituted nor any other could make this people accept. Indeed, no peace would be lasting if France cedes territory; for no time would make either the present generation or the future accept the cession. It would be eternal war. The ' Times' writes the contrary; but I have been forty years in this country, and know the people better than the ' Times ' or the French people themselves. I have in general no overweening confidence in my own opinion, but from the beginning of this war my anticipations have always been realized, and you may be sure that what I say above will turn out as I tell you.

" Now, what is doing about peace? I believe that the

foreign ambassadors are doing all they can. Our ambassador, Lord Lyons, knowing, as I do, the qualities which adorn his character, must be using every effort to stop more useless bloodshed, ruin, and devastation; but what is our Government doing? Has the Queen written to the King of Prussia? What is Lord Granville doing? Does he think that the majority of the English nation will ever pardon a government which shows culpable apathy at such a moment? You may be sure that a continuation of this war is fraught with danger to every constituted government in Europe, and to none more than to our own. Has France for the last twenty years ever been false to England, and will she ever pardon those who abandon her in her direst moment? Let Mr. Gladstone ponder on this. Starring in the provinces is necessary for singers and actors, but is it worthy of a Prime Minister at such a moment? Pray pardon me if I pour out my indignation upon you. I owe something to this generous and valiant nation, and if a forty years' residence in the country can give any weight to my words, it will be but a poor return."

There has been a fight to-day (Sept. 19th). It took place in rear of the fort of Vanves, which is between the fort of Issy on its right and Montrouge on its left.   It began at 6·30 A.M., and went on till 3·30 P.M. I am inclined to believe that this is the time from the march out till the fall back.   A corps of Mobiles was sent to occupy the wood of Clamart and the outlying covert of Meudon.   They soon found that the Prussians were in force in the Forest of Meudon (which was to have been burnt), and while still out of their chassepot range they peppered the Mobiles with their mitrailleuses and artillery.   Then they came to closer quarters, and the Mobiles held their own for a time.   Then the Prussians, reinforced, came on in force, got as usual on three sides of the enemy, and then I fear there was a regular "sauve qui peut" to the fort of Vanves.   Some thirty wounded were brought into Paris.

This is the verbatim account of one Mobile backed by several others, who were all in the action.   It is a bad beginning, but what we must expect at first.   It is young soldiers who have never fired a shot in earnest, *versus* the best drilled men in Europe delirious with victory !

Later—10 P.M.—The Baron de Billing has just come from the Club, and brings the worst account. It seems that the fight was of larger proportions than my Mobile imagined, several regiments of the Line and Zouaves being engaged.   And here comes the awful story—a story which sent one old officer back to his family exclaiming—" What have I done that I should live to see this day!" and caused many a soldier to shed tears.

"You have heard it already," said M. de M——, who had just left the field as he got off his charger at the Rue Royale Club. "You know it, of course," and the tears stood in his eyes. Then he poured forth his tale of woe.

The 76th of the Line and the Zouaves were in the front, and advancing towards the wood, when they were received with shot and shell. The 76th said that they were unsupported by artillery, and when the first shell burst among them they coolly faced about in spite of their officers, and marched off the field. The Zouaves stood fire a short time, and then bolted off to Paris. Mr. Hutton, an American gentleman, and two friends were nearly pulled to pieces in trying to stop their retreat.

The truth is, there is no discipline whatever: it has been sick a long time, but expired on the 4th of September. The present Government dare refuse the citizens nothing, and they choose their own officers. The officer who succeeded General Ambert (who was one of the most respected men in France, and who was dreadfully ill-treated yesterday) is a man returned from transportation, and he led his men into this mess to-day.

Yesterday also they withdrew a command from a friend of mine, a superb artillery officer—because the men of his corps would not serve under an ex-senator. "Give the command to whom you like, and I will serve as a gunner," said the senator. "Well," replied Trochu, "*perhaps* the men will not object to that." The fact is, the Government of Defence rules France, and the Socialists rule the Government of Defence.

Through a good glass you could see that active fighting was going on, and that blazing villages were illustrating the sad history of to-day. The only good news is that the forts are manned by sailors, who will fight like the gentleman who is not so black as he is painted. The fort of Mont Valérien made some excellent practice from its north front to-day, and ploughed up some heavy masses of Prussian infantry.

Then a word more of bad news. It is said at the Club that poor little Roy, who used to ride steeple-chases, and whom all our lot in the "shires" will remember at Melton and Grantham, was killed yester-day at Meudon. I trust it is not true: if it is not I will read him this entry.

The great fight to-day, and perhaps to-night, is to

get the position of Châtillon. If held by them, the Prussians can knock the Faubourg St.-Germain (including their own Embassy) to pieces. " You will see the scene of the cathedral of Strasbourg reproduced on the dome of the Invalides," said a Frenchman just this moment.

I fear that the official report confirms the statement of the officer rather than that of the Mobile, and that it was a disgraceful as well as serious retreat. " The Zouaves," says the " Electeur Libre," " have now to wipe out a stain more disgraceful than any defeat." I hope that many Moblots are not like one which we encountered last night. He said he left the field after firing away all his cartridges, and there being no more to be had. His rifle had never been fired, and his *giberne* was full of cartridges.

This is an extract from the report published by M. Gambetta. After describing the action much as I have already done, he states that early in the day the French were forced to retreat on Châtillon, and says that " a portion of the right wing effected its retreat with deplorable precipitation" (*i.e.*, bolted in a panic). At 4 P.M. General Ducrot " found it necessary to retreat under shelter of the forts. Having secured an open route to Paris for the horses and ammunition of the eight guns in position in the redoubt of Châ- ·

tillon, he caused the guns to be spiked before his eyes, marched, last man, out of the redoubt, and retired to the fort of Vanves. The General sustained his reputation. The artillery behaved admirably, and fired twenty-five thousand rounds, causing great loss to the enemy. The National Guard stood their baptism of fire staunchly. Orders are issued to the troops to concentrate themselves in Paris."

In another address Gambetta speaks of the deserters before the enemy, and says that a court-martial is assembled to try them. They must break up the 76th and Zouaves if what I hear is true. The " Electeur Libre" says that Ducrot had forty-five thousand men, and put his loss at four hundred wounded and a few killed; that of the enemy at six thousand killed and wounded (a grain of salt to be taken with this).

It strikes me it was a bad beginning to the Paris campaign, and unluckily officers, men, and Belleville are of the same opinion.

Rentes, 54,25. No business.

Tuesday, September 20th.—No papers or letters from London since Friday, but our friend Captain Johnson, the Queen's messenger, got through gallantly with despatches, being stopped by the Prussians, who, though no respecter of persons, were obliged to respect this resolute person. But on the way he was arrested as a spy both by Prussians and French.

The news of to-day is short, but makes up in unpleasant importance for its brevity :—"The Prussians occupy St.-Cloud : the bridge is blown up."

I think no minister has had to make a more humiliating statement since Clarendon was forced to acknowledge that the Dutch fleet was in the Thames, burning the British ships of war. One paper declares that there is " nothing to prevent the enemy crossing the Seine ;" and if that is, as I fear, the case, and the Prussians once get into the Bois de Boulogne, I assert, on the evidence of my eyes at 6 P.M. yesterday, that there is nothing to prevent their marching straight into Paris without firing a shot. There is no discipline, no organization, no energy, and " Ah, troppo tardi" should be inscribed on the banners of the " République Française."

Here is another true story. On Sunday the Garde Nationale à Cheval paraded for drill. The colonel was pleased, and said, " Very good. Now we will cross the bridge, and see if the enemy are in sight." With a few exceptions the corps refused to go out of Paris. Also a few days since there was a question of crossing a bridge near the enemy, when twelve men alone out of a regiment of Mobiles followed their officers.

I have just returned from Montrouge, the suburb of Paris which leads by the Boulevard to the Porte d'Orléans, and which was once celebrated for two very different things—its eating, drinking, and dancing *guinguettes* (Le Jardin de Paris being the Willis's Rooms of the whole suburb), and the guillotine of the Barrière d'Arcueil. At present it is, or was, a thriving quarter, with a railway station of the "Round-about line," a fine boulevard, and a bran new church with a tall spire and Lombard galleries. It is forty minutes' journey from St.-Lazare.

We went down by the train, travelling third class on the roof, to see what we could see. Indeed, we are now all "sister Annes" every day, and truly we see clouds of dust. It was interesting as soon as we were clear of the city and could see the fortifications, inside which we travelled for some miles. There was a certain degree of activity in the works, but, as I think, not enough, and the authorities either cannot get workmen or they do not understand employing strong gangs and finishing off one operation at a time.

There were plenty of materials—stone ready to hand for the strong works, heaps of sandbags, and stacks of fascines—but the men were wanting on the very day when every soldier not under fire should have been armed with a spade. This south-south-western side, too, is not strong in guns—but then the forts of Issy, Vanves, and Montrouge defend it. The guns are, I think, chiefly mounted at the St.-Denis, Villette, and Vincennes gates. The country under the walls from Auteuil to Montrouge should be admirable for the artillery of the defence. Now and again you pass a strong point where extra pains are being taken—pains and labour that should be devoted to the weak place.

We passed the "shady blest retreat" of Rossini at Passy. There was the house as quiet as ever, and the well-kept garden smiling in the sunshine, just as it did on the peaceful Sundays when the "Swan of Pesaro," as he was affectionately called by Italians—the greatest professor I have ever known of the art of "Il dolce far niente"—used to receive his friends. One hundred yards further frowned a very stern angle of the bastion, and that was being strengthened. I must state, however, that men were drilling in every shel- tered spot, and trains of waggons laden with supplies stopped the road as we steamed above them. Crossing the Seine at Point du Jour, near Grenelle, we found a new battery on each side of the river, the troops at drill, and their shelter-tents in old chalk pits. The great *pensionnal* of the Jesuits carries the red cross of an ambulance—trust them for safety. The manufactories are barracks, and the gardens, the pride of their recent possessors, food for cattle.

When we reached Montrouge we found it like a fair. Half the shops were shut, and the remaining half, which sell wine! absinthe!! brandy!!!! doing literally a roaring trade, for I have never heard such a noise : it drowned the mitrailleuses. Considering that we have a "levée en masse," it is curious how many able-bodied men escape military service, so of course there were a few loafers in the Rue Papillon and on the Boulevard d'Orléans ; but excepting these, every man was armed after a fashion ; while — always a saving clause in the difficulty of a nation—the children played at soldiers to the war cry of " Vive la France! " "à bas la Prusse !"

Every old woman was dressed in her best, and sat on a bench in the boulevard, talking war with contemporary old men who remember (as one observed) " ces Prussiens" here before ; while the generation who will next fight these hereditary foes were eating *galettes* and playing in the dust at their feet. Regiments marching up " to concentrate in Paris" (it is rather like the wild boar turning in his lair), advanced from every side ; some Liners, whose uniform told tales of Sedan ; many Gardes Nationales and Mobiles, bright and clean in all the bravery of just served out clothing. Long strings of artillery horses and empty *caissons*, returning from leaving their guns and ammunition on the fortifications. Now two artillery-men, hot, dusty, and loaded with every impediment *plus* two despatch bags, galloped past from head-quarters to the Etat Major at Montrouge. Then a field officer in a hurry, utterly distancing his two orderlies, cantered his weary cripple to the chief in command—the poor beast was an evident stranger to oats. Country carts with forage going one way, tumbrils full of cartridges going the other, and on each side of the road half-drunken soldiers singing out "between two wines" their desire to die for their country. If all I hear is true, they were in no such hurry for " death or glory" yesterday. It **was not** *one* regiment of the Line, but three that followed the **Zouaves** in their disgraceful flight from a fight which up to their " rapid act" was bloodless.

As it happens I can give you General Ducrot's own opinion of the fight of Châtillon :—" We were beaten yesterday on the heights of Meudon because all the old soldiers ran away at the first shot. The Mobiles are better, they did stand firm a short time.   As for regular soldiers, France now has none."

We went to the Porte d'Orléans.   Like other defences, it will be strong, but is not finished ; another stable door to shut upon the Prussian horse.   All this time the day was bringing

"Battle's magnificently stern array."

They were fighting all along the line from Meudon to Bellevue.   I was assured that the battle was under the walls, but I heard no guns.   There was certainly an awful noise at hand, and from no vantage point which I could reach could I see troops *en masse.*   I searched the country with a very good glass, and I believe I did see a division of Prussians entering the Bois de Sèvres.   I tried to pass the lines, but not having as yet General Trochu's military pass, I was refused. . The observation of one of the officers amused me :—"It is not amusing either.   Shells bursting, needle-guns knocking off the legs, and that forgotten-of-heaven mitrailleuse raining balls all over."

Every now and then a faint sound told the practised ear that the great game was being played.

Then we strolled up the street towards the new church.   There I saw a sight such as can only be sed in times of actual war. The yard round the church was like everything else—now open to the people. Outside were standing a white ambulance full of wounded ; a hearse—to use the horrid *argot* of the driver—" waiting till it was time to take up ;" and a waggon round which Regulars, Zouaves, and Mobiles were fighting for casks of beer. Two boys were wrestling in the street, and an old woman selling " La Patrie en danger, deux sous !" Inside the court, with their backs to the walls of the sacred building, a party of Mobiles were celebrating a high mass to Ceres and Bacchus, by consuming bread and wine. Some were sleeping, others singing and smoking, but the most striking party was one which, with intense and pallid eagerness, and with oaths such as can only be heard in a Paris *tripot,* was playing at " pitch and toss" till the *rappel* should sound and send it off to " manslaughter," for which I suppose it was equally ready.

Just as the drinking, singing, gambling, and swearing were at their height, the door opened, and the little white coffin of a very young girl, followed by a small procession of children, was carried by a man of the Pompes Funèbres across the court. At that moment there was a mob, and a cry of " Prussien I Prussien !" I looked across the street, and there was a fine-looking young man, about twenty-five years old —a good specimen of a German officer—disguised as a working man. He was in the hands of four of the National Guard, and was showing such fight that more than once he nearly got away from his guard; luckily he did not, for if his escort had not shot him the people would have torn him to pieces on the spot. A well-dressed woman rushed by, pushing me out of her way. "Let me pass," she said with a perfect feminine fierceness. "He is a Prussian! A Prussian I tell you! Let me get up to see him." One elderly man, who should have known better, thrust his face into that of the prisoner, who, I rejoice to say, "got home with his left" to the visible damage of the inquisitive individual's beauty. Then that episode ended.

I have deep sympathy for all prisoners of war. I little thought I should have such tender respect for the next that was taken.

My wife and myself were strolling away towards the station, talking, in English mixed with a language of our own, about the sight we had just seen, which is one by no means the least of the horrors of war, as the "spy" is generally the victim of enthusiasm or reckless courage, when an important little man in full National Guard uniform—that is to say, a wide-awake with a tricolour cockade, a brown great-coat, red stripe down the trousers, a " Brown Bess," and a most ferocious, bloodthirsty bayonet—came up and said :—" Monsieur must come with me to head-quarters over the way." I replied, " Anything to oblige a National Guard; but is it permitted to ask why ?" " Monsieur will know !" said my hero sternly; and then, with a guard with fixed bayonets on each side, we proceeded into the presence of the officer in command of the district. He was a fat general with a staff of about twenty officers, mostly fat also, two of whom spoke English after a fashion, and the rest only understood French. They were all in full uniform, and looked fine, if not imposing. It was a droll scene. Somebody at once offered my wife a chair, and she sat down, looking so amused that I dare not look at her for fear of breaking out into indecent laughter. I said, " I am an English resident in Paris; here is my passport."

" What's the matter with you ?" asked a military secretary, rather surprised at the sudden announcement of my country and my residence—" and what do you want ?" " Not much the matter," said I, " only the military gentleman in the brown paletot has been good enough to arrest me, and I suppose he knows why. I don't."

Then my accuser came forth! Lucius Junius Brutus could not have denounced a traitor in grander tones, or in a more patriotic and striking manner (allowance being made for his dress and stature). With one hand resting on the muzzle of his musket, and the other free for action, he spoke as follows :—"Citizens! I have caused this person to be arrested" (he had done it himself) "because he has been for three hours on the ramparts, sometimes alone, sometimes with that other person in the chair!"

"Stop, my dear citizen!" I said. "You are a bad judge of time. It is now five o'clock. I left Paris at three o'clock, and we were an hour coming down, so how could I have been three hours on your ramparts?"

"But," interrupted a full (judging from his size a very full) colonel, "what business had you there so late?"

"None, as I well know; and so not wishing to be shot, I never, though I have a very good 'pass,' tried to go there."

"Humph!" (Accuser, looking smaller and less important, comes to "attention.")

"Your papers!" says military secretary No. 2. (Accuser "grounds arms" and smiles.)

"Here is my passport."

"Cré nom d'un chien ! it is very old. Ten years !" (Accuser shakes his head.)

"Seventeen I think," I said, and showed Earl Clarendon's well-known signature ; but my citizens did not seem to think much of it.

I then put in a private letter of the Prefect of Police. "This looks better," says another officer ; and then the thirty all talked together like a Greek chorus.

This will give you some idea of the Babel : Solo—"Monsieur has no business here" (a bow from the "spy"). "Monsieur has no arms and no glass ?" (a shake of the head of the Prussian prisoner). Then a "trio"—

1st colonel—"Monsieur has the Legion of Honour !" (Bow.)

2nd colonel—"Monsieur has the Turkish Order." (Bow.)

3rd lieut.-colonel—"Monsieur has the Cross of Savoy." (Bow.)

Colonels look benignant ; others stern and determined to do their duty—drum-heads, blindfolded eyes, and a letter to your grandmother.

"Sir ! You say you live in Paris ! Where ?"

" 1000 Rue Quatre-Septembre !"

" We don't know it !"

" But I do."

" Monsieur must remain till we send to Paris to assure ourselves of the fact." (Accuser "shoulders arms," and grins with delight: he has deserved well of his country !)

" Very good, but do me the favour to be as quick as you can, as I am going out to dinner. I can't dine at home because my dining-room is full of Mobiles and their beds, which interferes with our British hospitality, of which you have heard."

I fear that the fat commander began to think I was *intriguéing* him, for he got very red. The rest seemed as if they did not know what to do. Presently I thought of my card-case. " Here is my card, and the printed address"—and lo! what neither prefect nor passport could do was effected by that small visiting card. It was handed round like a curiosity, and then the military secretary, raising his cap, said—

" Monsieur et Madame sont libres ;" then I, knowing how the French like claptrap, turned at the door and said—

" Messieurs ! I love France, and hate Prussia. If I can serve France in any way, the Minister of Foreign Affairs has my address. Vive la France !"

They received this speech " avec effusion." All

rose and uncovered. I bowed, covered, and left the head-quarters, to the utter disgust of the mob, who had their "à bas les Prussiens!" all ready.

On our road home we saw a great fire in, as we thought, the Bois (it was near Sèvres), but when we went at night to the Avenue Ulrich—late Avenue de l'Impératrice—we saw no signs of it.

A party of Mobiles were encamped in one of the pretty flower beds by the fountains at the Rond Point, had burnt the shrubs for firing, and had trampled the whole to dust! Poor Haussmann!

A speech in the train:—"What place is this?" "Auteuil, where that gross hog Pierre lived."

"Galignani," "that blessed piratical print," has ceased to appear, and the Paris papers are only half their usual size! No communication with London for four days.

Rentes, 54,60.

Wednesday, September 21st.—At 5 A.M. we were all awakened from the sleep of the good and tired by a dreadful drum beating "to arms," which produced at the windows a plentiful crop of gentlemen in odd garments, and old ladies in their night-rails, and those horrible *foulards* bound round their ancient heads. It was nothing; only an *alerte.*

Jules Favre returned last night from Ferrière, Rothschild's place near Meaux, where he went to see the King, and did see the King's king. We are to have full particulars to-morrow; so to-day suffice it to say that the terms of possible peace were so hard that Favre returned, held a council of war, which published a dauntless document declaring that they will fight to their last man, and will not "yield an inch of their territory nor a stone of their fortresses." I knew the terms three weeks ago, and so did the Duc de Grammont, but now they are a little more severe.

So it is evidently war to the knife—guerre à outrance! I believe the volunteer army of Paris will fight as well and as savagely as it knows how, but, alas! fighting against a victorious army is desperate work. My great hope is in the forts—if they have not "forgotten to send the guns, which ought to have been here yesterday," as happened at the important position of Châtillon. These forts are seventeen in number, and present ninety-three fronts. Their cross fire is supposed—we shall soon see—to be most effective.

In Paris to-day there are four hundred and eighty thousand armed men.

. It is curious how little is known in Paris of the skirmishes which are going on within ear-shot all day. It is true that getting outside the gates is impossible, and the sentries keep watch so strictly that their own soldiers are often turned back. This is excused by the fact that the spies come dressed as Zouaves and Liners, and only on Monday the Prussians seized a lot of French uniforms at St.-Cloud.

Fighting was going on from 5 to 6 P.M. to-day. The fort known as the Couronne du Nord, to the north of St.-Denis, kept up a steady fire of big guns, the enemy evidently being in force in the woods in rear of the battery. I dared not use my glass, so could not get at any idea of their strength. It was a strange and interesting hour. We were sitting among some score of groups of idlers (nobody in Paris now does anything) at the foot of the old Roman Mons Martis, the summit of which is crowned to-day with a new style of Temple of Mars in the shape of a strong battery, while on every side were companies of Belleville volunteers in all stages of drill, from "goose step" to "ready—present— fire!" Every three or four minutes the "Crown of the North" sent forth its thunder, and a faint rattle of rifles was wafted to us in a distant chorus. It was a lovely day—it always is—and a splendid view towards the two Prussian positions of Pierrefitte and Dugny; but there were blots in the picture—deserted villages, ruined houses, and burning woods.

I must give you one or two incidents of the affair of Châtillon. A French orderly while receiving orders had his horse cut in two, and escaped unhurt—only got up looking rather "out of time." An English volunteer *éclaireur*, while carrying orders to the general, had his horse's head carried off clean by a round shot: he himself got off with a shake and a few bruises. It is said to be Sir Culling Eardley.

To prove the hatred of the natives to the Prussians, I must tell you that a boy aged fifteen caught a Prussian soldier in a lone spot, knocked him down, then killed him with his own rifle, and despoiled him. The boy was reported to the Governor of Paris, who authorized him to keep his spoil. His name is Gabriel Vinety, 18, Rue des Vosges.

I was nearly arrested again yesterday, in consequence of information laid by a little wine-shop keeper close to the market in the Place de la Madeleine. I saw him looking; then he spoke to a soldier; then he got an officer of the National Guard, and they followed me, escorted by some twenty *gamins*, to my own door. I took no notice, but they examined the concierge, who pointed to the flag which braved the battle and the breeze for so long a period, and so my wine-seller and bibber went home, looking like a greater fool than Nature had made him. It is a bore! But they arrested Trochu the other day.

There is a French proverb about the propriety of washing your dirty linen at home, which this Government does not seem to regard. The authorities have found and seized the whole of the private correspondence of the Emperor and Empress. It is very voluminous and confidential, and ten thousand persons compromised are mentioned by name. It is all to be published by M. Barthélemi Haureau, Chief of the National Printing Office. The first volume is to contain the details of the late Duc de Morny's dealings in Mexican bonds, and the correspondence of the Emperor with Margaret Bellenger.

I dare say that the private correspondence of Napoleon III. will no more stand the test of publicity than would that of many men leading professedly strict lives. But why give the chance? I once heard Sir H—— M——, who has been well called the Bassompierre of his day, asked how it was he had never got into trouble about his liaisons, and he said, as if speaking of some extremely virtuous act, "I never write to them, and never keep their letters."

The publication will only produce gross and useless scandal.

Poor Emperor! To-day he is accused of giving information to the Prussians; of having uttered forged notes, and of being "as tyrannical as he was cowardly." Hit him hard! he has no friends: only don't go too far, for fear of reaction!

I confess I was rather astonished to read the following notice in the "Constitutionnel:" — "As material for the history of the last days of the Second Empire, we give you the recollections of Blanqui concerning the affair of Villette, in which he was rightly considered to be concerned, and those papers which attributed the affair to Prussian agents were deceived, or lied knowingly. It was not Prussia, but the citizen Granger who supplied the money; his whole fortune, without reserving a centime—seven hundred and twenty pounds.

"Eudes, condemned to death by the Council of War, is now elected chef de battalion of the National Guard, Faubourg St.-Antoine, and his fellow-citizens chose him solely on account of the affair of Villette. At Montmartre, Blanqui has been elected to the same rank by acclamation. These men wished to do this on the 14th of August. They made a mistake no doubt, but in such grave affairs men must

not make mistakes. The 14th was too late or too
soon.

" M. Blanqui's excuse is, that he acted under the
effect of the surprise caused by the startling news
from Alsace; but when men are concerned in serious
politics they must not allow themselves to be taken
by surprise. But, after all, a man is not sold to
Prussia because he was delayed against his will, and
chose his time badly. The chief authors of the attack
of Villette were Blanqui, Eudes, Granger, Carta,
Piènes, ex-representative of the people, and Flotte,
who had just arrived from California; Tridon, who
was ill, was not able to be on the ground."

It will be remembered that this was a cold-blooded
attack on some innocent fireman, in which one or
two lives were lost, including an innocent little
child.

There exists a regular government here within the
Government. Twenty delegates waited on Jules
Favre, and put leading questions to him which must
embarrass any government; but then, in fact, one
council has as much *raison d'être* as the other. These
are the names of the delegates, chiefly unknown men
even in the next parish:—Ch. Beslay, Camélinat, Ch.-
L. Chassin, E. Chatelain, A. Claris, Cornu, E. Dupas,
E. Duval, Johannard, P. Laujalley, G. Lefrançais, Ch.

Longuet, L. Michel, Mollin, G. Pagnerre, J.-B.
Perrin, G. Ranvier, E. Roy, Toussaint, Vertut.

Bourse—no business for cash or account; 3 per
cents, 54.

Thursday, September 22nd.—There was a great demonstration to-day at the Hôtel de Ville ; we presume
it was in honour of the anniversary of the proclamation
of the Republic of the 22nd of September, 1792.   At
any rate, every battalion marched down to the hôtel
during the day, and without the slightest orders from
head-quarters.   We took boat (for three sous) and
steamed up from the Hôtel de Ville to the Bridge of
Bercy, passing by miles of wine in casks and in bond.
It is the land of evil spirits and good wine !   All the
river-side was gay with soldiers, but sad from the
sight of the many commenced structures which will
now never be finished.

The fine bas-relief of the Emperor on horseback is
taken down from the new Louvre, and the legend is
effaced by a coating of pitch!   It is clear that " Art "
and the " Beautiful " are crimes in republican eyes,
and that life must go back to the practical plainness
of the days of the Commonwealth.

We found Bercy by far the strongest place we have
yet seen.   One arch of the bridge is blocked up, and

piles are driven all over the bed of the river. The fortifications rest on the left and right banks of the river, and two gun-boats are so stationed as to cross their fires with those of the Bercy and Charenton batteries. While we were looking on, a strange little steam-tug glided by : it was half covered with an old tarpaulin, and the stern hidden by a shabby green cloth, but at the prow appeared the brass muzzle of the mitrailleuse with its little black *capote*. They have cleared a large space which was "encumbered"— military term—with a beautiful wood and some fine houses, and are mining the Bercy road at three points. The trenches to conceal the wires are nearly complete. There are many guns in position, and many mitrailleuses out of sight, and the position is very strong. We returned to Paris, thinking we had seen a better defence than had as yet rewarded our searches.

In the evening there was to have been a great demonstration, but except that one of my prophecies came off, and a Moblot playing with his chassepot forgot that it was loaded, and so blazed off his cartridge into "the brown" of us, there was no movement. Indeed, the evening ended by a select party, consisting of two ladies, an Irish gentleman, a French advocate and colonel of National Guards, a French nobleman, and myself, sitting on the benches of the Place de la Madeleine and drinking what the lawyer-colonel called " pickups."

By-the-way, he is a serious man, an ex-deputy, who never voted for the Emperor till his Majesty gave constitutional government, which alone he considered might be able to save the dynasty. He is indignant at the behaviour of the Senate and Chamber of the 4th of September, and asks, " Why are we not assembled and protesting, in some provincial city, against this accidental Government ?" He is all for a " serious republic," but believes that it is much more likely that France will have the " riotous republic," which, for the sake of Prussia, Bismarck said last week he so much desired.

The National Guard now wish Blanqui—a conspirator by profession—and Louis Blanc—who in politics is certainly " contrarius albo"—to be added to the Government Council of Defence. " We had better take them," said my friend ; " and even Mégy, the murderer of the Sergent de Ville : they would add to our strength to resist the enemy. I know that this means fighting among ourselves later, but in this supreme hour we must forget that."

Now I must give the little war news of the day. One of the peculiarities, and one of the greatest horrors of this war is, that it is so close to Paris that when an action is over an officer gets leave for a few hours and comes up to dine at his Club. To realize this you must imagine chargers in St. James's Square, and hurried officers in full but dirty uniform eating hasty dinners before they gallop back to head-quarters at Hampstead.

I hear wonderful accounts of the mitrailleuses; it seems that Vinoy protected his retreat entirely with this arm, killing hundreds of Prussians, and losing few men. From the forts, round which the defenders have measured every inch of ground, both mitrailleuses and artillery are playing awful havoc with the Prussians—six thousand wounded were at Versailles on Wednesday. Three hundred Prussians were blown up at Châtillon by a torpedo, and seven hundred surprised and killed ·by the Mobiles. As fast as guns are put in position the French knock them down.

The French have as yet suffered little. So far so good; but they are behind walls, and the enemy has not attacked in great force. A new explosive compound is invented, which, it is said, can destroy a regiment at a *coup*, and there is a talk of Greek fire. "For you see," said General X., "it is a war of extermination."

Three fine new corps are raised—"Les Amis de

France " (a foreign legion), " Les Gardes de Chasse," armed with the Remington rifle, and finally, the three thousand Sergents de Ville, all old soldiers, who are at the Ecole Polytechnique.

The ludicrous side of this sad state of Paris is the confusion of classes. The Baron de B——, who is of one of the oldest families in France, and whose ancestors' names are to be found earlier than that of the Duc de Broglie in the "Golden Book" of re-publicanism at Mulhouse (13th century), is a private in the regiment commanded by the secretaries of his club, and last night, when we were saluting the officer on guard at the "National Palace," he returned the salute, and said, " Bon soir, M. le Baron " (not " citizen "); " bon soir, monsieur." It was one of the waiters at the Petit Club.

The French have not yet shot a prisoner, but the Prussians have shot M. Vallentin, just named Prefect of Strasbourg—an old 1848 man—who was carry-ing letters to Metz ; so reprisals may now be ex-pected.

A Zouave was shot for mutiny to-day.

Friday, September 23rd.—Jules Favre has published a long account of his interviews with Bismarck. The terms for an armistice included Mont Valérien—it is the last feather that breaks the camel's back. "You might as well ask us for Paris," exclaimed Jules Favre, who confesses that he was between fainting and crying. It was a rude experience, and "Væ victis" is evidently the motto of "the pious master" of the astute Count.

It was an unequal contest—conqueror against conquered; diplomatist against lawyer; aristocrat against democrat; man of the world against theorist—and the result was certain. It has been proclaimed—it is "war while there is a Frenchman left!" Jules Favre and his party do not despair, and profess (especially since Châtillon) to be of the opinion of the first Napoleon, that raw recruits fight better than veterans, because they do not know the danger, and so are not alarmed. We shall see.

To-day Emmanuel Arago, Garnier-Pagès, and Gambetta are added to the Committee of Defence. If ever any army marched "Left" in front, it is that of Paris to-day.

Now I am not going to write any "scandal about Queen Elizabeth," or any other queen or king, only to relate some little stories which I have just heard, and which amused me. A report has got abroad in the best educated classes, which has created a very bad impression on the now vexed and irritated political mind of Paris. It is believed that Queen Victoria has written an autograph letter to King William, urging the claims of the Orleans family to the throne of France. This is seriously credited and severely commented on.

The other historiette is as true as ludicrous. A friend of mine passing yesterday through the Place de la Concorde, saw a friend of his own in evident dispute with another person who spoke English. "Come and be my interpreter," said my friend's friend. "I want you, who know all about it, to assure this gentleman that the Queen of England is not lending large sums to King William." "It's no use telling me," said the man; "I have just returned from England, where I have been in exile sixteen years, and never missed a political meeting, and I know it as a fact."

Last night we were talking of De Morny and his speculations, when a well-known banker said, "Oh ! he was nothing ! The only real grand speculator I ever came across was the old King of the Belgians ; he had the best information in Europe, and never failed to use it."

A great failure was hinted at last night, and I fancy it is premature.

I forgot I have another royal anecdote. A year

ago to-night a party of some of the big people, among whom were H.R.H. the Duke of Cambridge, Colonel Clifton, Mr. Arthur Otway, M.P., Mr. Constantine Phipps, Mrs. Phipps, the Duchesse San Arpino, Viscount Torrington, Mr. Huddlestone, Q.C., &c., were asked by his Excellency Lord A. Loftus to come to his villa at Baden. The Queen of Prussia was there, and repeated that which she had said at a dinner given to royalty and diplomacy the day before, which was to the effect that she had but one desire, and that was " Peace," and that she admired the Emperor Napoleon and his grand career above all things.

The statue of Strasbourg, in the Place de la Concorde, is to be re-christened "Statue de la Résistance." Very proper too. The statue is that of a French woman, and who knows better than a French woman how (long) to resist ?

Mdlle. Bellenger, about whom the tide of scandal is now at the flood, is the niece of the proprietor of " Voisins." Six years ago she was very handsome, now she is so fat that she has lost all expression. She used to dine frequently at " Voisins," and blow up her respected uncle before the party if the dinner was not good ! I believe she is now a respectable married woman, and fled with all the rest of her former world (demi-monde) to London or Brussels. I hope we shall hear no more of her or her affairs.

This is true—it came direct from the chef de cabinet of M. Jules Favre, who was walking up and down the room while his chef and Bismarck were skirmishing. In an arm chair in the window sat General Moltke, reading one of Dickens' novels. M. T—— took the trouble to look: it was "Martin Chuzzlewit."

Nothing can exceed the politeness which I have received from all the ministers of whom I have required anything—MM. Jules Favre, Gambetta, and de Kératry. To-day I had an amusing letter from the secretary of the former. After sending me the passes for which I had written, he says, "In a word, I am at your service, and the minister also; but all the passes and papers which we can give you will not prevent you being arrested. They take up some of us every day, and bring us back here (Prefecture of Police) in triumph."

I am beginning to have greater faith in the power of resistance of Paris. Some points, notably the Avenue Ulrich—*i.e.*, the old gilded gates into the Bois—are weak, but the others are very strong.

Hearing that there had been heavy firing from 4 A.M. till 9·30 A.M. in that direction, we took heart

and carriage and drove there, this time armed with a
"passe-partout." We were too late for the fight,
even for the end of the fray, which had been the
heavy shelling of the enemy by the fort of Bicêtre, to
the west of the hospital. The Prussians were again
hit hard, and retired. We saw several prisoners,
many ambulances, of which only a few held wounded,
a balloon, a great crowd, and hundreds of Moblots, and
one wounded Liner in the ambulance of the Round-
about station in the Avenue d'Italie.

At Montrouge we found a capital fellow. Two
hours before the Prussians entered he left Rheims in
his four-wheeled "shay" (a wonderful vehicle), and a
white horse—so old that he might have been with
another white horse in the Ark—drove direct to
Paris, and enlisted in the Paris National Guard.

We walked from Montrouge to opposite Bicêtre.
This side of Paris I should say is impregnable.
They are making two very strong trenches and
earthworks within the fortifications. Most of the
guns are mounted, and the sandbags are ready
built up for the chassepots. It was a lovely day,
and the whole scene was like a fair, though the
dead were lying within gunshot; the prisoners, those
living-dead, and the wounded constantly passing
by, and beyond the usual scene smouldering cot-

tages, trampled gardens, and burning woods. All sorts of reports were abroad, but the result of the day was unimportant.

The question was mooted among us to-day—how long Paris could be fed? It was asserted that it could hold out for three months ; and surely after that, with sixty thousand regulars, Vinoy would imitate General Webb at Wynendael, and give battle in order to conceal the advance of his supplies. We fraternized to-night in the train with many people, blouses, broadcloth, and uniform, and found the confidence and enthusiasm immense. The cry is, " Prussia was in the right when fighting the Empire; now she refuses reasonable terms from the Republic she is the aggressor, and the opinion of Europe will be against her."

Very queer news from Rome : great opposition to Italy.

Rentes rose twenty-five centimes.

Saturday, September 24th.—There seems to have been rather serious fighting yesterday afternoon beyond St.-Denis, but according to an account—and I trust that the present men do not allow them to be cooked—it ended in favour of the French. If all reports are true, their continued losses must tell seriously on the Prussian " corps d'armée."

The "Official Journal" to-day contains—Firstly, a notice that a large body of citizens are very eager that M. Louis Blanc should return to England and enlighten public opinion on the true spirit which animates the French Republic, and excite the sympathies of the English people in favour of France, and that the Government entirely accords itself with this idea. Secondly, a decree summoning M. Devienne, late first President of the Cour de Cassation, to stand his trial for having gravely compromised the dignity of a magistrate by acting as arbitrator in the Bellenger affair. M. Devienne is out of the jurisdiction of the court, having wisely gone away. Thirdly, a series of extracts, of no great interest, from the private correspondence of the Imperial family, over which the Paris public will gloat. Lastly, an admirable "request" (under any other form but this "Jack's as good as Tom" Government it would have been a "General Order") that the National Guard refrain in future from empty demonstrations and street processions, stay near their quarters, and prepare for serious fighting. This is excellent advice. A regiment is now passing singing like lunatics, and their rifles filled with *immortelles*—cartridges would be better.

It is rather a curious and not an unpleasant change (for a short time) for people who have been for years living in the centre of the most restless society of the noisiest capital in Europe, to find that society reduced to *nil*, and the noisy capital a deserted village—dull as Newmarket in January. It is quite a rest. The half-dozen friends still remaining are very affectionate, and you talk to the stranger in the streets as if you had known him from boyhood's happy hour.

To be sure, republicanism has its spots, like the sun. I do not see how it adds to the good of one's country to have all the beggars in France "come to town," not "some in rags," but all in rags; nor, except to the animals themselves, do I see how freedom is advanced by letting the myriads of Paris dogs go unmuzzled! On the other hand, the papers are reduced to one sheet, and only those who have had for years to wade through their platitudes and digest their three days' old news can know what a blessing this diminution is! When I saw the "Official Journal"—which consisted frequently of twelve large sheets—is reduced to one small one I could have wept for joy.

At last they have got together a small body of police, but only for the markets. For this especial service the prefect was forced to use experienced men, and so had to fall back on the old Sergents de Ville; but they are so detested that he dare not expose them without precaution, so he has changed their dress entirely, and caused them to be clean shaved. As this is duly published in the papers, I rather pity those policemen.

Paris to-day presents a curious spectacle—a city which has proclaimed itself to be France, governing itself without a government, and defending itself without an army.

I have just heard that Louis Blanc is quite taken by surprise at this national invitation to him to return to England. They had better have sent him as ambassador, as was first proposed. "Un vaut bien un autre" in these transition times.

We have a bold Queen's messenger—Captain Johnson—trying to fight his way back to London. He seriously proposes a washerwoman's cart and a donkey, of which he has the refusal. The despatches he is carrying are of the utmost importance. By-the-way, why do they dress Queen's messengers like King George the Third, or the old twopenny postmen, in the Windsor uniform, and stick " V. R." in their caps? What does V. R. suggest to any one but an Englishman? And what a feeble diplomacy it must be which cannot contrive to pass a British messenger through the lines of such allies of England as France and Prussia !

It ought to be recorded that the last despatches before the siege stopped all communication with England, were brought into Paris "vix et ægrè" by Captain Johnson.

I called at Messrs. Rothschild to-day, and was told that M. le Baron was doing duty in the forts.

You ask what is the opinion of the resistance of Paris. Well! Dr. Shrimpton, who has served for years with the French army, gives us three days before the Prussians are in Paris. Mr. Parker, who has been at Arthur & Co.'s for years, says the Parisians will cry out for peace at any price if victuals get scarce; and Hill, an English shopkeeper here of thirty years' standing, says the Garde Nationale will run away when it comes to the point. On the other hand, M. Treitt, a Parisian ex-deputy, ex-colonel of Garde Nationale, and a lawyer of sound judgment, believes that the people of Paris can beat the soldiers of Prussia. I don't.

The Crown Prince is at Meudon, and if they erect a battery there they can bombard all Paris. N.B. It is said that Meudon is mined.

"Up in a balloon, boys; up in a balloon!" I don't know if it is "jolly," but there were some of our etters up in a balloon to-day, preys to every idle wind. I wonder where they are now.

There was firing to-night (5·30 P.M.) to the north of Meudon. Latest quotations, domestic and financial:— Butter, ten shillings per pound; no veal; no fish. Rentes, 52,75; no business—a rise of twenty-five centimes on yesterday.

Sunday, September 25th.—Three weeks to-day have elapsed since the collapse of the Empire, and even yet it seems like a dream. Paris is so changed that no one would recognize the " Haussmannville " of September, 1869; but even that is nothing to the change in the people.

This was generally one of the gayest weeks in the year as far as strangers were concerned: Baden was over, the autumn races beginning at Chantilly, all the reverend crew of wide-awake covered parsons, provincial tourists, and lawyers, pleasantly relieved by a large admixture of racing men, were in the flesh and in spirit in that now deserted caravanserai, the Grand Hôtel, where yesterday one elderly lady sat enthroned alone. We heard all the German baths' scandal, and what was going on in London; and to-day you see nothing but a crowd of Mobiles, a gang of beggars, and a quantity of contractors who offer to supply the Government within forty-eight hours with anything, from an iron-clad to a tent-peg. Writing of those

"gents" (the right word), I saw poor F—— L——
yesterday, looking the shadow of his former self, and
the very reverse of the ghost in "Hamlet," who had
no speculation in his eye. Query—which is the
greatest nuisance, a man with an idea, a man with a
grievance, or a man with a patent?

France has purchased a large quantity of "Reming-
tons." I hear that there are nearly three hundred
wounded French at Calais, and many more in the
Great Hospital of St.-Omer, and they are so utterly
destitute of the commonest articles required by a
wounded man, that they were compelled to get a
friend of mine to apply to Lieut.-Colonel Loyd-Lindsay
to send them stores, which he did by return of boat
to an extent that astonished them. Charity is a very
fine thing, but Europe seems like Paris—one large
ambulance, and the wounded are made so comfortable
at other people's expense that pious William and
ambitious Bismarck do not care how many thousand
men are returned "wounded."

By-the-way, according to the saintly telegrams of
the King, and the epithet applied to him by his head-
piece, his Majesty should be called "Pius 10th," and
his motto should be—"Never is the Landwehr more
heavy than under a pious king."

My friend at Calais asked the authorities, "Am I

to understand that the French army went into the field without making any preparation for the wounded?" "Monsieur, effectively it was so!"

To keep up our spirits we last evening met a large *roulage* waggon filled with deal coffins. What for? A " memento mori" for civilians I suppose, for soldiers in a time of war are buried with their martial cloak around them. It is not a subject to joke upon, but I know a very curious and true story about these last homes of poor. humanity. In Evans' Spanish legion there was an Irishman named Tim McCarthy; one day his captain looking over the books of the men, found Tim charged with a coffin. " What's this?" asked Captain C. I. " I'll tell you what it is, captain ; it is a great shame! This is the third I'm charged with. I should not care if I was dead, or had the coffins." It was true; he was "Dr." three deal coffins.

The " gamins de Paris " from eight to thirteen have been formed into a corps for the purpose of carrying messages, &c. ; at least it will give them something to do.

All is calm this morning: perhaps a day of rest.

On Friday they tried in action the new coil mitrailleuse, and the effect was terrible ! No wonder ! There are one hundred and twenty-five barrels of larger bore than any yet used, and " practical officers believe, that fired into masses they could kill three thousand in a few minutes."

There was a naval action under St.-Cloud yesterday.   What next ?

It is stated that the Government has planned, by reduction of the salaries of officials, allowances to royalty, senators, &c., no less a saving than two million four hundred thousand pounds a year. I regret to say that the citizens of Paris are fast losing caste, not only with Englishmen, but with the more serious of their fellow-citizens.   Mr. Henry Labouchere, who is liberal enough, Heaven knows, thinks on reflection that they are a parcel of children.   The Inspector General of Hospitals (English), who has just been here, described them as " a lot of idiots, who, while the Prussians are preparing positions under their very eyes, are picking the N's off the buildings."

A balloon has just passed, apparently dropping parcels of letters into Paris : it really was carrying news to the provinces of the postponement of the elections.   When a Queen's messenger arrived at Louviers the other day, he was taken prisoner, of course as a Prussian, and when he produced his de-

-spatches to the republican Government, they were addressed to " His Excellency —— ——, accredited to the Court of his Majesty the Emperor of the French !"

Colonel Claremont thinks Paris can make a fine defence, and he is one of the best judges I know. He says it is all " bosh" about the great range of the Prussian guns : one league, that is, $2\frac{1}{4}$ miles, outside range ; if they tried a further, the elevation would be so great that the guns would be dismounted. The real superiority of Prussia was in having the proportion of eight hundred guns to two hundred French.

M. Ring, secretary to Jules Favre, and who has been attached to Vienna and Berlin (where Bismarck picked him out as a rising man, and wished him, as a Baden subject, to go into Prussian diplomacy), went with his chief to Ferrière, and had a long conversation with Bismarck and the staff, all of whom he knew. He was told that the Prussians entirely depend on street fighting among the Parisians to get into the city. They will not attack Bazaine. They say he has typhus and dysentery, and must give in. This is false. They admitted that the mitrailleuses twice (at Gravelotte, and in one other action) fairly confounded them ; and they owned that the " Bismarck Regiment " went into action full strength, charged up a hollow, and came out with one lieutenant, one trumpeter, and seven troopers.

The National Guard have elected nearly all their old officers, and, *mirabile dictu*, Baroche and C. Walewski among them.

I went to-day to see Captain Hore, R.N., our naval attaché, who has been ill. I found him better, and I rejoice to say, as I respect his opinion, with a firm conviction that the Parisians will fight and inflict much damage on the Prussians if they do not finally defeat them. It is a curious fact, that for years Captain Hore and Colonel Claremont have said that the French navy and army would, when put to the test, prove fitter for show than work. They were pooh-poohed, and were right.

Dr. C. A. Gordon, Deputy Inspector General of Hospitals, is here to report on the French system. We told him that the way to get at the actual republican system was to get the hospital statistics of the Empire, and reverse them entirely, as where the Empire prescribed a bandage or a poultice, the Republic was bound to order amputation or a blister.

Such a bear garden as the Champs-Elysées to-day I have never seen! The people sat just where they have been told not to sit for years. They have destroyed every flower, trodden the turf to dust, and scattered old newspapers and empty bottles all over the ornamental parts of the show-thoroughfare of Paris. It was like a bad fair. Goat-carriages and go-carts, merry-go-rounds, Mobiles playing billiards for almond cakes, nursery maids neglecting their tender charges for the tender passion (of course "Mars" in the ascendant), an arrest here, a fight there, a chorus of "Mourir pour la Patrie" from half-drunken lips, and when there was a lull the cannon of Mont Valérien murmured hoarsely in the distance. This cannot be Paris!

More Bismarck! He said to Ring, "We have been so hard hit that we cannot go back to Germany without very great compensation." They have 300,000 men within twenty-five miles of Paris, 200,000 watching Bayonne, 100,000 keeping their lines, and at least 10,000 watching the 100,000 French prisoners now in Germany. There are to-day 580,000 men in and near Paris, including 72,000 regulars and marines.

Bismarck is very savage about the delay: three months ago he said, "God in Heaven! don't let us give the Gardes Mobiles time to become soldiers."

I can answer for the truth of the following anecdote, which all here think accounts for the easy triumph and entry into Paris which the Prussians have openly declared they anticipated. The Comte de Solms,

who was chargé d'affaires at the death of poor Comte
de Goltz—who, had he lived, would (I believe), with
the aid of Lord Lyons, have prevented this war,
which seems likely to end as fatally to Germany as
France—remained on here ever since, fêted by every
one, and most politely treated at the Tuileries. He
was just that man whom you would always expect to
see first when you entered a *salon* " cis," or " citra,"
Seine. When war was proclaimed it was noticed that
he did not leave. The Emperor left, and Solms was
still in Paris. Fighting began, and still Solms
lingered. The Baron de Billing saw and spoke to
him ; M. Laporte saw him lounging on the ramparts,
and I also saw and spoke to him. Somebody said he
was astonished to see him in Paris under the circumstances, but he took no notice. Later he told Comte
de Moltke, the Danish minister here, that he should
not leave till he was told he must go. He examined
the fortifications carefully, and it so happened that up
to the time of his being diplomatically forced to leave,
the culpable neglect of the then executive had left the
defences of Paris not incomplete, but untouched, and
literally " in statu quo ante bellum." It is seldom a
trite old phrase is so truly and unhappily applied,
and it would apply to so much of the Imperial expedition. Solms then went to Berlin, and reported that

Paris was open, and that there was no idea of fortifying it; therefore the army of the pious King anticipated a "walk over," where perhaps they will be "beat on the post" after a severely contested race.

A friend of mine goes to-morrow to Meudon, to see the Crown Prince. I hope they will not set fire to the nitro-glycerine when he is there, for he is a good fellow.

There seems no doubt about this mining, and I always sleep under a conviction that I shall be shaken out of bed. I saw a mine at Bercy last Thursday, which, if ignited, will blow a regiment into subdivisions and sections. "C'est l'extermination, mais ce n'est pas la guerre!" to slightly alter the speech of the Russian general to Edward Fellowes.

I now go to my rest praying for rain, though I fear "it is no use praying while the wind is in this quarter," and with a murmured wish that the Prussians may be confounded. In about two hours there will probably be an *alerte*, and the day will dawn on us to an accompaniment of drums and bugles.

Monday, September 26th.—The very dullest day since the beginning of the state of siege; but the pressure of siege is already on us, and though nobody is fighting to-day, yet Paris is in low spirits.

There is always a ludicrous side to all events. The other day a very old English resident said to me, " Mark my words, the people of Paris won't stand being pinched; they will never wait till we come to our dry stores: the eggs and butter will beat them." We laughed; but there are no butter or eggs to-day, and the " Electeur Libre" calls for a sally and an attack on the enemy, mainly because of the want of eggs and butter. " We pay high to live like anchorites;" so "to the battlements," and " hang up the banners on the outward walls," for we cannot have an *omelette*, or indulge in a *tartine*. Oh! they are droll dogs, these French!

In the dullness of this Monday I feel inclined to solace myself by translating a serious story from a standard evening paper :—" We cannot be too careful about the signals which may be made to the enemy, only sometimes we go to extremes. Here is an example. Lord A——, anxious to observe the attitude of the people of Paris during a siege, and not wishing to leave Paris, hired for his own use a house between Charenton and Vincennes. Now, on Friday night, the Mobiles on duty at the fortifications seeing signals glimmering from his windows, immediately placed a cordon round the house, and sent a picket to examine the chamber of our eccentric one, whom they found plunged in the deepest possible sleep. That which our Mobiles had taken for a signal was a pillow which was burning at the end of the room. It must be known, in order to understand this, that the carelessness of Lord A—— is proverbial, and that he always reads himself to sleep. When he finds he is dropping off, he throws the lighted candle on the floor, and then takes a shot at it with his pillow. When there is no shooting, he finds that it keeps his eye in. Sometimes he hits, and sometimes he misses. Sometimes he puts out his candle by simply sticking it under his bolster. (Mark this!) At Badminton and other country houses where his ways are known, a servant always sits up till his lordship goes to sleep, to see all safe."

I have looked over the names of the thirty-two of the " nobility of the United Kingdom " whose titles begin with the first letter of the alphabet. I see that they range between Lord Avonmore and Lord Athole, so the affair must rest between them, the alpha and omega of age. At any rate, I shall never ask my " Lord A." to stay with me at Castle Nowhere, N.B.

In the event, which seems probable, of our soon being able to get very little money and still less food—for even if one is lucky enough to possess a new republican hundred-sous piece, with "Liberty, Equality, and Fraternity" on its front, you cannot eat it—it is well to prepare for the worst, and seek out spots which offer cheap food to the hungry. Such a spot is the Bouillon Duval, at the corner of the Rue des Fiacres, and there are thirteen others in Paris. They are the property of Duval, the largest butcher in Paris, who, in Imperial times, paid fifteen hundred pounds a year for his shop in the Rue Tronchet.

We entered a brilliant restaurant on the ground-floor—well lighted, and not hot—in which hundreds of ladies, gentlemen, professionals, and swarms of soldiers were dining at little marble tables. As you go in you are given a card with a list of all you can have, and as you order it the waiter makes a mark, so that at any period of the meal you can see how much you have eaten, and how much it has cost. Having an appointment there, we went upstairs, and found a second gorgeous *salle à manger* equally full of Mobiles and marble tables. We had an excellent dinner —in fact, the potato soup was worthy of the Windham, and the meat equal to any you could find in London. We were luxurious, and expended three halfpence in a table cloth and two napkins; but the usual rule is to dine on the white marble table. The whole cost per head was—bread, a penny; soup, two-pence; roast mutton, fourpence; purée de pommes de terre, twopence; haricot beans, sauce blanche, two-pence; pint of Macon, fivepence; waiter, a penny; total, under eighteenpence. Now, be pleased to re-member that I am not talking of cheap and nasty, but of cheap and excellent food, and if Paris is ever Paris again, and I catch H——h B——y, or Mc——t here, I will take them to dinner and make them confess they have dined, and dined well. If you dine every day, two halfpenny napkins will last you the week. You laugh! You "English gentlemen who sit at home at ease" ("Boomb!" there goes a big gun), but we are in the presence of the enemy, and he will perhaps eat up all our soup, meat, and vegetables, and leave us to give the penny to the waiter.

Forty deserters from the Line were taken to-day.

The gun-boats off Le Point du Jour had a lively afternoon: they amused themselves by sending ex-ploring shot and shell into the woods of St.-Cloud and Meudon, to dislodge suspected troops. If any were present they retired. Every shot which crashed among those beautiful trees, which even the next generation will never see as they were last week, drew forth a demoniacal shout of delight. It was the destruction of property, so Vive la République! everything is everybody's! Long live Destruction! Down with the Beautiful! Live the Deformed!

An officer has to-day got through from Metz, and brings good news—-verbal ; and listen to this, my republicans,—he detests you, but loves France, and having once escaped from the jaws of death, has started to force his way back through them with other verbal despatches.

A memorandum—Louis Blanc was utterly frantic to-day about his reported alliance with Blanqui. He said to a friend of mine, " Why, I assure you I have never seen that man."

Thiers is absolutely raising and organizing armies in the south. A man got through to-day from Tours, and told the news to ——, who told me. After this, talk of steering the Channel fleet ! and now they say that the " intrepid veteran " is going to Russia.

I heard a strange story to-night, and I do not hesitate to say that I believe it. It seems that on the night of Friday, the 2nd of September, the Empress had signed the order of arrest for Jules Favre, Gambetta, Ernest Picard, and the whole of that party. The Emperor's police were good enough to find out the plot to establish the

Republic, but the republican spies were clever enough to find out that they were found out.

When we think how happy and prosperous Paris would have been but for the "Government of Small Unknowns," one is tempted to wish that there had been a female *coup d'état.* Louis Blanc considers the Republic of the 4th of September the postponement for years of republicanism.

Rentes rose forty centimes, and left off 53,15.

Tuesday, September 27th.—No war news this morning. It is reported that the King of Prussia is making an entrenched camp at Versailles, not finding the apple of Paris fall into his mouth so easily or readily as he expected.

The Prussians make war very like savages: the other day they captured twenty-five French Francs-Tireurs, and on the march kept taunting them with the unpleasant news that King William had determined to shoot all Francs-Tireurs as peasants in arms. Luckily they all escaped during a scrimmage caused by the guns of a French fort, and got back here to tell the tale. I fear it is very French, but I have to record that the National Guard is getting a little tired of its last new toy—the fortifications. They are already beginning to say that they have homes, and that sleeping at the sign of the " Fine Star " is rheumatic and unpleasant. They now call on their government to form an army of a hundred thousand National Guards and fifty thousand Mobiles, and assume the offensive. They forget Moltke, I fear, his strategy, and his victorious army; also that they themselves have no officers. If the Emperor said, with evident truth, on the 25th of July, that there was not a general in the French army who could- handle a hundred thousand men, where has he sprung from since?

I believe the Parisians are in awful dread of famine, but the Government declares we are good for three months. This is the state: there are in Paris a million and a half mouths to feed, and the *matériel* in store seems to be 24,000 oxen, 150,000 sheep, and 6000 pigs (I confess that I hope " with power to add to their number," or I too should feel, like Oliver Twist—a craving for " more "). Besides this the Defence Committee has stored a quantity of salted meat, and is also strongly recommending horse, shops for the sale of which viand are being opened every-where. I suppose we shall come to " gee-gee " at last, but oh! my friend ——, you who have with me stood on your head in every field in Northampton-shire, Huntingdonshire, and Bedfordshire, I swear by St. Thomas of Wansford the first mouthful will choke me. I shall think of "The Creeper," and "The Jewess," of "Whitebait," "Merchant," "Royalist," and "Hermit," and the taste will be as aloes in the mouth.

Well, thank goodness, in their lives I have often nearly cooked them, but I never thought of eating them *à la chasseur* at 7·30.

The first part of the Imperial private correspondence is published. It is a little quarto pamphlet, and does not contain (as yet) any of the Bellenger scandal. The second part is to be out to-day. By-the-by, as somebody will tell the truth of this story, I may as well. It was an intrigue commenced out hunting at Fontainebleau, where the lady, who looked very well on horseback, had gone with her "amant en titre," to whom it was remarked in the field— " You must be nearly tired of la belle Marguerite !" " Quite," laconically replied M. de ——; and so he ceased to be recognized at the court of La Bellenger. The dispute which the Judge of the Court of Appeal was called in to settle was about the age of a child— the age settling the question of paternity. The lady was nonsuited.

At one o'clock there was a great alarm. It was a bright day even for this exceptional summer, and suddenly Paris was covered by a dense cloud rising apparently in the direction of Vincennes. There was of course a panic: some said Paris was on fire, others that it was smoke from a great action, and we thought it best to trust our own eyes and so see what it really was. As we walked up the Rue d'Amsterdam we heard nothing but such broken sentences as "Prussians at Vincennes," "Forest on fire," "Bondy burning," and other lamentations. Very little more and it would have been "The eastern part of Paris on fire," and then indeed there would have been a "sauve qui peut."

After trying Montmartre and the heights round the Tower of Solferino—which is not at all pulled down—without seeing anything, we at length made for the top of a dust heap near the Place de St.-Pierre, and there we saw what was the matter. It reversed the proverb that there is no smoke without fire, for there were volumes of the densest black coal-pit-looking smoke, and no gleam or glimmer of visible fire. The Buttes de Chaumont have been closed for some days— nobody knew why. But we made a pretty good guess at it, as through a strong glass we saw curious looking stores which suggested *pétrole*. It was so;

and that *pétrole* caught fire to-day. It is said to be the work of a Prussian!

"Çà va sans dire." Every crime committed "a du Prussien dedans," according to Paris, and really I believe that Paris is right this time. No harm was done except that, as I am given to understand, there is a great loss of defensive *matériel*. I believe that is all *blague*. There is plenty more in Paris. What is not *blague* is the improvement in discipline and drill of the National Guard of blood-red Paris. I saw all the Belleville divisions to-day. They were, as to drill at least, as good as a militia regiment in England after a year's constant training, and are composed of men so superior in height, strength, weight, and appearance to the French line, that an observer is struck dumb, and is utterly puzzled as to where the "Grande Nation" could of late have recruited her soldiers; what could have been the system which has ruined at once, and for at least half a generation, a dynasty, a country, the prestige of an army, and the whole moral worth and responsibility of France. I could tell you, but you are so republican in England that I dare not. Well, well! The wafer may be carried to England yet.

Wednesday, September 28th.—I had a bye chance of

sending off letters to-day by Captain Hall, an old
Indian officer, who had volunteered into the French
éclaireurs, both horse and foot, but has left because
they had little organization in one and no horses in
the other service ; so I was awakened early by a messenger with letters from Baron A. de R———. I was
just going off to sleep again, when the wife of the
concierge rushed in, "les larmes aux yeux," and
sobbed out, "Monsieur, I can get no meat!" So it
was. The butchers are to have a certain quantity of
meat to sell at a price fixed by Government every day,
and the second day the system is at work you cannot
get a scrap of any sort of food at 7 A.M. The scene
outside Duval's in the Rue Tronchet, the largest
butcher in Europe, was curious. The crowd had been
gathering since break of day, and was kept in order
by two National Guards. Two women had fainted
from exhaustion.

The scene at the opening of the *halles* is terrible :
the people are actually fighting for food, and no real
pressure is as yet felt. What will it be this day fortnight? What I fear is a starvation panic, as any row
in Paris would be fatal to France. We live in
strange times. Thackeray says that "when, in the
month of March, anno Domini 1815, Napoleon
landed at Cannes, and Louis XVIII. fled, all Europe

was in alarm, and *old John Sedley was ruined.*" This comes home to me when you see that because the Emperor, Bismarck, and King William have con-spired to uncivilize, degrade, depopulate, and ruin France and Prussia, we modest people cannot have a boiled leg of mutton and turnips for dinner.

I think I remember an Irish distich—

"If you had seen these roads before they were made,
 You'd have downed on your knees and blessed General Wade."

I am so grateful that I too will write a couplet:

"If you knew the void in French larders and bowels,
 You would see why we English cry 'Bless Messrs. Powell's!'"

Without their preserved food I declare we should have starved, or, like the Parisians when besieged by Henri IV. in 1590, have to eat roast rat, find car-cases, and "grind their bones to make our bread"— a gigantic proceeding even more striking in real life than in a nursery rhyme.

Well, there is alleviation in everything. Thank goodness! our last servant left us yesterday. She had an appetite which was only equalled by her capa-city for doing nothing and her love for Moblots.

There is no war news, but a report of a great council of generals at Versailles, which, if authentic, would mean action. French officers believe in a sudden attack on three points at once—St.-Denis, Montrouge, and St.-Ouen.

The Garde Nationale and Mobile are now under the strictest military law, and so we shall have more discipline and less demonstration—that is, if the citizen soldiers do not mutiny. Why should they not? Is not citizen Bobot, drummer to the 8th Corps of the 99th Legion, fully the equal of Generals Trochu, Du Flô, or Vinoy?

The Mayor of Boulogne (in the wood), having seen the last man out of the town, has left that suburban city utterly void of supplies, and come, the last man, into Paris.

Government has fortified Lord Hertford's late residence in the Bois—Bagatelle, and his legatee is strengthening *his* position in the Rue Laffitte, where are the mines of artistic treasure which he has inherited. By-the-way, he has even the Irish property.

Saw Fred. Hankey to-day, wandering about in the original white trousers which he used to wear in the Guards in 1848—period of last revolution.

Balloons are now regularly established for the post. I dare say our letters go somewhere, but where, and how are we to get replies? I fear balloon correspondence, like bad speculations, will not answer. Mr.

Lewis Merton has sent off a private one, and so has the American Press.

It is said that four thousand barrels of petroleum were destroyed by malice a fortnight yesterday. Happy thought, ten thousand barrels were stored there, close to the powder magazine! There is also a vast dépôt in the Parc Monceaux.

The British Charity is doing wonderful good to the English here, but it is in great difficulty. It wishes to establish a kitchen, and feed the applicants for relief; but though there is plenty of money, no useful amount of food can be obtained. The Hon. Alan Herbert works like a slave—coolness in danger and charity, which neither begins nor stops at home, comes natural to that family.

I have just returned from a very long walk and a sort of tour of inspection from the Porte Courcelles to the Porte Maillot, and I rejoice to say that the improvement in the means of the defence of Paris is so rapid that you see the happy change every twenty-four hours.

We saw some perfectly wonderful drill of Mobiles under the tuition of old Zouaves, who were instructing them in that quick drill and rapid movement which distinguish that corps. The men were in a very advanced state of instruction, and were all armed with the chassepot. We wandered through that strange neighbourhood which flanks the Parc Monceaux, which is neglected in a horticultural sense—barred and double locked—in a word, a mere grave of petroleum, the resurrection of which will be a bad "Last Day" for the unholy men of Bismarck.

Courcelles is an artillery camp! and to think that a year ago we used to be asked to tea there! We never went. We saw thousands of pounds of powder and waggon loads of charged shells, and in the interest of Paris—I am only a lodger—I wish the volunteer artillerymen had more respect for the explosive qualities of gunpowder. Sitting on a barrel of powder I have no doubt rests you, and smoking we know is soothing ; yet the man in the street may be blown up, and though you take the leap in the dark with him, my dear artilleryman, it is but small consolation.

We walked from Neuilly to the Porte Maillot. You must get used to the enormous size and strength of Paris before you can appreciate them. I have seen several strong places, but a stronger than this, never—if they are prepared. Porte Maillot is now defended by an inner stone barricade which—if the enemy carried the earthworks, which are defended first by a frieze of jagged growing trees, then by an earthwork faced by planks bristling every inch with tenpenny nails, the summit crowned with short, sharp pegs and twisted, almost invisible wire, then escaped drowning in the fosse, or being killed by the big guns—he would find defended to the death by the red republicans of the Barricade Committee. They come much from Belleville and Montmartre, and will fight and die as boldly and gloriously as their grandfathers of other days of horror. Yet honour to bravery where honour is due.

Nothing since Sebastopol has, I think, exceeded the strength of the north-west front of Paris. So far so pleasant; but the sight from Neuilly to the Porte Maillot, outside the walls, is dreadful. Everybody remembers the pretty suburb, the quiet little restaurants, the country-looking wine-houses, the villas, and the gorgeous gardens. To-day all the space they covered is as desolate as the Sahara, and I walked through one of the prettiest of the gardens, and beneath bricks, mortar, and desolation recognized the beds where we used to gather early salads, eat strawberries, and pluck violets for the ladies who loved us. I might have picked a violet to-day, but, as Whyte Melville says, " What is the use of a violet with nobody to give it to?" Eh, bien! We went home perfectly satisfied with the defences and those who are to defend them. We met Captain Hore on our road home, and he is more sanguine than ever. Colonel Hoffman, the American Secretary, believes that the Powers (how can he know it?) are striving eagerly for peace. Nonsense! France cannot concede humiliating terms, and if Prussia retires from France, the prestige of this ruinous war is lost. Hoffman believes that the delay looks like peace; Hore that it is only caused by Prussia waiting for big guns; both think the delay in favour of France.

I note here a curious fact. We English are so disliked by the existing republican Government, that when Mr. Wodehouse (and I will appeal to all who know him, to say that he is the most pleasant and conciliating person possible) applied for a flag to get Captain Johnson, Queen's messenger, through the lines, he was met with such difficulties that he had to ask the assistance of Mr. Washburne, to whom the favour was granted at once. After this I think the Lion had better cut his claws, and the Unicorn (like poor Imperial Vivier here now) cease to depend on its horn—shut up and be no more heard.

But again I repeat that nothing can exceed the civility of the Government of Defence to myself. It may be that the members were struck by my offering to go as an amateur, and not the least a republican, to certain spots where they could hardly venture. They are so slow, however, that I fear the event will not come off.

There was a curious scene on the boulevards to-night at 6·30. When the hungry traveller arrived at Duval's, he found a great crowd waiting, as at the pit of a theatre on a first representation. Forcing his way in, he was told that "All was eaten." They would not even give cards. Having heard this, we went on to the Grand Duval, Rue des Fiacres. There we were (at 6·30) offered·ham and vegetables. Finally, we made another Duval's, and got in. They had soup (very good) and roast beef. "But," I remarked, "the beef is raw—blue!" Answer, "Of course; they would not eat it cooked!"

It was a droll sight to see hungry Mobiles come in, take their ticket, and ask, with the air of Captain and Lieutenant-Colonel Lothaire de St.-Sybil, nulli secundus regiment, "What have you got to give us?" Answer, "Soup, dried herrings, and roast beef." The expression of countenance during the soup and herring phase was gloomy, but it cleared up with the beef. "Beef then, and as raw as possible!"

A period of five minutes is supposed to elapse, when returns the waitress (the attendance is female in the

Rue Montmartre), and says, "That gentleman has eaten the last of the beef!"

We apologized, and shared a cheese. I confess that my dinner consisted of a half-pennyworth of Paris bread—a compound I detest at all times, ten pennyworth of chablis—very good, and a remnant of an uncooked ox, which would have been underdone for one of the banqueters on the late lamented Captain Cook, R.N., *éclaireur*. But there is an unpleasant side to this question: if the people once get it into their heads that "les riches," who can pay a franc, or a franc fifty centimes, for their dinner, cannot get it, food must be short. Then will come the popular assault on bakers, and any others who have grain or meat in store. It will be a repetition of the history of Milan in the "Promessi Sposi," a scene I have seen repeated since at the Porta Tosa (and was very nearly shot for my pains)—first, a rising against all holders of food, and then a starvation assault on all proprietors! There is a slang phase—"We are at the beginning of the end." In truth, we are but at the commencement of the beginning.

The weather lasts perfectly wonderful. Prussian troops, which for discipline's sake sleep in the gutter, may be quite comfortable here such a season as this. But what are the Prussians doing? Is it a case of "reculer pour mieux sauter?" is it a sudden know-ledge of their isolated position? a slight panic at a series of slight defeats? or a great surprise at the way in which they are opposed? I confess I do not like this deadly calmness and quiet.

I opened a book to-day, and read, "Never is an army so near and so threatening as when it has entirely disappeared." Now for four days we really know nothing of the Prussians.

Thursday, September 29th.—Here's a pretty Michael-mas, when you can't buy a goose for a guinea. Lovely weather ; it is like July; but then it is such a satire on existing Paris.

"Troja fuit," I think we were taught at school. That Paris has passed away should be the text of to-day ; blotted from the map of Europe. Not that they will be disgracefully beaten here ; on the con-trary, good authorities believe that Paris can resist. I believe so myself ; but must it not be the resistance of volunteers against regulars, and so a mere question of time?

Mr. O'Sullivan, formerly United States Minister at Lisbon, started about a fortnight ago on a "mission purement volontaire et officieuse" to see Bismarck and the King. He got half way, and saw the Duc de

Mecklenburg, and then had to come back. He had much talk of the tall order with the Prussians, and writes—for he has rushed into print—" Yes, sir; they laugh at the volunteer defenders of Paris; say the French army was worth nothing, and that their own losses are comparatively small." Mr. O'Sullivan had every description of pass and permit that the republican Government could supply, but, in spite of those defences, he was attacked all along his line by the French, who declared he was *ipse* Bismarck, and treated him in a manner which requires the pen and the experience of a Sala to describe.

Mr. O'Sullivan had that treatment and his journey for his pains, but from his statements I am more than ever convinced that the Prussians have two stories— one for private friends, the other for Paris consumption. Bismarck says they shall not attack, but starve out Paris. The staff declare they have lost no men, that the French artillery is poor, and the mitrailleuses no use except to defend a narrow passage. That is the story told to Mr. Mallet, and later to Mr. O'Sullivan : but they told quite a different tale about their own position, supplies, and the effects of the mitrailleuses to their old acquaintance of Berlin— M. Ring, formerly chargé d'affaires at Berlin, now secretary to Jules Favre.

We were to-day for a long time at the Embassy. England is now represented by Mr. Henry Wodehouse and Colonel Claremont, who have a rough time, as every English individual left in Paris wants one of three things—if not all three—advice, money, and a pass through the lines. Our advice was, "Let them draw on you for the first." There is, I regret to say, a gradually increasing idea that we are to be starved out. The Prussians are said to be in retreat towards the coast; in fact, an American declared that he "heard them packing up last night, and knew they were gone," just leaving a curtain of troops to deceive the Parisians. They are supposed to be victualling themselves, and, when that operation is effected, they will come and sit down quietly till we are starved.

The Socialists are calling for an equal division of all the food in Paris, and to-day Government has demanded all supplies except those purely domestic. We have, I hear, plenty of meat, corn, and breadstuff; but the weak point is the meat : five hundred oxen a day is a great drain, and to-day you cannot get a cutlet. I have seen a small town left with fifty thousand men and a pound of potatoes, but to wander about at 7 o'clock on an autumn evening through all civilized Paris, and not be able to buy anything but Bologna sausage at five francs a pound, and dried cod (oh, so nasty!) at one shilling and fourpence the pound, is, to say the least, more practical than poetical—more curious than pleasing. Butter to-day cost eight shillings a pound, and lard four shillings a pound.

We went to Tattersall's to-day. Out of a nailer's shop I have never seen so many screws. The first eight lots, comprising four warranted and a thorough-bred hack, which can step and jump, fetched on the average eleven pounds a head. A friend who was with me amused me by saying, "Look at all the butchers"—they were the small farmers of the environs in blue blouses. He thought we were to dine to-morrow off "Zani, cheval bai, s'atelle seul et à deux, sans garantie." He reminded me of the Reverend B—— A——, who years ago went to Tattersall's, and on his return said, "I thought I should have been the only parson present, but there were forty or fifty. I talked to several pleasant, easy-mannered fellows." In those days your small coping dealer much affected a white tie and a black coat and waistcoat.

Friday, September 30*th.*—Heavy fighting in several directions, and, as usual, numerous, various, and untrue reports.

I forget if I have written that a workman at the

Buttes de Chaumont thought he would take some tobacco and "put that in his pipe and smoke it." As he lit his lucifer he found himself surrounded by an atmosphere of fire, so he rushed away and got home scorched; but that pipe of tobacco cost the French Government six thousand barrels of petroleum.

I have another pleasure of republican life to record. The landlord of his lodging called on a Russian gentleman, a great student, philosopher, and writer, and asked for his rent. The Russian under existing circumstances asked for time. The landlord, a National Guard, went away, returned with four of his corps, seized all the furniture, destroyed manuscripts of unknown value, and finally arrested the poor Russian professor, who was only let out yesterday morning. This is no *canard* of siege times, but a stern fact, which will do this Government great harm, for the Russian Embassy has taken it up very seriously, and De Sayn Wittgenstein, the military attaché, has been with Jules Favre this morning on the subject. It is just when France requires friends that too much zeal, too much rapacity, and too great suspicion raises enemies on each side. Our representative was nearly arrested to-day.

All sorts of accounts of battle, murder, and sudden death reaching us from all quarters, we took train for Montrouge. We rode on the roof, and our society, which was cheery and talkative to a degree to bring on deafness, consisted of the fattest female I have ever seen, with a face like a plain turnip with a vacant expression; her friend, who was as thin as Miss Miggs; the most inquisitive man I have ever seen even in France, and an aide-de-camp who had crawled on his hands and knees to within a hundred yards of the Prussian lines at Maisons, and seen them in the flesh and their helmets. Conversation lively and instructive. When the French advanced on that post the Prussians had retired.

The fortifications along the line are going on very rapidly, and the weak point of Point du Jour has become very strong.

Before I come to our day, I must record two facts —one gunner has dismounted forty-seven Prussian guns : he is a sailor, and never misses. They have also "one to follow," another salt almost as good. Both have been decorated. The marine artillery is doing everything. At one of the late actions the French general found it necessary to " battre en retraite," and leave a battery of mitrailleuses. Suddenly it entered into the head of one of the gunners that one of the mitrailleuses was loaded, and that the Prussians had only to reverse its position and fire on the retreating French. He galloped back, reached the battery as the Prussians were ascending the hillside, began "playing the Barbary organ," and literally mowed down some two hundred Prussians, and got off untouched.

In one affair a French regiment went into action three thousand strong, and came out three hundred weak! There is great talk of Gallifet's charge.

But to hark back to our day. When we got to Montrouge there were the evident signs of a battle— long, melancholy lines of carts, carriages, and ambulances, with the dismal white flag and red cross, crawling slowly into Paris. The report—serious affair, and many wounded on both sides. I spoke to our aide-de-camp fellow traveller, who was a private soldier, and probably a duke, and said I had passes to the fortifications, but I wished to go beyond. His reply was laconic: "I should say impossible;" but he added, "You are English. I think you are very well known in Paris on both sides of the Seine. You will ask, and you may obtain." So we went off to head-quarters, and got there just in time to see a private of the Line (35th) in a nasty fix. He had left his regiment in face of the enemy at Villejuif, having on him eight out of ten packets of cartridges, and an ominously clean rifle. Moreover, he had heard the "retreat" sounded, which no one else had, and did not know the name of his captain. He was sent to Paris, and the campaign of 1870 will not be "dulce et decorum" to his family. "And now what do you want?" said an official. Then turning he saw my wife, and said, "Ah, par exemple! I know you and your husband. We arrested you for Prussian spies about ten days ago." To which we replied, "Effectively you did so, colonel;" and then came roars of laughter. I thought that a little round deaf man would never have recovered—have "cracked," in fact, as they say here.

"You know you were arrested," he said. Of course we knew it, and so did the "gallery," which knew us again, and had been attracted by the previous capture of that poor, hazy deserter.

"But," said the commissioner, for it is to civil rather than military authorities that we are recommended, "what can I do for you?" I said that I really was ashamed to ask, but having a pass through Paris and the environs, like all persons to whom much had been given, I wanted more, and so I wished to go to the field of to-day's fight.

Having satisfied the scruples of the commissioner the necessary pass was given to us, and we proceeded on our way, to be stopped twice in the streets of

Montrouge proper—that is, between the Quartier Général and the fortifications.

The *consigne* is very strictly, and even over strictly kept, for on Thursday they shot a drunken peasant for not knowing the watchword, and kept an old female of eighty in a ditch from damp and rheumatic eve to dewy morn for the same reason.

At the fortifications a French gentleman who spoke English, and who had been one of my examiners when I was arrested last week, made a desperate effort to stop us. "At least," said he, "Madame will remain in safety with us ;" but Madame preferred a walk.

Montrouge, but a month ago a very flourishing suburb of Paris, and really a pretty-looking village, with good houses, shops, a great distillery, the Villa d'Orléans (where to-day a French general was lying in the agony of death), and a large dreary girls' school, is now a long, deserted street, with four barricades at intervals of about an eighth of a mile. As we passed out, except the sentries there was not a living soul. On our return there were a few soldiers cooking in the middle of the street. Not only are the houses closed, but entirely deserted. Of course there was a little military movement at each of the barricades, and we were duly arrested at all of them, which gave us the opportunity of making the acquaintance of several of Vinoy's men, and also of studying the composition of these truly French defences—the barricades. The soldiers, who had all been engaged in the morning, said—"Yes! all had fought well. It was but a reconnaissance in force, and they had to fall back before overwhelming masses. The Prussians brought up thirty thousand, and but for the resolute stand of a French division, which barred the route from the Marne, they would have had another "corps d'armée" in support. "And the losses?" we asked. "Terribly heavy on both sides," was the reply.

I was waiting to show my pass to the officer in command of the last barricade, when a sentry addressed me and said—"Do you speak German?" This being a very nasty question just now, I hastened to say—"Chinese, Russian, Irish, Dutch, even Portuguese, which the natives themselves cannot speak, but not German." "I have been long in Alsace, and I do speak it," replied my private friend. "But," I said, "you are Italian by your look and accent." He grounded arms and pointed with his right hand. "This was the most thriving suburb of Paris eighteen years ago. I was born in that house; left there in 1852; have been all over the world, and see Montrouge to-day for the first time since, when I am on duty to keep out the Prussians!"

The component parts of a barricade are peculiar : say for "pièce de résistance" casks filled with stones and stable litter, and embedded in litter; then a quantity of old tin cans, a tree, a broken warming-pan, more stones, a stove, a broken ladder, an old straw hat, and a pair of most dilapidated boots ; many cart and carriage wheels, vehicles of all descriptions, loads of earth, and this curious medley makes a serious barricade, though I confess I believe that the late Lord Cardigan, on the horse he rode at Balaklava, would have gone "on and off" any of them and landed safe in the middle of his foes. These people's defences are strengthened by six feet stone walls, ten paces to their rear, and with sand bags; and wherever there is a line of houses or walls—and they are very lucky in that at Montrouge, as they have in one place three sides of a square—every two yards is pierced for infantry.

I do not think I shall ever forget the extraordinary impression produced by walking through the last barricade and entering on the open country. All life was shut within those defences. The silence was oppressive, and the flight of a sparrow produced the effect of a cock pheasant or a cockney. As we walked along the paved road to Sceaux and Palaiseau we looked over miles of desolation ; every crop destroyed, every tree cut down : there was one curious exception—a large garden of standard roses.   All the houses desolate.   Through a glass might be seen sentries now and again, and several roadside inns were evidently now head-quarters, in which troops were reposing after action—" the weary to sleep and the wounded to die."   Every ten minutes the pallid flag of the ambulance announced the passage of more of Bismarck's victims, and we saw that awful expression of pain resisted which is so habitual to soldiers.   To-day almost all the wounded are hit in the head or the left foot.

We advanced, challenged at each post, to the hill of Montrouge.   It was a strange sight.   The desert around us, the total absence of life, the two great forts of Bicêtre and Montrouge, whose fires would cross exactly on the spot on which we were standing, the lovely woods of Meudon glittering in the sun, and to the left the scene of the morning's carnage, the beautiful vale of Arcueil, shut in with those wooded heights which even then were bristling with Prussian bayonets.   It was a day of July, and truly " all save the presence of man was divine," for men and women were picking up the wounded and plundering the dead.

We reached Arcueil, which is, I rejoice to find,

celebrated for having two arches of a viaduct built by the Romans, but which will be better known as now possessing the great modern railway viaduct on the Versailles line. It was a few days since a very pretty village, with a church of the fifteenth century—a Dominican school—and an ambulance, into which I saw enter a melancholy train of wounded, including two Prussians.

Hundreds of retired citizens had bought houses, and pottered about in black silk skull-caps in these suburban gardens. There was an "Authority," a café for snuff and dominoes, a doctor, an avocat, and a priest; to-day there was one old soldier, who opened the doors of the ambulance. Before us was the plateau of Villejuif—a strong position, to gain which was the Prussian object. The battle—for in such it terminated—originated in a French reconnaissance, consisting of the 35th and 42nd of the Line (which have suffered awfully), some National Guards, Mobiles, cavalry, and some, but not enough, artillery; and it was made in order to discover what the Prussians had been doing for the last four days, where were their positions, and what their strength—questions now answered.

They had thirty thousand men in the field at least, many guns, and were barricaded in the villages, and even in the houses of Chevilly, Hay, Thiais, and Choisy-le-Roi, where, in a sort of street fight, they slaughtered many French. The French, however, drove them from each position, although, "by order," they did not hold them.

The end of the day was in fact this—Nothing lost or gained as to occupation on either side, a material falling back on former positions, great loss for such a small action on both sides. The French confessed that they had to fall back, and that they had had heavy losses, including General Guilhem, who was wounded in three places. The mitrailleuses again did good service. I fear, however, that the day was not to the advantage of France. I think that public pressure caused Vinoy to advance, and that Guilhem and some hundreds of soldiers were sacrificed to the exigences of excitement of the National Guard, who are getting bored with sedentary service. In fact, the Government is sadly hampered with advice and orders. It must be so in a Latin republic: the troops command their officers, and the officers the Government, while every writer on the Paris press— and truly "their name is legion, for they are many" —who can point a pen or shoulder a pencil has a strategical theory of his own which he prints in black and white, and woe to the general who does not obey his superior. Eh bien ! If the sovereign people will officer their own army, the sovereign people must put up with defeats generated of popular strategy.

On our return all was quiet along the line, but I was struck with the present strength of the Point du Jour—the holes full of spikes which occupy the foot-path (piéges à loup), while the guns sweep the cause-way, are as pretty devices as I have ever seen. I believe the invention is as old as Julius Cæsar.

Is not this like the French ? The division which stopped the advance of the Prussian supports returned to head-quarters in such spirits that, " finding a deserted ball-room, they stopped and had a little dance, no Sergent de Ville interfering !" and this while Bismarck is saying " non perdidi diem" !

OCTOBER, 1870.

Saturday, 1st.—A quiet night : I wish I could say a quiet morning, but my drummer began to play up at 6·30. If he had been at the front yesterday, and had only dry food for supper, he would not have been in such a hurry.

As I write the "relief," about two thousand strong (National Guards), is going out. The citizen army, which has a tendency to corpulence (especially the majors, who I believe are promoted by weight) and comfort, is followed by a military train of phaetons, broughams, Victorias, and Potel and Chabot carts, which carry coverings for the outside and lining for the inside of these civic soldiers.

It is diverting to see that the Socialist republicans have already suggested a decoration. Ribbons and crosses are dear even to the people and to the people's servants, and no wonder ! It is the national army, and we are assured an army of tradespeople. What more natural than that they should like to get orders ?

I have been wandering about the streets of Paris—

boulevards, Grand Hôtel, Rue de la Paix, Madeleine, Rue de Rivoli, and Palais Royal—for three hours, and to the best of my belief have not seen an Englishman. My barber received me with a shout of, "You here!" and he would have cut, curled, oiled, and scented me for nothing. At 4 P.M. I was his first customer—I beg his citizenship's pardon, "client" of to-day.

Paris the beautiful is a disgusting sight. The garden of the Tuileries is a very untidy artillery camp; the Palais Royal a bivouac of Mobiles, and the streets are crowded with old women, that fossil specimen of a Frenchman who has a snuffbox, a coloured cotton handkerchief, and pokes his nose into everything, all the beggars from the provinces, and all the dogs from the suburbs. I get up from my writing to see a curious sight—rather useless and very theatrical—fifteen hundred boys, "les vrais gamins de Paris," who are enrolled in a sort of commissionnaire corps. It is odd to observe how natural marching and drill come to the French. There were corporals,. whose entire uniform was a red cotton stripe on a shirt which had seen more service than its wearer, facing their companies, marching backwards, and forcing their front rank to keep time to the movement of their sticks.

The "Official Journal" declares that the Government is in a position to prove, by certain and reliable evidence, that every one of the reported plots, "which did so much to consolidate the fallen dynasty," since 1863, were concocted by M. Piétri, M. Lagrange, and the police. I simply do not believe it. Orsini and Pianori are honourably mentioned as bonâ-fide would-be murderers.

Another specimen of the justice and equality of a republic. At a meeting in the Salle d'Aligre, Citizen Toussaint made a fraternal observation about a young fellow citizen of whom he knows nothing, and probably has never seen. Citizen Toussaint states that he knows that there is in the artillery a lieutenant named Conneau, a nephew of the physician and friend of Bonaparte, and in consequence calls on all citizens to watch attentively over this lieutenant, such relationship being a bad recommendation. According to republican law the sins of the uncles shall be visited on the nephews. As to M. Toussaint, I feel inclined to say of his all-holiness what Charles Lamb said of the parson whom that old woman would praise, and wound up by saying, "I know him, bless him!" "I don't," said Lamb, "but damn him at a hazard."

Food in Paris is to-day ideal. I could not even

get a wink ·through the bars of a butcher's shop at a beefsteak I had ordered; but it is one thing to order, and another to be obeyed, as our military friends of the Republic have already discovered.

We dined at Duval's at six, and got a capital dinner for two francs. As we went out we found Frank Lawley and Labouchere in search of meat, and sent them on Mr. Goringe's recommendation to the Rue St.-Marc—capital dinner one shilling and ninepence. Mr. Goringe will be known to all our lot, to whom he never laid more than "six to four," and is a capital fellow, as is Mr. Jones; and why the deuce are they to lose all sorts of hard-earned property because six lawyers, with "power to add to their number," declare they are a Royal Commission appointed by Heaven (and Radicals) to rule France?

Sunday, October 2nd.—Quiet again, but all kinds of reports—Universal Republicanism the order of the day. We hear of an actual revolution in London, and a threatened revolt in Berlin. Louis Blanc has written a letter to the English—Why the English?— which is claptrap worthy of Richardson's show at a fair. I pointed out the fact to a great friend of the illustrious exile, and he said, " You call that nonsense !

Just wait till you see Victor Hugo's effusion." As "Argus" said of Admiral Rous, "Can no one keep them from an inkstand ?"

The sovereign people should be called the halfpenny people, as they propose to melt down the statue of the first Emperor Napoleon, which is in the Place Vendôme, and that truly historical relic, "Le Petit Caporal," which was then and is now buried at Courbevoie, and coin them into sous. Confound their sugar-selling souls! Can they read, and is there no future history of France? I have seen Italian republicans, but they did respect the glories of the grand peninsula. As for the people of Paris, it will serve them right if the pious King makes them sweep the streets of their own capital.

Yes! republicans are hard to rule. The Government, poor over-worked, willing, and under-fed beasts of burden, have done their best to defend Paris. They have even subjected themselves to the chance of being killed with their own weapons, for they have sanctioned the erection of barricades, and, what is even more dangerous, the election of a committee to raise them—President, Rochefort ; vice-president, Flourens, and secretary, that M. de Fonvielle who could not cock his pistol.

Then the sovereign people again come to the

front, and erect private barricades opposite their own groceries, as a rule just in the line of fire of the forts ; and I was much amused when I read the announcement, "by order of Citizen Rochefort," that really the people had nothing to do with barricades, must not erect them, and must in fact leave all that to the Committee, which will communicate with them by letter through the secretary, or briefly according to *non*-cocker.

The general feeling seems to me to be this, and it is the expression of a *salon* nightly haunted by the ghosts of Paris society, French, English, Russian, and American—"We will see the siege out, and then adieu for a decade to a city which is no longer Paris."

The boulevards were crowded to-day with idle *flâneurs*, going about grinning, with the guns of the "Crown of the North" thundering above the streets of this idle, frivolous city. They have got a nice little bit of news for their evening papers, and will say "Tiens ! tiens !" several hundred times—Strasbourg and Toul have capitulated or fallen. It must have required great strength of mind in the ministers to give us this news on Sunday evening. It was to be expected, but when it is come the effect is awful. If Mégy is in office to-morrow, with Blanqui as Foreign

Secretary, and Victor Hugo Ambassador at the Court of St. James's, I shall not be astonished.

Toul and Strasbourg are serious losses to France, for Prussia once having put her paw on them, will never take it off.   Toul was only a fourth-rate fortress, commanded by an inexperienced cavalry officer, and that made a gallant resistance.   Yet it is a great loss. As for Strasbourg, it is a jewel taken from the diadem of France, which has held it as its own since the end of the seventeenth century.   The worst is, that once the Prussians have taken some armed place, they will want to take, and will take more, and I fear that we shall have a great fight for Paris and then shall lose it.

The Prince de Buron says we are safe for eight days.   Are we to have continental Europe Prussianized entirely under the pious rule of the Emperor William of Germany?   Has not Russia a Cossack, Austria a Croat, Italy a *cacciatore*, or England—well England, that is difficult—England, say a Greenwich steamer to stay the advance of Bismarck, and the swamping of Europe?   As for France, c'est fini!   Send for Edmond About, and order another new map of Europe.

Monday, October 3rd.—I look in Johnson's Dictionary, turn to the word "uniform," and find that it is "similar to itself," "regular," "the regimental dress of a soldier." That is all the "sage" knew about it! I wish he could have walked up the boulevards now—he could have counted the kiosks, and touched every other stone as he did in his own dear Fleet Street. I fancy after two walks he would have revised his Dictionary, and said that "Uniform" signified any dress or disguise which was like no other. I saw hundreds yesterday, and shall see scores to-day. One man has a cap with No. 1002 on it, and the rest of his dress is civil; another has, like Theodore Hook's Bow-street runner, "rather a red waistcoat than otherwise." No. 3, has a military superstructure, but ends basely in a dusty civilian. One man has a sword—indeed, cne man has mine, and a very good one—and an epaulette; the next only shows his military ardour by the varicose stripes down his trousers. Uniform signifies deformity, or an arrangement which should not exist.

I noted yesterday that Strasbourg and Toul had fallen. What do you think the Government of Defence proposes to do? Turn the stone statue of Strasbourg into bronze! They wish to make guns and halfpence out of the effigies of the departed Empire. Had they not better hold their stupid tongues, make a large cannon, and let the "Statue of

Resistance "—a " resistance " which, like all France, has collapsed—stand in the Place de la Concorde in its natural stone till some other jealous stone-hewer knocks it into remnants because it is "so like his wife ?"

I have just read a pamphlet—"Le Sieur Louis Bonaparte : sa Vie et ses Crimes." I should like to kick the writer. And is republicanism so moral ? Suppose I instituted a black cabinet, printed private letters, and retailed secrets ! Would Louis Blanc particularly wish his citizen brothers to know how he was wont to borrow the bedroom of M. T——, in order to intrigue with a married woman between the hours of " ten and four, the husband being in a government office ?"

Victor Hugo has written a letter—I really think that it is worse than that of Louis Blanc. When cannon wake us at 5 A.M., when we are starved at home, and chance being riddled by amateurs in arms if we go out to seek meat, when the enemy is not only at the gates but inside them, we really don't require poetry written prose-fashion, and printed in large type ! And then, fancy, appealing to the " good feelings " and the " poetic tendency " of Prussia !— Prussia, which is as hard as a stone ; the King, who is as stupid as an owl, a man with a military idea ;

Bismarck, who belongs to the flint strata—still Victor Hugo appeals to sentiment, humanity, and general fraternity! Bosh! The victorious Hugo's description of winter is minute, though scarcely novel:—"Winter is, so to speak, snow, rain, frost, white frost, rime, and ice." As if we did not know that on the 3rd of October, with coals at eight pounds per ton. No! When I am in a blockaded city, and wish to be defended from a foe, may Heaven protect me from poets!

"L'Electeur Libre" says that M. de la Guerronière, ex-minister at Constantinople, was arrested when he set his foot in France. Ergo! to be a clever man, and "deserve well of your country" under any régime but that of the tyranny of the people sovereign and detestable, means loss of liberty, and perhaps loss of life. The sovereign people is indeed putting back the clock. It is a pity we cannot return to the days of fig-leaves instead of Poole, signs instead of letters, roots instead of a dinner at "White's," and become savages—that is, republicans.

We went up to the Trocadero, but saw no signs of movement, though with a good glass you can inspect Issy, Vanves, and the whole curtain of woods which now screen the Prussians. I mention as a curious fact, that we met two people we knew. Firstly, M.

Odiot, a great swell in his way, and a capital fellow : unluckily his family business is racing-cups and other articles of luxury, and so is dead and buried for years. Secondly, the Baron de Beylus, Belgian Minister, who looked, as he said he felt, just awaking from a dream.

The "Correspondence" scandals have missed fire. The scandals and the letters are too old, and though dates are altered and suppressed, yet the fatal memory of man exists.

Tuesday, October 4th.—" Terrible and trying are days of waiting," as Mr. Dicey says in his admirable memoir of Cavour. We go on waiting, but there must be a period to it, and in spite of the noble feeling of the people, one of these fine October mornings the Prussians will walk into Paris, and then what terms will they require?

I come to this conclusion—from the action of troops in the field, from the feeling of serious people who literally weep over the degradation of France, from the solemn aspect of the general population, and from the inexorable logic of fact, that three hundred thousand regular soldiers are worth nine times an irregular force of that strength. Keep the people of Paris inside the walls of Paris, and they can hold out for a certain time; but even idiocy must confess that the larger is greater than the lesser, and that strength must win in the end. And then discipline! A friend of mine, who for years commanded a battalion of National Guards, was at St.-Denis yesterday. He says that they have quantities of half-drilled men, but no officers, and that those they have can make no stand! Yet St.-Denis is one of the keys of Paris.

Our accounts from Versailles are terrible, but, let us hope, exaggerated. It is said it will be totally destroyed. The only hope that France has is that Prussia may be starving; but one can hardly think it—they have an open country, railways, and resources.

Madame de Gallifet is nursing at an ambulance; M. Paul Daru is serving as a private soldier on the fortifications. The house where I last met him (that of the Marquis de Caux) is now blocked as for a private siege of its own.

"Byron's Tavern," too, the "angulus" which was really England—where you got English food, English drink, and above all English cordiality, welcome, and politeness, is working half time, and giving no dinners. The Café Anglais is half closed, and the Café Helder says it has nothing to eat.

Day dawned, as it always does this year, with perfectly lovely weather, but with the dawn came three explosions—either very big guns, or blowing up of bridges.

A maire at St. Cloud, offended by Prussian terms, produced his revolver and knocked four of Bismarck's young men out of time. The maire, however, who was seventy years old, was taken out and shot.

According to the latest reports, the ex-Emperor has a credit of 933,000*l.* sterling with Baring Brothers. I wish I had, I should at once, though no artist, take to drawing.

Sixty-two generals gave up their swords at Sedan ! I am told, however, that resistance was vain—they were surrounded, and would have been killed to a man.

Bill of fare of yesterday's dinner at a meeting of Commissioners of Health :—

> Croûte au pot of horse soup.
> Boiled horse and cabbage.
> Horse cutlets à la mode.
> Braised ribs of horse.
> Roast filet of horse.
> Cold salt beef and horse.

Are spelling books still printed? If they are, I

suggest that " wholesome" be substituted for " noble" in the text, and that the youth of England read that " the horse is a wholesome animal."

A practical objection always seems to me to arise as to eating your stud—the meat would be so dear. Knackers would not be good even curried, and if you are to eat a horse—"a good hunter and hack, quiet in double and single harness, has carried a lady, rising six, and what will any gentleman give for him?" (I quote the departed Tattersall)—the flesh would be about two guineas a pound.

Went to see Countess Rapp's private hospital for the wounded. I saw eight patients, who must really thank the "God of Battles" for getting them shot. The house, in La Rue Cardinal Fesch, is wonderfully airy, cool, and comfortable. The Countess sits up three nights a week with her patients, and they are attended by international surgeons. France ought really to be very proud of these semi-French, who do so much for them.

There was a report that the Americans had a messenger "going straight through" to-day. It turned out that it was General Burnside, who went yesterday. Then I heard that the Hellenic Legation was likely to have "a little cove running into the opposite shore." As a rule "Timeo Danaos," even when carrying letters, but his excellency the Hellenic Minister assured me that he would willingly take all my despatches if it was not diplomatically impossible. He had pledged his honour not to carry a line. He goes to Tours to-morrow morning.

Happy thought!—not my own. " Why not raise the standard of Siam if you are denied that of England?" I believe it is a white elephant, and most people have got one of them.

Paris was duller this afternoon than I have ever seen it. The utter silence of usually noisy streets; shops which we all frequent shut at 3 P.M.; hotels, the *rendez-vous* of those who are condemned to remain here, closed; families which we know fled, and friends disappeared. Well, I can keep up my spirits pretty fairly, but there are limits, and I nearly came to these limits this 4th day of October, 1870.

Wednesday, October 5th.—I knew they would do it. Trying a blank-cartridge torpedo yesterday at Sablon-ville, they contrived to ignite the charged one, and so killed eight or ten persons. Never mind; we must die once. I wonder if there is a torpedo in my cellar, and if it will *débouche* itself in the dead of the night. To be sure, if it does, it will blow up several lower lodgers. I do not speak of their social status, or their rent, both of which are no doubt more elevated than mine, but only wish to suggest that I live *au cinquième*.

We had a wonderful story last night. De B——, Madame de X., and an inspector-general were with us, and we heard that the Duc d'Aumale was advancing from Havre with an army which is to make Prussia look more blue than ever. But where is the Duc d'Aumale to find his army? We have also a letter from the Queen of England to the father of Fritz: it says—at least, they say it says—"In the name of God and humanity, if your Majesty can, without compromising the dignity of your victory, spare a greater effusion of blood, do so, and spare the lovely city." To which Prussia remarks, that he would not kill a Frenchman on any account!

A propos—the Duke of Wellington said one evening at a private party—indeed, it was at the Cinque Ports head-quarters—that at Vienna, in 1815, there was a serious question of dividing France into the three parts recommended by Cæsar!—"Omnis Gallia in tres partes divisa est." Heaven and earth! are we in 1870 coming back to Commentaries and the Tzar who wrote them?

We hear the most extraordinary accounts of the bread in the city. But then you will say that "man cannot live by bread alone," but the French doctors tell us that he can live on bread and wine, and the supply of the latter is, thanks to " Bacchus, Apollo, Virorum," enormous !

" Le Figaro" kindly gives us the prices of our food. But "Figaro" is naturally a *farceur*. We pass over the soup, which you get cheap, good, and in any quantity at Duval's, and come to fish. A pike, which is like a paper of pins, costs from 5*s*. 10*d*. to 11*s*. 4*d*.; a barbel, 3*s*. 4*d*. to 5*s*. 10*d*.; a good eel ranges to 12*s*. 6*d*.; and a tench—imagine a small tench, which is, in fact, mud—10*d*.; a " friture de goujons" cost half a crown before they are fried; butter, 3*s*. 4*d*. the pound; while vegetables are at fancy prices.

So says M. de Villemessant. I find that you can get nothing at any price. Butter costs the price of a lawyer's letter. Fish is as high in price as in flavour. Your butcher utterly ignores you, and to-day my supplier of salt pork is " de service," and perhaps killed. A chicken costs 7*s*. 6*d*.; a duck, 8*s*. 4*d*.; and a goose, 15*s*. 2*d*. !

Oh! if they would but bombard us! We are getting quite dull. To keep up our spirits we went off outside, and visited the hospital established at the Dominican College at Arcueil.

Our arresters of last week were very polite, snubbed a National Guard on duty who declared no one should go out or come in. "This gentleman," they said, "will do both. He has special privileges, and goes where he likes." Then he gave me a pass also for a friend.

After we passed the last barricade, we saw not a soul. The two great forts were silent, but there was a lively little fight in our front. As we turned into the lane which leads to Arcueil, we suddenly ran up against the 42nd of the Line, bivouacking under the shelter of a naturally strong position. Each man had a straw mattress, very light, easy to carry, and which must be very comfortable. Some of them were cooking. We in Paris shall soon envy such rations. The colonel was there, and evidently expected an attack.

The College of Arcueil is, as far as position, air, buildings, and gardens are concerned, a splendid establishment. It was formerly the great naval college; it is now an ambulance, where we found ninety wounded. They chiefly belonged to the Line (Vinoy's division).

According to English ideas there was neither air nor cleanliness enough, but I confess never to have seen wounded looking better, and though one was at the point of death, another shot through the body, another with a doubtful leg, and several hit in the head, they were reading republican papers, smoking their pipes, and looking as jolly as possible. I must not forget to say that the kind manner of the "International" attendants to their patients was very striking.

But here was the interesting point. We have seen and spoken with a real, live Prussian soldier! He was slightly wounded in the head by a splinter at Villejuif. He is getting well, and the French feed him and pet him so that he must hope never to be sent back to his friends. He is a Pole, of the 23rd regiment.

Coming home we had an amusing scene with two Mobiles, who had had a few hours' leave to go to Paris. One admitted that he had taken "the land-lord's bottle," and he had! but "il n'avait pas le vin mauvais," and evidently he and his comrade were gentlemen. They insisted on knowing us quite well, —had let us through the lines, &c., and so, as there was no drink to the fore, we shook hands for a quarter of an hour, and parted such friends that Private 93, Pierre Petit, said to my wife—"If I see you in danger I will shelter you with my body!" He was a nice-looking youth, and carried a very tame white cat on his shoulder.

I hear that the Crown Prince says that we lost a victory at Villejuif by not having artillery. He also states that he must, to save their honour, take Paris by storm. Prince Wittgenstein heard this. *A propos*, I wonder where is our little friend Obreskoff. De B—— has been on duty round the Bois de Boulogne, and says there is a strong battery on that very strong position, the "One Tree Hill" below the Lakes, which commands St.-Cloud.

"On dit" that the Senate and Corps Législatif are asserting themselves at Limoges, and that Red Republicanism rules at Marseilles, Lyons, and Toulouse. Even here the Government has again had to protest against the "orders" given by armed battalions of the National Guard.

Thursday, October 6th.—The weather changed to-day—a fog and cold wind. Now, as we cannot buy coals, coke, or any inflammable media, we are distressed, and think of taking to our beds (Thanks to Witney, we have yet blankets) and staying there till the siege ceases.

Things seem queer. A citizen, from whom I think

I may have once bought a bundle of asparagus, stopped me in the market and said—"We are in a bad state. Can we be worse?" I observed that the question was embarrassing for a lodger. "Well," he said, "if they had shot half a dozen loafers to-day we should have had a chance. But Monsieur is busy." I remarked, "Never too busy for such conversation, but I go to the hospital with a professor." "Go then, Monsieur, but return." I said, "Yes;" and we parted "avec effusion."

This was essentially a man of the people, but of the trading—that is, reasoning—class. The fact is, that to-day great deputations have again gone to the Government to tell them that they must do "telle et telle chose."

Gustave Flourens required ten thousand chassepots for his Belleville and Montmartre Nationals. General Trochu says, "No, I have an army in the field, and I *must* reserve arms in case of a reverse." Then the "Patriot" resigns his command—it was of the dangerous division of Paris.

Another day of hospitals—the Senate. There is the splendid building, half blockaded by sand-bags, and the rest by turf still green, while the treasures of artistic wealth are sent to the cellars.

Friday, October 7th.—The Comtesse de Montfort was at the Señate yesterday. She is " grande dame s'il en fût." She went out during the Italian campaign, and at once assisted at the hospital at Milan. She has two sons wounded and prisoners at Sedan. "Ah !" she said, "I come here to help somebody, and hope in doing some service I shall forget some of my own sufferings."

We are told to-day that we are to have our siege raised through the attacks of two or three "corps d'armée," which are being organized in the provinces. But if the French army could not beat the Prussians in August, why should younger and less experienced divisions be able to beat them in October ? Thus, with all their dangers around them, and when it is still quite possible that France may be an "annexe" of Germany, the people of Paris go about with bouquets in their muskets, singing the Marseillaise, governing their rulers, commanding their armies, not the least dying for their country, but upsetting the ministers of their own choice, and destroying the beauty of their own capital. Why should they destroy a statue of Prince Eugène, or call a street "Jules Favre," when he may be to-morrow the most unpopular man in Paris, as he is to-day in Belleville and Flourensville— that is, Montmartre ? And again, the female citizen (we have now of course no *servants*) who is kind enough to visit us one hour a day for a monthly stipend which would keep a powdered footman in Belgravia, has just informed me that the Mobiles are encamped all along the Boulevard Haussmann, and are burning the trees (as well as shrubs out of the neighbouring gardens) to cook their food. If " beautiful, gay, charming Paris" has in ten days any element of beauty, joy, or fascination left, at least it will not be the fault of its citizen soldiers.

Count de Kératry is going to commit official suicide. He advises Jules Favre to do away with the office of Prefect of Police, as Brummel advised Palmerston to do away with Brummel's consulship. But surely Paris must have a police, and a head to that body ! *A propos,* " Le Figaro" says to-day that there are so many ruffians now in Paris, that property is safe nowhere, and life only in certain quarters.

The Prussians do not advance, and Captain Hore says they must regularly besiege any of the larger forts to get even the outwork. Had the Prussians advanced from St.-Cloud on the 19th of September with a hundred and twenty thousand men, and a resolve to lose twenty to thirty thousand, or even more, they might have got into Paris, and once there could have made terms. Now they will, according to the generally received opinion, try starvation, and that system, observed a well-informed man last night, " Will not take them long."

I have not yet, except *en passant,* alluded to the " Imperial Correspondence." Nor shall I do so to-day. The scandals are not very amusing, and are very old. Witness the letters of Miss Howard, whose son, Count de Beauregard, was in Paris on Wednesday.

Henri de Pène has a capital article about the resignation of Flourens. He says that any arm is better than none : if there are no chassepots, the National Guard cannot have them; but they must not cast down the muskets they have at the feet of the Prussians ! " But," adds M. de Pène, " it is an odd world. Republicanism, which is a month old, is already out of fashion, and even reactionary. You must cry out for Communism. All we republicans ask are arms and a general !"

Half our gas is cut off.

The Socialists forbid ladies to play on the piano ! I wish they would try to sit on an early drum or two, and put them down.

We had a most successful expedition to-day, when we went to see the American ambulance in the

Avenue de l'Impératrice, close to where Duvergier used to live and give breakfasts, as perhaps W—— P—— may remember, he having once called on me at midnight (I had got home at 5 P.M.) on his way home from one.

The whole of the American arrangements are admirable, and especially should be mentioned their waggons, which carry four wounded in perfect comfort. There is one at Greenwich; perhaps it will be found before we enter on the second Crimean expedition. As for civility, it is unequalled, whether you have to do with American diplomatists, civilians, or military. They cannot be courteous enough.

An observation was made by Mrs. Ward, an American lady, to Mr. Washburne, the minister, who was there with Dr. Swinburne (who went all through the American war), Il Professore Ranzi (who was one of the Romans in Rome in 1848), Dr. Gordon, and ourselves, that two doctors were called in by the Americans, in whom the French put no faith—Dr. Fresh Air, and Dr. Cleanliness. The ambulance can be packed up bodily in a few hours and taken to the field.

Mr. Washburne is very much annoyed with Mr. Sullivan, who made himself a sort of amateur ambassador between the non-existing government of the 4th of September and the Prussians.

England has not recognized the Government of the 4th of September, and dates her passports the 2nd of September. She has given here about two thousand in six weeks. It often strikes me that if De Goltz had lived, and Lord Lyons been ambassador here, we should have been spared this great and scandalous war.

Saturday, October 8th.—The first thing which the Provisional Government ought to have done this damp Saturday morning, should have been to shoot Gustave Flourens; instead of which they arrested me. M. Gustave Flourens is in open mutiny : commander of a division, he resigns his command, and resumes it because his division voted his return. I wonder what Condé, or Napoleon, or " the Duke," would have said to a division voting that a cashiered officer should return to his command ! Voting ! Good God ! As if soldiers should ever even be allowed to think ! I should say *not*, as thinking is evidently antagonistic to fighting.

Very cross I got up before my usual hour, and went to be examined by a republican policeman in the Rue de Provence (which used to require as many policeman as the Rue St.-Nicholas). I asked, "What is the matter? If you wish to give me orders for food, we are two and a servant, and for choice should like the best of everything, and as much of it as the sovereign republic will allow us." "Halte là!" said my policeman—no, say police gentleman, for he was very civil. "It is no question of food. You are denounced as having constant relations with the Prussians."

Then I said, "My dear sir, here is my passport. I have lived here eight years. I have written three times to 'le Gouvernement actuel,' as you call it; but as we don't yet call it, to offer to help you, though you will not admit it, and you are not civil enough to reply to my letters. On the contrary, I have been three times arrested, though you are obliged to let me out, as I have special permission to go where I please."

Then the authority confounded himself in excuses, and I confounded him inwardly for making me get up at eight o'clock.

Mr. Hutton, an American gentleman, was also arrested: he was taken from his bed by grocers armed with bayonets, and kept prisoner for five hours. I admit, however, that there was some reason. Hutton and the Duc de Castries had penetrated into the Prussian lines and spoken with the enemy.

Rothschilds' was an odd sight to-day. Instead of the constant pressure of the tubes of the electric bells, and the swing of the two doors which used to bring, from one moment to another, the latest news from all Europe—all the world, there was a silence, and the Baron, in uniform, was waiting till it was time to go on duty on the fortifications.

As I write, more fools go by with flowers in their muskets. I begin to hate a Parisian who does not belong to the Jockey Club or the *halles.* Defend us from the respectable middle classes.

Sunday, October 9th.—There was rain last night, but I fear that the Prussians, in such good quarters as Versailles and St.-Cloud, did not care much about it. The report to-day is that the Prussians are prepared to pass the winter here; but then even if we are put on rations we cannot hold out till Christmas.

A friend of ours was at Bicêtre yesterday, and was told by the naval officer in command there that, as soldiers, the Prussians are splendid. "We know that those woods are full of them, but we never see one." Our friend detected one sentry behind a tree, and he never moved for two hours, when the relief came round.

Questions of the day :—Where are the Corps Diplomatique, and the detached ministers of the Republic one and indivisible? Where is the manifesto of the Emperor? What is the existing government of France, and who rules Paris?

There was a great "advanced," or "commune," demonstration yesterday, to tell the Government that the people "decreed" that the municipal elections should take place at once. However, the united people were on this point divided, and so there was a counter-demonstration, which ended of course in speeches and cries of "Long live every one who agrees blindly with us, and does what he is told to do." So the affair ended ; but it might have been most serious. "That which is postponed is not lost!"

Facts of the day :—·Eggs have risen in price twenty-five per cent. A man went into Potel's and asked for some at any price. "Very sorry," said Potel *père*, "but we can *only* offer you plovers' eggs !" I never heard of them in October, but I suppose there are plovers, and plovers.

This reminds me of what was once said to us in Rome. "We have no champagne, except some nasty dry stuff which we got for the Russian Prince Swallowoff." We tried it, and when the time came to leave the Eternal City, I can answer that there was not a drop left. The bottles were then dryer than the wine.

The new police have appeared. As the English were christened "Bobbies!" these should be dubbed "Gambette." They are such guys! like a child's idea of "Bogey!" Military cap, civil coat and cape, with republican decorations; the latter being little cockades exactly like the carrot and turnip ornaments with which, in the early period of civilization, people in the districts "between Mesopotamia and Russell Square" were wont to adorn tongues at evening parties. These agents of safety go about in threes. The rulers might have made it "fours," and then when they went to their café to play whist they would not have been obliged to play dummy.

Big guns at intervals, but it's only the republican army knocking down the works which the despotic army is raising. The French have the best at this game.

I have seen several very well informed Englishmen, quite experienced in Paris life, and they shake their heads and say, "Cut off the supplies, diminish the menu, stop the soup, or reduce the roast, and it is all over with Paris. Le Colonel l'Estomac will give in," probably advancing with a clean napkin as a flag of truce.   Anglo-Parisian trade is utterly ruined, and nobody makes enough to pay his concierge.

"Le Réveil" has come out with an anti-government-of-national-defence article, which, if Jules Favre swallows, we may certainly serve him up the rest of the "dîner du jour." He will probably make a speech, and ask some subaltern's permission to put a general order in the order book, to say that France is now heaven, and will continue so to be as long as the troops do exactly as they like, and take a pot shot at a Prussian if he is well within range. If they wish to go home when it rains, why, naturally, they must do as they like. So pray Heaven for fine weather, and in case of an atmospheric reverse, Fortune and umbrellas protect the army!

A duller Sunday I have never passed, and I have been both at Exeter and Edinburgh.

Monday, October 10*th.*—No news, and bad weather.

Yesterday one Sapia, who commands the 146th battalion of National Guards, ordered a parade, distributed cartridges, and proposed to march on the National Government at the Hôtel de Ville. Luckily his own men arrested him, and he is sent before the Council of War. I pity the ministers, who mean well, but are hampered on every side.

People are getting very low in spite of the assurances of the Government. Three people, English residents of years' standing, said to me yesterday, " It is not the Prussians, but the Socialists we fear. We know them of old."

Trade, except in wine shops, cheap restaurants, outfitters of the mildest order, where "affaires marchent" very rapidly, is a history of the past—a reminiscence. The only transaction I have to report is the exchange or barter of a tin of boiled mutton against x (quantity to be settled by arbitration) boxes of sardines. Strasbourg beer is dearer than pale ale: wine alone keeps its nominal·price.

The American General Burnside came from Prussia —*i.e.*, Versailles—to Paris, and has gone back again, carrying all the American Legation bags. In fact, if you are American you can do anything, and carry anything. At the Russian Embassy they are very angry. Our Embassy is calm, cool, and bored.

The French Home Office to-day was a curious sight. "Is M. de Z. here?" "Mais, non; certainement, non! Nor anybody else!"

Having dined, we were going home, when we met a friend: "Deuce of a row at Belleville and at the Hôtel de Ville. Come down." Now the countenance of the boulevard had been threatening—little groups, murmurs, orderlies galloping, dinners eaten in hot haste, and other signs known to the frequenters of revolutionized cities. So off we went. At the Hôtel de Ville was a regiment of National Guards, " with the customary signs of solemn" joy—their rifles loaded to the muzzle with laurels and other greens, and evident signs that they were prepared either to favour Favre or save Sapia. It is always difficult to know who Paris favours. No disturbance.

Then we drove to Belleville and Villette. They were as calm as a good man's conscience—as dull as a droll book. The citizen who kindly " conducted " us, at two francs twenty-five centimes the hour—with a " to drink " of course—was a good, if morose fellow. " Row !" said he; " well, if not to-night, to-morrow. I don't wish for bloodshed, but for my part I'd shoot them all. Why should three parts of Paris be ruined, starved, and blockaded because this *quartier* wants to select and give us our king ?" We had no row, but it is evident that the whole thing is rotten. The most we can hope is that six months of republicanism and six weeks of socialism may bring back the tran- sient calm of Orleanism — unless, indeed, France becomes a dismembered state, and ranks with Hanover.

As unlikely ships have come to shore, as unlikely predictions come true. " Figaro" makes very merry about Flourens. It believes that he is going to "name himself colonel-major of fourteen regiments of cavalry, six of artillery, and two of baggage-train—of course with trumpets."

Tuesday, October 11*th.*—Weather bright, but cold, especially towards morning, and some of the Mobiles have begun to feel it. Gambetta, who has gone to raise provincial France, and show the Red Cross, has got safe over the Prussian lines. I did not see him leave the Place de St. Pierre, but I hear that when he got "on board" the balloon he was in a Prussian-blue funk, as we used to say at school. Some Americans, too, have "aired" off for Havre to get arms from America. How on earth do they expect to get them into Paris ?

We hear of great rejoicings at St.-Cloud and Versailles—feastings, reviews, music, and decorations. But as a set-off we are told of great suffering, cold, and want of food. Probably one report is as true as the other—that is, not the least true. All I can say is, that we have no music but drums ; no reviews but drills. Now drums are too spirit-stirring when taken on an empty stomach at 6·30 A.M. ; and as for drill, it is the devil! to which wicked Blackness at daybreak this very Tuesday I wished that an adjutant might march his regiment and get permanent service.

On the whole, I think that a siege is very like a general's uniform. Seen outwardly it has a deal of the pomp of war; turn it, and it is only a common cloth garment with a cheap lining.

Food? Oh! yes, there is plenty of food, only you cannot get it. Beef and mutton in times of siege go as kissing does (I am told) in times of peace. Duval, however, continues his cheap dinners; but, to quote the play bills, you must " come early," or the play will be played out. The "house" is crowded, and your Mobile is a noble eater, who dines soon.

I have seen to-day many shops and two markets full of "horse." In the shops, cut up, it did not look so nasty, but I confess a whole side of horse is a spectacle. The meat was dark in colour. A medical friend who was with me objected both to the colour and to the smell; but it was quite fresh, and prime parts were fourpence a pound. They offered it cheaper if we had a large consumption. Prices vary with the skirmishes: yesterday they killed a good many Prussian horses near Bondy.

As we were walking home Dr. G—— said to my wife, looking into a shop window, " Well now, there is food! Do for breakfast—capital sausages." Where-upon a lady, a total stranger, passing by, turned round, and said, "Bah! horse! don't buy those." (I think not!)

Dr. G—— does not approve of the sanitary state of the miles of canvas barracks which line the boulevards of Paris. He says that there is no ventilation, and not even an attempt at drainage. "Look," he said, "at the position of those cooking places, the un-drained and fetid space round them, and the want inside the barracks themselves of two elements—air to breathe, and water for ablution—and then it will require no great prophet to predict typhus." As yet, I think there is little sickness.

Are we to be attacked or starved? Report to-night: An attack to-night or to-morrow. It could only be on a fort; and the St.-Cloud battery seems, in fact, an established fact. Per contra, Bismarck is said to be against attacking, and in favour of treating, the King and Moltke opposing him.

It was a curious scene at Montmartre to-day. Few soldiers, no Mobiles, but a large idle crowd staring at St.-Denis, to which spot ten thousand regulars marched at 9 A.M. with waggons, &c. There was some heavy firing at Courbevoie.

Wednesday, October 12th. — Weather suddenly changed, and after quite a warm evening such a cold night and morning as will sorely pinch patriotism, and let us hope also Prussians.

The balloons are all very well, but we want some slight return for our kindness in sending out so many amusing letters, and at this present writing we have not had a letter, paper, or telegram since the 18th of September.

Home news is scarce to-day. Flourens is "said to be going to be" tried by court-martial and civil process. He proposed to attack the Hôtel de Ville yesterday, and, from what I hear, is likely to assault it to-night. He lives at his private residence, where he is guarded by his men, and the papers to-day state that one thousand men are ready to rescue him if he is arrested. Now, one thousand would attract another thousand at least—nothing truly against the force which the Government can command, but yet sufficient to upset Paris, and that signalled to St.-Cloud would produce a movement. Bismarck has cut into the Prusso-French rubber, and got Flourens for his partner.

Monsieur (late Count) de Kératry has resigned his post as Prefect of Police, and is going on a " mission."

He is succeeded by a '48 man—M. Edmond Adam. Query—Do these many missions mean peace, and is the existing Government prepared to give up a stone of its forts, or an inch of its territory ? Time—a very short time—will answer the last question.

The gardener from Meudon has escaped into Paris, and says that the enemy is destroying the whole of the beautiful gardens and the celebrated avenue. It is very sad certainly, but it is the work of an enemy, and we know that nothing is so cruel, so tedious, and so expensive as to make " war and water." War must be neat—devastation, destruction, murder, and desolation, so the Prussians are right in mutilating magnificent Meudon ; but what excuse is to be made for the people of Paris, who have made the capital of Europe—as they were so fond of calling it—the dirtiest and dullest town in Germany ?

I was going to make a remark about the " patient angler," who has lately very much amused me, who not only raises my respect for the disciples of Isaac Walton, but my envy, for I never see a man fishing with a float without wishing to sit down beside him. But Théophile Gautier has been before me : all he says is true. There, under a tree and a heavy fire ; here, on a wall, sits the fool who submerges the worm.

Gautier writes:—"Notwithstanding this agitation, the fishers with the rod are quite undisturbed. They are philosophical, and cold blooded. The other day we saw many of them between Bercy and the Point du Jour; some knee deep in the water, some sitting in boats, and some on walls, never moving their line or taking their eyes off their float. These brave men are not the least afraid of the Prussians, and when a shell falls close to them, they only exclaim, 'Those sour cabbage eaters will frighten the fish!'" I will myself confirm all this.

Another phase of this state of siege—we have got a society which I call "Le Club des Frondeurs," because we are all opposed to the existing Government, and throw our stones at it. We meet every evening, but we don't always talk politics. Last evening a National Guard told me a statistical fact: he said that living in Paris was cheaper since the siege!

"Yes," he said, "it is!" I doubted; but he insisted. This was his argument:—"Lui" is obliged frequently to give a little supper to "Elle." Up to the day of the legal Government he was forced to go to the Maison Dorée, order "hors d'œuvres," soup, cold fish, game, truffles, and Cliquot "à l'indiscrétion." Now he writes—

"Dearest Jeannette,—

"Come to Brébant's at nine : he has promised
me a horse-hoof and a bit of cheese.

"I place at your little feet

"Your Alphonse."

Well, when it's over it will be droll to remember.
No meat, no money, no servant (God is ever merciful,
and made our "help" impertinent), only one fire, and
the supplies kept in a drawing-room cabinet, to which
we apply ourselves, like Sarah Gamp—"when we
are so minded."

It would not even be very tiresome if they would
only shell us ! I dread a bored Parisian, especially if
he lives at Montmartre ; and he may take to shelling
us ! Eh bien ! mon cher, I hope they will never try to
improve any other government under which it may
be my lot to live.

A great force, with baggage-waggons, stores, and
ammunition has just marched by. Surely they are
not going to try the fatal folly of attacking ! If so,
the Magazin de Deuil is likely to have a good time.

Poor people at Villette and Belleville decline to eat
horse, and an Italian servant told me to-day that she
had heard that " quella povera carne " was good,
but that no one in her quarter of Paris would eat it.

Thursday, October 13th.—There was a good deal of heavy firing from the forts yesterday, and our reports say that the Prussians were driven back on two, if not three points. I confess that, like the rest of the " Frondeurs," I cannot make out the Prussian game. A month ago they might have walked into Paris. They did not; now they cannot; but surely the Uhlans should beat our best Eclaireurs à Cheval, and the infantry which I saw reviewed not long ago must be stronger than a Moblot-volunteer force, and yet the " Fritz " does nothing. He can starve us out before Christmas, to be sure, but that will be a very tame conclusion to this ferocious campaign.

" Le Figaro " has to-day a wonderful article on Prussian *espionage*. According to M. Ivan de Wæstyne, no boudoir, or even bedroom, is safe from Bismarck. Even now treacherous washerwomen from Versailles go to and come from Paris, bearing much more than shirts and shifts—even, it is hinted, the wearers of the latter.

I have small faith in spies, and ever since I have known Paris there has been a lot of fair women with blue eyes and attractive manners, about whom the world always said, " You know, mon cher, with whom you were flirting last night ? Madame de Sablotoff—a Russian spy." Later it was " the Graffin von Badenberlingerhoff, a Prussian spy, and the lover of Bismarck's third private secretary."

What really did an immense injury to the Empire, was a clique of *soi-disant* clever women, who gave breakfasts to mature members of the representative bodies, who talked false politics, retailed true secrets, and intrigued for concessions.

The eighth volume of the "Correspondence" is very interesting, and proves the great trouble which was taken to keep the Emperor in the dark. Fancy the little "Pourtalés," the most charming of countesses, a patroness of short dresses, coming out as a politician! .

Five of the Liners who ran away at Châtillon are sentenced to death. They will never dare to carry out the sentence.

They really are forming female legions! Yet are Parisiennes no race of Amazons, but formed for all the witching arts of love; and the whole party should be whipped and put to bed, like the scions of that house, the female representative of which "lived in a shoe." "Le Figaro" calls them "foot Amazons who have eaten their horses."

The fighting to-day has been again serious and unsatisfactory. A reconnaissance in force, and a retreat to former positions. Unluckily these natural, but perhaps I may be allowed to say exhaustive, tactics are not understood by volunteer and irregular armies, which think that when, as to-day, one hundred and fifty men have been killed and three hundred wounded, and they " retreat in excellent order," that they are no great gainers.   As a proof of this I will mention, that where we dined to-night there was a fierce discussion between two people who had both been all day on the field, as to whether we (the French) had been victorious or defeated.   The fight was to the south and west of Paris, the forts of Montrouge and Issy protecting.   That plateau below Villejuif is our cockpit.

The French fought well, and seem, if our present returns are correct, to have made an example of the Prussians, about one hundred and fifty of whom were taken prisoners, and several Prussian, or rather Baden and Wurtemberg officers are now in the private ambulance.   On the French side the loss was less because they were really all day under their own great guns, which were admirably worked.   Still, great holes were made in every rank of Paris life during each succeeding twenty-four hours, and if you meet an acquaintance you dare not ask after his relations.

To-day we lost Count de Dampierre, one of the great men of clubs, of the turf, and a master of staghounds, who fell shot through the heart by the first Prussian bullet fired as he was leading his men against a barricade at Bagneux. A few days since that revolting radical "Rappel" hinted that he was a coward, and said that he treated his men like dogs. He was foolish enough to be annoyed, and exclaimed, "If I get a chance they shall see if I am afraid, and how a Dampierre dies."

Yes, I know, my dear Mrs. Grundy, that it is just as dreadful when Pierre or Julien dies; but then, you see, perhaps we don't know Pierre or Julien personally. Dampierres too have been writing, fighting, and dying for France since A.D. 1500. The last time I saw him he was booking 1000 to 600 in the Bois.

To-day is an unholy day. The beautiful Château of St.-Cloud is destroyed. Become a "nest of Prussians," it was bombarded, and purposely set on fire. An English resident in Paris, by no means given to the melting mood, has just left me literally "les larmes aux yeux." The fine building, frescoes, tapestry beyond price, pictures, the gardens, old trees, flowers, are wreck and ruin. It was a splendid place, and is now a barracks from which Prussians have been driven out.

I shall not easily forget the last time I saw St.-Cloud. It was in July of last year. The Emperor gave a private party, at which he discussed the coming "constitution" (confound it!). We walked about under avenues lighted "a giorno" by electric lights; talked about everything, from the constitution of a government to the construction of a crinoline. Later the thoughtless danced and the heedless of to-morrow supped. "I do not like the tone of this senatorial society," said the friend who drove me down. "Most of the people should have been *outside* the *grille*."

It is a curious fact that this week we have had *two invitations to dinner*. The note now usually runs thus:—"We have got some fresh meat: come and eat it at eight."

We had so curious a party last night that I must make a note of it. Our hostess was an English subject married to a Scotch nobleman, but by birth and connection also French and Dutch. Her mother, who was there, is Dutch and German. M. X., who was opposite to me, is an Alsatian, married to an English lady, and with English children. He is the great international lawyer. The other was a French baron, who is half English, something French, something Corsican, and who represents one of three great houses which are entitled by birth to sit in the Parliament of Prussia. The language spoken was as peculiar as the occupations of the party had been during the day. The lady of the house had been up all night at her hospital, and had just cooked the dinner, her only assistant being an old soldier of the first Empire.

The Countess R—— drove straight to dinner in an ambulance waggon from the field of fight, where she was gathering wounded for her private hospital. One man, with thirty thousand pounds a year, was limping about in uniform as a Mobile private; and the Baron de B—— had carried despatches to General Ducrot. After a long ride he found him at Argenteuil, but though he rode across country he could not see a Prussian.

Captain Hore, attached to the British Embassy, was sent back by the Prussians at Epinay St.-Denis, and the enemy even refused to receive a letter from the Nuncio for William the Pious. But is not the Republic slightly insolent to England?

Friday, October 14th.—The anniversary of the battle of Jena. I think I have already written in this diary what King William said at Homburg to Lady ——: " He would not die till he had avenged Jena."

He has done so now; but we were promised a pretty little battle to-day. I fear it will not come off. *Vado vedere*—but all is as yet silent. In fact, there was a truce of six hours to bury Prussians.

The last pleasure of living under a republic! I was very anxious to see my " Official Paper" to-day, and sent the aid for it. She was away about forty minutes, and when she was slightly rebuked (we dare no more now), she said, Yes, she was a long time, but the concierge had not finished reading the paper ! N.B.—It comes " sous bande," which actually is an envelope.

They say that De Kératry goes to St. Petersburg, and Louis Blanc to London. The chief recommendation of Louis Blanc to diplomacy is that he is related to the late Pozzo di Borgo. That is about as good reasoning as that evolved at " White's," where somebody said that Sir Robert Peel was made a Lord of the Admiralty because he once fell into the sea.

I wish I could tell you some little stories of the siege ; but I cannot. Not the least too coarse for the ladies left in Paris, they would make the hairs of England, male and female, resemble " the *fruitful* porcupine."

There seems little doubt that Bismarck and Burnside have been treating for peace, and about peace. Bismarck mildly suggested a six weeks' truce, during which no troops were to move out, and no provisions or ammunition' to come in! France naturally said that active was better than passive blockade. Bismarck and Burnside were yesterday called the "two busy B's."

I had a visit from a brave soldier and clever man to-day. He dined on Wednesday with the King of Prussia at Versailles, and being on a mission of charity, passed the lines without trouble; but he was arrested this morning by the French, though he was in English undress uniform, and wore (I think) the "Légion d'Honneur." His opinion is that the Prussians mean attacking, and are only waiting for guns. They are, as I expected, perfectly jolly at Versailles.

England may well be proud of the following announcement, as she may well be proud of the Guardsman of whom Kinglake wrote—"It was for the resolute stand made here" (a handful of men opposed to the majestic Vladimir column, in fact) "that Lindsay received the Victoria Cross":—

"The English Colonel Loyd-Lindsay has just arrived in Paris, bringing to the Minister of War the sum of five hundred thousand francs for the relief of the sick and wounded French soldiers under treatment in the ambulances. This sum is the result of subscriptions collected in England.

" A committee will be appointed to dispense and watch over this fund, and Colonel Claremont, the military attaché to the embassy of her Britannic Majesty, will be requested to accept the office of president.

" The Minister of War has, in the name of the army, offered his thanks to Colonel Lindsay."

It is so pleasant to see England give some sign of life !

I dined last night in the Rue d'Enghien. As all the ladies were on duty in the hospitals, and the men at different posts, we broke up early, and I, being a " bearer of despatches," walked across half Paris. It was the most lonely, dark, and deserted walk I have taken for many a long day.

At dinner a servant burst into tears at hearing I could send a letter to her lover. The very day the banns were published, that is, the names put up at the Mairie, *Lui* marched, and has never been heard of since ; but *Elle* knew the number of the regiment.

St.-Cloud, it seems, was destroyed accidentally by a shell fired to test distance. I hope this is true, as it would rather strengthen my conviction that they do not intend to destroy Versailles. To-night it was positively asserted that they had learned the dinner-hour of the King and his staff, and meant to blow up the whole wing in which they live, eat, and smoke, and have their beer and being. As sure as fate, if the King, the Crown Prince, and the Count live to come into Paris they will be assassinated. Young Duval, the son of our great butcher, was to-night "de service" (not dinner service, but as an Eclaireur à Cheval); he came in his brougham with *two* beds.

Saturday, October 15*th.*—I said that I had a truly lonely walk last night; indeed, I met ten cripples and beggars to any one else—cripples armed with crutches, and beggars with bad language; so it is consoling to read in this morning's paper that—" At a public meeting held at the Cour des Miracles, it was resolved to order the Government to discharge at once the keepers of the public peace, as police is an Imperial system."

According to the " Figaro," there are four hundred and seventy-five thousand armed men now in Paris.

Lieut.-Colonel Loyd-Lindsay got off quite safe with a company of about eight. Two officers sculled him over the Seine at Sèvres, and an escort of Uhlans was waiting citra-Seine to take him to Versailles.

Paris to-day was duller than I have yet seen it, and shops are closing gradually. There were about two dozen chickens in the market, each costing as much as a second-class return ticket to Brighton, and a fair supply of vegetables at war prices.

There was no fighting I think, but great military movement of stores, &c., in the city; and I see that non-alarmists are becoming alarmists about disturbances in Paris.

Sunday, October 16th.—When Sir Walter Scott walked through Pompeii with the classic Gell, he said nothing but "City of the Dead! City of the Dead!" Had the author of "Waverley" been at the Grand Hôtel at ten o'clock this morning, I think he would have looked up the boulevard and made the same remark. The inténse quiet was broken later by the march to the "front"—which means the Point du Jour—of some three thousand Nationals—mounted officers, vivandières, colours flying, and drums being beaten; for "drums beating" must be false English.

We have a quantity of reports, chiefly derived from the "Standard" and "Times," which an American lady has smuggled in. Among other stories, it is said that Garibaldi has actually arrived at Marseilles. Now I have a deep respect for the great guerilla General, and wish him well; so I wish him back at Caprera. Red republicanism seems rampant; if so, it is all up with France, for those who can will leave the country.

Burnside's mission missed fire. It is very odd, living in the centre of great events, and knowing nothing more of them than what comes from the vaguest reports. Probably, of all the Franco-American reports we have heard to-day, not one is true. But if true, what does Garibaldi's mission portend? The French Republic assisting at a later period the erection of the people's government in Italy?

Four o'clock. Definition of utter dullness!

A wet Sunday in a city in a strict state of siege!

Two visitors, who tear linen into lint as they talk hospital!

All existing club Paris was present at Dampierre's funeral.

We dined with the Hon. Mrs. ——, and met Viel-castel, who was on guard at the funeral, and said it was a splendid spectacle. In these times I never go to funerals. Besides, I hate to see a sportsman "go to earth!"

Yes; we had horse for dinner, and I was tremendously laughed at for having last Wednesday declared that I could not touch it, after I had dined off it! It is very good, but I declare that I will never eat it again if I know it. Of course it is prejudice, but no more "gee-gee" for this child. A mule's cheek is,

I am told, excellent, and I dare say it is ; but I shall take the advice given by young Bailey to the Misses Pecksniff—"Don't have none of him."

All sorts of wild stories about a battle at Orleans. Mr. Washburne's valet, who came to-day from Versailles, says that he saw a large number of wounded brought into Versailles from that direction; and Vicomte de Flavigny (head of the ambulance movement here), who was to have seen Bismarck on some mission of mercy, was stopped on his road, and told he could not be received for a day or two.

Roy is not killed, and Obreskoff has come back to Paris, only he says he will not stay.

One of the balloons which were to have started yesterday "bolted before it was mounted," and got clear away. The Prussians fired on another, missed it, and killed four Moblots who were missing a target in a drill yard.

It was distinctly stated to-night that many letters of the Imperial correspondence are forgeries. I give you all my news, "under reserve the most strict."

Monday, October 17th.—Lovely weather for campaigning, and about five thousand Mobiles marched at 10 A.M., towards Vincennes. They were in heavy marching order, with tents, bread, &c. Looking like work, they went by singing, and seemingly very happy, and if I thought they knew how to fight I should not be much alarmed; but if they get into the " open field " I fear their want of drill and discipline, the strong points of Prussia, must beat them. You require a Clive to make great sorties with untrained troops.

I called on Colonel Claremont, who is solicited to be president of the British Fund Committee. I hope sincerely that he will accept the office, as he is the proper man, and would give satisfaction to both French and English; but I do not envy him the task. It is resolved to give no money, only stores—coffee, chocolate, flannel, tobacco, with good wine. I have a letter now before me from the Comtesse de Montfort, President of the Luxemburg Ambulance, saying that at that ambulance they would prefer money's worth to money. The Vicomte de Flavigny, head of the "International" here, was proposed, but I fancy he is not popular; besides, a civilian president would not do.

We had a most interesting walk—very long, but certainly the most war-like march we have had this siege season. We started up the Champs Elysées, which was of course bare of carriages, and even " piétons," but every five minutes there were some signs of military movement. The only foreigner we encountered was Mr. Labouchere, in high spirits in spite of the prevailing dullness, amusing as usual, and making to himself friends of the Mammon of republicanism by wearing a truly truculent hat of the date of the Great Revolution.

The Arc de Triomphe presents a curious, if not a pleasing sight.   Like the rest of Paris to-day, all the space around it is very dirty, not having been swept since the German soldiers came into France, and the German " sweeperesses " left; and the whole circle round it is now a foot deep in earth and sand.   This is piled up to diminish the danger of shells bursting, and is to be seen in the courtyard of every house.

They are putting up strong boarding over the great " alti-relievi ;" but, by a curious error, or oblivion, they have covered up the side of the Arc looking down the Champs-Elysées, where even a chance shot can hardly come, and have not yet touched the side facing the Avenue de la Grande Armée, which before the anniversary of Leipsic is over may be within range of French forts fallen into Prussian hands, and which looks stark into St.-Cloud.   The usual crowd of those idle gazers into space who always see nothing, and who mistake the fall of a camp-kettle for a big gun, was ranged at the head of the Avenue.

There are changes there within the last week. Now,

the first barricade meets you two hundred yards from the Arc, and you are opposed by several more before you reach the poor Porte Maillot, which I am sure its dearest friend would not recognize. All the way down the Avenue the houses are empty, except the " English Ladies' Boarding Schools " and the " Pensions pour Demoiselles," which are occupied by Zouaves and Mobiles in force. Every other house is prepared for an infantry post, and the end of each street is strongly barricaded. The desolation outside the Porte Maillot has, I should say, now arrived at a climax. Paris, seen from that point, looks like some strong place in a desert. Luckily it looks like a *very strong* place.

As for the Bois, it does not exist: the whole of the trees which grew inside the lines between Porte Maillot and the Avenue de l'Impératrice are cut down, as is for two hundred yards wide all the fine forest which ran parallel with the Avenue Porte Maillot down to the Jardin d'Acclimatation, where there is a strong barricade. That prettiest bit of the Bois is now one large "cheval de frise," while the ditch along it is cleverly covered with the cut-down boughs, and makes capital Mobile barracks.

We mourned over this ruin, and turned into the high road which leads to Neuilly and Courbevoie—

that hill which we have so often seen from the Arc de Triomphe, and on which, when the "Petit Caporal" was deposed from the column of the Place Vendôme, he was set up on a granite pedestal. Nothing but granite was strong enough to testify to the firmness of the love of the French for their Bonapartes, yet the pedestal to-day was occupied by three men "on the look-out," and there is a talk of coining the "Caporal" into "coppers."

I complained that a walk from the gates leading to Bercy or Arcueil was the extreme of silence and depression. It was not the case to-day when we got back into the Courbevoie road. The barricades became more frequent, the houses more fortified; but there was at least a "corps d'armée" of regulars, chiefly drilling or cooking, and Mobiles singing and playing pitch and toss. From the Rue d'Orléans to the Rond Point of Courbevoie it was one long bivouac. That would prevent silence, but in addition there was a perpetual visiting of guards by field-officers, occasioning much drumming, relief of sentries, galloping of aides-de-camp and orderlies, strings of chargers, a long line of stores, ammunition waggons and ambulances going out; literally a legion and a half of country carts loaded with everything conceivable and inconceivable, waggons full of straw and vegetables, and now and again a wounded man in a cab—coming in. These were ranged four deep, and impetuous aides-de-camp could hardly get along.

The crowd of country carts and the rather rare private carriages coming in struck me. For six weeks they have been streaming in; then we had a lull. To-day they were pouring in as from a panic, bringing in everything down to vegetables and the last bunch of autumn flowers they will probably ever gather from the gardens of the houses in which they were most likely born. It was sad to see! but then, you know, war has its exigences as well as its glories.

I fancy a big fight is imminent. At any rate, the scene on the bridge of Neuilly was very striking. It was a lovely day; the river on both sides was running like liquid silver, and the autumnal tints were in great beauty. It was a military masquerade: every man was (and so were some women) in uniform—Moblots, regulars, sailors, vivandières, priests, a man like " Figaro " (I mean " Figaro quà, Figaro là "), Zouaves, Turcos, and a good-looking girl dressed as a Mobile.

A general officer is galloping up to a post, and "Guard turn out!" puts about a mile of men in motion. A regiment of cavalry is watering its horses. All is life there, but war again peeps out in the distance, where all was desolation, and the broken bridge

of Asnières carried us back to the horrors of the hour.
It was here that, on the 15th of December, 1840, the
body of Napoleon was landed under the inspection of
the Duc de Joinville—when Horace Vernet's daughter,
being asked if she was not affected, said, " Yes, by
the cold ;" and when Soult knelt before the coffin, and
burst into tears.

We proceeded to the hill—the extreme outpost,
and close under Mont Valérien, where we were within
easy reach of the Prussians; but as they were in a
good temper we enjoyed the view and examined the
vast strength of the position in utter tranquillity.   In
a battery facing the west are three very large guns;
on your left hand is Mont Valérien, a shell from
which is said to have been sent so directly that it
killed General Treskow, who was standing at Montretout; and on your right stands the now strong
place of St.-Ouen; between these two forts are three
batteries.   All the guns are worked by seamen, and
only yesterday they fairly cannoned down the Prussians who were repairing the bridge of Argenteuil,
supported by a masked battery.   It is a splendid
position, and I think the Prussians will never get in
on that side ; and I should say that they keep threatening the west defences of Paris to take off attention.

As we were looking at the view, and thinking how different it all was since we last passed it on our way to dine at Bougival, we heard a mighty rush as of a large Etat Major. We walked over the road and saw General Ducrot gallop up, followed by his staff and by a troop of the mounted skirmishers. He had been out on a reconnaissance. He halted at the head-quarters of General Berthout; then he, with all his staff, came out. In the mean time cavalry, infantry, and artillery defiled along the road to Paris. The infantry had been " looting " vegetables, and many a good soup was eaten later no doubt on the Neuilly road! All of a sudden three swells from the staff of Berthout, and three privates of Ducrot's escort, all men one sees daily at clubs, in salons, at races, or dancing furious cotillons, came over to us, as pleased to see acquaintances as if they had been at Kentucky instead of Courbevoie, and the first words —" You here still! What is new in Paris?"

The Eclaireurs à Cheval are well mounted, and some of them can ride!

Oh! my poor bones, what a cropper one of Berthout's fellows got! He fell off, too, standing still!

Tuesday, October 18*th.*—It is settled that Colonel Claremont is to be president of the British fund, and

Dr. Gordon, Deputy Inspector-General of Hospitals, and Dr. Wyatt of the " Coldstreams " are invited to be on the committee.

We have no war news to-day, and only a few reports worth repeating.

I am assured that De Kératry resigned and went into the provinces to take a command, only because he found in the now famous Imperial papers the names of many men of the extreme Left who had received large sums of money, and the receipts for that money had been found and suppressed. He insisted that they should all be published; but the Ministers said, " No! we dare not publish them; if so we offend them all." " Then," said the Comte, "I will resign;" and he did. This is his own cousin's story. The fact is, that the Ministers are dreadfully encumbered. Flourens laughs at them; Sapia spits at them, and Portalis will end in being a martyr. Ah! those ready-made martyrs, what thorns they are in ministerial sides! With Rochefort's " persecution" still on their tongues, how could these men *prosecute*?

I fear too that the Ministers are either slow, or not backed up. It is certain that the tickets for meat promised ten days ago are not given out yet in many, if in any, districts; and I heard it openly stated that the cannons supposed to be getting ready for the walls were not even ordered. There has been a hitch; but what does it matter? If Prussia intends to starve out Paris, the tickets for soup will not delay dire famine a fortnight; and if William the Pious intends to bombard, he will scarcely grant an armistice till such time as mitrailleuses abound on the fortifications and a thousand new guns are handed over to Trochu.

By-the-by, the papers here have killed the Crown Prince of Prussia, and to-night state that Dumas *père* is gone to his Dumas *pères*.

A few words about the Bellenger scandal. I am told, as a fact, that the lady in question never was confined, but that she accepted the maternity of an infant ("for a consideration" as old Trapboys said) who was supposed to be born of the Purple, if not for it, or with any chance of it, the actual mother being the pretty Mlle. V—— H——, since married, and who certainly did "winter in Italy, A.D. ——." Thus scandal is fed when we are starving.

Wednesday, October 19th.—Those who expected that the Prussians would attack on the 17th or 18th—the anniversaries of Leipsic—were deceived. They have done nothing, and now it is said that they will do nothing; on the other hand, the papers very foolishly hint at a great attack to be made by us. Trochu is to command, with Ferry and Rochefort as staff officers! I believe in the attack; as to the staff— well——

I hear that the "Légion d'Honneur" is to be abolished, but of course the Orleans Prince will restore that Decoration, which dates from 1802. It is to be reserved for the soldiers of the Republic.

Yesterday the first shot was fired from the walls of Paris. The Auteuil bastion sent three shells in the direction of Montretout; so at last the city itself is attacking. "Good luck to her," say we, for the people are beginning to be a-weary of their confinement, and already prices are to be considered rather than appetites.

I have just been informed by a desolate housewife that there are but few eggs, and those are threepence each, and that butter costs eleven shillings and sixpence the English pound. I am bound to say that the Paris tradesman is a great protectionist—to himself. They have raked up everything that used to be cheap and nasty, doubled the price, and left the quality "in statu quo ante bellum."

At a table d'hôte yesterday they rang the usual

bell when the repast was ready. "They should have borrowed a trumpet and sounded 'to horse,'" said a diner. The right thing to eat now is donkey. This is not a joke : they say it is excellent, and I heard it asked for in a restaurant.

The Boulevard Haussmann was last night, by a paper placard at the corner, named after Ulrich. This is not fair, as the gallant general has already got his avenue. I am sure that if the poor ex-prefect could now walk down this great thoroughfare, he would feel glad it was no longer his, and hope that the general godfather who succeeds him will get his bantling cleaned, dusted, and freed from nuisances. At present it is as dirty as St. Giles's; soldiers are gambling on the pavement, boys revelling in "tip-cat" in the street, while sheep feed in the gardens, and bullocks roar at you through the rails.

The pretty garden of the Chapelle Expiatoire is as bare as a common. It used to be a treat to walk in Haussmannville ; it is a punishment to pass through Peoples-Town.

The cathedral of St.-Denis has given its bells to make guns.

Went to the Arc de Triomphe, and found that the inside portion was protected by a wooden screen, a little stronger practically than brown paper and string, but that not even a plank was prepared to cover the most exposed position of Paris.

They say that two hundred Prussian spies were arrested here on Friday. I don't believe it: I believe but little, but I dare say there are many here. One was being brought into Paris the other day in a carriage, and, as usual, there was a crowd of carts laden with stores, &c., in the way. The prisoner could not speak a word of French, till suddenly he said, in pure Parisian, "We had better have gone down the Rue St.-Honoré."

It is proposed to do away with religion and long petticoats. "To believe in anything degrades human nature, so pull down the crosses and de-crucify the Christs," says a *he* patriot. "To regenerate the female citizens," says a *she* patriot, "you must remodel their dress. Let us assume, then, the uniform of the Zouave!" These are public meeting views. If the latter reform is carried out, let us hope, for the sake of Young France, that Paris in 1870 may have a Bloomer Ball, like that of the Hanover Square Rooms of 1851.

Thursday, October 20th.—Yesterday morning before daybreak the Government got two "dépêches de pigeon voyageur" (carriers), which gave evident satisfaction.

At 9 A.M. the Eclaireurs à Cheval were called to parade, and twelve were selected to carry thirty-six despatches to the outside fortifications and forts. I saw the bearer of three. He went two leagues beyond Vincennes. He had an escort of a non-commissioned officer and six spahis. The leader of the escort could hardly speak a word of French, but suddenly he rode up to my friend, Private ——, and said " Prossianes," and there they were in force at Rosny-à-Bois. There was a sharp outpost skirmish going on, but the little party delivered their despatches and got home safe.

We rather thought that these thirty-six notes from head-quarters meant an attack last night or to-day, but till now all is as "calm as moonlight sleeping upon snow."

Thousands of troops poured down the Boulevard Ulrich between 7 A.M. and 10 A.M., and I am inclined to believe that Trochu is massing troops at the front previous to an attack in force. Nobody can deny that the attempt is very bold, but I believe the General is very sanguine. The Mobiles look very well, and improve rapidly, but the National Guards are the finest men. Unluckily I have been told, and in several quite different quarters, that when the last hour comes they will think of their shops, their cafés, their wives, and their children, and propose peace. In saying this I nothing extenuate, nor set down aught in malice, but tell that which is told me by many Parisians, and several English who have been the unwilling witnesses of several revolutions. Nobody doubts that the Mobiles will fight, and they are better drilled.

Here are one or two boyish follies of the young Republic. One M. Mottu orders that in his Mairie the Christs and crucifixes shall be taken down, as they are too indecent to be looked on by young girls. On this subject the " Patrie en Danger " writes :—" As to the image of Christ, we render sincere homage to an historical personage animated by the purest intentions, and whom the spiritual ancestors of the Royalists (I wonder they did not say Bonapartists) caused to be crucified."

M. Blanqui believes in nothing, which is perhaps the shortest way. As for the majority of Parisians, they may be religiously divided into two sects—those who follow the miner whose theory was that " it was a long time ago, let's hope it isn't true ;" and those who say with Foote—" No, I never go to church, though I see no harm in it !" And we must not believe that all immorality was confined to the Imperial quarter of Paris. There is sin at Belleville, at the Faubourg, among the tradespeople, and the Orleanists—everywhere.

And now for a " casus belli." A citizen rejoicing in the appropriate name of Belly (it should be spelt with an " i"), insists on raising this band of " Amazones de la Seine "—this phalanx of fighting females. I don't suppose that they will be as well worth inspecting as the regiment of " Amazones du Bois de Boulogne," which used to parade between 5 and 7 P.M., when there was a " Bois."

There were two curious coincidences on the 4th of September. Mr. George Augustus Sala was the last person arrested by a " Sergeant of the City," and was released by the last decree of M. Piétri, Prefect of Police, who signed it almost as he was putting on his hat to escape with Conti.

The Baron de Billing, of the French Foreign Office, and who was much about the Imperial Court, where two of his sisters were in waiting, volunteered, like every one else. He is a private in the Eclaireurs à Cheval. His first turn of duty was at the Tuileries, and he had been just two hours in the palace when an orderly came to tell him that the Empress, whom he was " on guard" to protect, was deposed, and the Imperial Government, whose commission he held, was dissolved.

There goes another battalion. One captain evidently means work : he is marching in front of his company, with his sword drawn and his chassepot slung over his shoulder. The squad of Nationals who have not yet got their uniforms offer a curious study of the "levée en masse." I saw in one squad a sweep, a grey-headed old soldier of sixty, a commissioner, two " blouses," a swell in polished boots and " gris perle " gloves, and my own butcher.

There is merely nominal business on the Bourse : no one stays there later than one o'clock. Rentes to-day are 52,90.

Friday, October 21*st.*—The more one reflects, the more one is puzzled as to the game the Prussians are playing. We have been invested now thirty-two days, and if they had marched on Paris on the 19th of September, or even the 1st of October, they would have found no resistance ; but now Paris is as strong as Sevastopol. I presume that they are going to starve us out ; and that, I think, is also Trochu's opinion, as he says that he wants ten days more to finish his preparations for defence, and that till then he shall not attack. If he expected an assault he dared not wait, as the men—" his commanders "—are crying out for a sortie in force. If that which I hear is true, Prussia is deceived if she expects to starve us very soon. We are good for three months (Mr. Blount, the banker, an authority, says six); but I confess that by that time short commons will be the order of the day, and that his Grace the Duke Humphrey will give a series of "dîners à la Prusse," nothing being put on the table.

The thirty-six despatches to which I alluded yesterday were sent to warn all the generals of the Prussian attack, which was made yesterday morning before daybreak, and of which Trochu had got wind. Finding that they were expected, the Prussians, who were in great force, retired. The attack, no doubt, was intended to be made on Issy, which Bismarck declares he will have, if "he leaves the trenches full of dead." This he told an American who has come back here from "interviewing" the Count.

M. Bonaparte Patterson remains in Paris, and, in spite of his name, commands a battalion of National Guards. His opinion is that no army could take Paris except by starvation or treachery.

The following paragraph would have read drolly two months ago, when there was a train from the Rue du Havre to Versailles every half-hour:—"They did not blindfold the Papal Nuncio when he passed through the Prussian lines, but they bandaged the eyes of the Columbian Minister."

The Ministers of Monaco and San Marino have demanded free passes in very threatening terms, so Prussia had better beware!

The spy mania still rages.   Last night the National Guards picket forced their way into the house of a French friend of ours, himself a National Guard, and arrested his servant, who was from Alsace.   M. —— knocked down the sergeant in command, and then took him off to the nearest post, where he will get "toko," this being no time to be hard on Alsatians.

It is calculated that there are 1500 Americans, 40,000 Belgians, 30,000 Swiss, and 5000 English still in Paris : 2000 of the latter are fed by the Embassy. The Americans are able to get away, but Bismarck says he will not let out another mouth which can consume fruit.   And right he is.   "Romance of War" is not worth a shilling edition.

They had a hottish fight to-day west of Paris.   It went on for hours, and yet nobody seems to have known anything about it, or heard a gun!   My conviction is that the enemy tested our strength, found that they were like the first Reform Parliament Ministry, in a "dangerous majority," and so retired into the woods which protect their positions, and which our side has not yet been clever enough to destroy.

We have as yet no official return, and all that an observer can say is, that there was heavy firing on both sides, that the mitrailleuses were more murderous even than the Emperor once told me they would be. "They roar like wild tigers," said a looker-on ; and I fear that the to-morrow's return of ambulances will really mark a " red-letter day "—and nothing gained !

I was amused by the remark of a Scotch gentleman of singularly kind and mild manners, who dropped into the "Cercle des Frondeurs." He was sipping a little weak sherry-and-water, and quietly observed— " That's my nineteenth bottle !"

The heroine of the day was the American ambulance ! Dr. Gordon speaks of it in the highest terms, and he tested its merits even to being jolted out by himself and jolted back with the wounded—only he says it does not jolt.

Saturday, October 22nd.—Here we are, with a day like May—May poetical, not actual : sun shining, a bird singing, nobody drilling, and only a gun now and then.

We had a delightful drive to Courbevoie, where we found all the staff in great spirits ; but I also found that yesterday was just as I expected—a drawn battle, with great loss to both sides. The Prussians caught it early in the day, and were driven back, or, as I read it, retired on Malmaison. When the French advanced into the park of Malmaison, they found nine thousand Prussians opposed to their three thousand selves; and then, as an old Guardsman—Frederick Hankey— observed, of course "they retired in the greatest order."

The Berthout division lost two hundred and seventy-three men, killed and wounded, including twenty officers. Our coachman told me that he had been talking to one of the men of the 35th of the Line, and had been told that that regiment alone had lost thirty-six men.

"It is not over, this affair," said *cocher* No. 1109 to my wife. "Monsieur is talking with the staff, and will hear so; but it has not commenced."

Hear a man of the people. We passed some time at the extreme outpost at Courbevoie. We found some officers "looking for Prussians through a glass," just as you would look for an eclipse. I lent one my glass, and said, "I have been looking for a Prussian for days." Then said a soldier, "It's a pity you were not here yesterday, for we could have spared you several."

Sunday, October 23rd.—The thirty-fifth day of the siege, and the second wet Sunday.

Rather like giving out the Psalms, is it not? *A propos*, I once heard the parson of Hornchurch give out—"The hundred and nineteenth day of the month, and the third Psalm," and saw an invitation sent to him to come and dine on the hundred and twenty-second. But this is beside the subject. Let us go back to our fighting, and forget such peaceful times as those—when we had invitations to dinner, plenty to eat, and no appetite.

> " Nessun maggior dolore,
>   Che ricordarsi del tempo felice,
>   Nella miseria."

Dante is right. The memory of a beefsteak makes me to-day feel as tender as that delicacy ought to be.

The French had 6350 men engaged on Friday, with a squadron of cavalry and forty-eight guns. The reserves were 4600 men, two squadrons of cavalry, and forty-six guns. But George Irisson d'Hérisson, who was in the thick of it, tells me that the Prussian troops in the park of Malmaison alone were at least 9000, which is only 1350 less than the French attacking force and reserves. The official return gives two officers killed, fifteen wounded, and eleven missing;

32 men killed, 230 wounded, and 153 missing : total
hors de combat, 443—a large proportion out of
10,350 men. Two guns were also lost. The Zouaves
and Mobiles fought like devils.

On the 6th of September the mob was pleased to
hoot and hiss the Jockey Club, and denounce the
members as "useless mouths," but these "bouches
inutiles" have a curious greed after fighting. Every
man who can carry arms, and is not exempt by reason
of his age, is on the fortifications or in the field, and
to-day I have a list of those who are over age but yet
will serve. They are—the Marquis de Berenger,
Arthur de Bonnechose, Vicomte Daru, Comte Charles
Dillon, Comte Charles de Fitz-James, Achille Moris-
seau, Baron René du Pille, the Marquis de Radepont,
and the Marquis de Saint-Vallier.

As for the Little Club of the Rue Royale, I found
them all up at the Rond Point de Courbevoie yesterday. Ashton Blount, who, as an English subject,
cannot of course serve against the Prussians, tearing
his hair because he could not canter that very neat
thoroughbred right up to the batteries, "merely to
look on ;" and little Weh galloping for hard life with
despatches.

An American gentleman—Mr. F. Kay Pendleton—
breakfasted yesterday between Malmaison and Rueil

with some officers of the Prussian Guards. They gave him an excellent breakfast, including butter, fruit, coffee, and good cigars; and when in their cups (coffee cups I mean), they confessed that they were beaten, and frightfully "mauled" by mitrailleuses on Friday. "We have never suffered from the accuracy of your aim so much as to-day," said a captain.

Many people (and I am of the number) believe that the Government has suppressed a considerable number of killed and wounded.

Signs of the times. We saw Garnier-Pagès going up to Mont Valérien in one of the landaus of the Empress, and Henri de Rochefort was at the Foreign Office to-day, where he said, "Of course everybody cannot now expect a 'château-brillant aux pommes' for his breakfast." "But," said a friend, "Henri, thou lookest as if thou gettest it."

Everyone is saying that M. de Rochefort is the pleasantest and least self-asserting of all the existing (on sufferance) Cabinet. He would, they say, never have been the radical he is if he had got a start in life; but he was an aristocrat by birth, and an *employé* at fifty pounds a year by position. His *cheval de bataille* was attacking Haussmann. Perhaps if Haussmann had given him a portfolio—a very small one—a mere "carnet," we should not have had the Revolution of 1870.

It is curious the savage delight with which the press of Paris records devastation. "We rejoice to say that the hôtel in the Rue de Courcelles, lately inhabited by Mathilde, is now a barrack of Mobiles." Now, considering that they have proclaimed it "National Property," I confess I think the nation might take better care of such a treasury of art as that house. "Le Figaro" suggests that, instead of pulling down Imperial statues, they should find a Red Republican something like them, and give each figure a popular name. "Le Petit Caporal," for instance, might be "General Trochu," and so on.

We saw a great battle to-day! Result—0 killed, 0 wounded, 0 missing. The position assaulted was the Government dépôt of Dutch cheese. The action was still raging when my servant was repulsed. We hoped for a dinner of game—to wit, a Welsh rabbit; but we shall get a dinner of herbs, and grumbling therewith.

Conversation between two Nationals :—"Do you like it?" "No." "Don't say so, but no more do I." "Coming off guard?" "Yes; and you?" ."Going on guard." "Where?" "To the mortifications !"

We were amused yesterday by seeing Mr. Washburne refused admittance to the American ambulance. He would have gone away, only that I knew the gate-keeper, and pointed out what he was doing. They keep the public out; and yesterday, with some fifty wounded and two serious amputations going on, all was as quiet as the sick-room of a private house.

I have just seen M. Grandhomme, the "James Weatherby" of Paris, and he gives me the following "list of engagements" of the members of the Jockey Club. One hundred and sixty-three members have been and are under arms; out of these there are five killed, eleven wounded, and twenty prisoners. Fancy that happening at Mr. Thomas Percival's establishment, 38, St. James's Street.

We dined out to-day! A Sunday to be marked with chalk. We were asked to meet—and she came, a little late perhaps, after the soup—a goose! a most satisfying encounter. One of the party has thirty thousand pounds a year, and he "had not tasted meat for three days," to use the beggars' formula.

Monday, October 24th.—They were firing heavily towards the south-west of Paris at 3 A.M. Possibly we shall have details later. The King of Prussia and Count Bismarck are still at Ferrières, where they pass the day shooting the Baron de Rothschild's pheasants, and the evening in emptying the Baron's cellar. I have no doubt that they " annex " a good deal of the celebrated " yellow seal " Johannisberg. I know I should.

Captain Hore thinks of trying to go away. He has the Prussian pass; so has Mr. Corbin, but the French will not endorse it. By-the-way, the last time Captain Hore attempted to depart, he got to Epinay, and sat just out of range of a heavy fire for five hours. Then he saw a Prussian captain coming towards him, and felt that he was repulsed. He was so. " Very sorry, but my orders are that you return." Captain Hore, the best tempered fellow in the world, was determined not to show to the Prussians the slightest sign of annoyance. " Many thanks," he said, " I return with so much pleasure. There are many worse places than Paris, even during a siege, and I shall sleep comfortably in my own bed this night. But I should be much obliged if you would get me an escort at once, as I want to be back before the gates are closed, and we have a little dinner—rather artistic—at the Café Anglais."

I am assured that the blank look of astonishment of the Prussian officers, who thought that they had intercepted important despatches, was worth " a tenner" (that was the expression I heard from a ribald who was present).

I saw yesterday the artillery camp in the Tuileries Gardens. It is dreadful. They have taken no steps to shelter their horses, and they are perishing from cold and want of food. There will be "plenty of carcases in the market" if bad weather sets in; but eating one of these gunners' knackers will bring back the old gambler's idea of "rattling the bones and gaining nothing."

I begin to think that Alexander Dumas was right when he said, with almost his last breath—"I have lived three months too long." Three months ago he would have died in the odour of Imperialism. He breathed on to see that all was not only "dust," but "dirt" (and no scavengers).

The Government has made a great mistake about the allowance of meat, which, be it said, has not even yet been universally distributed.

Not many months ago the most extravagant man in England proposed to his lawyer to pay his creditors fivepence in the pound. "Ah! captain," said the legal adviser, "your ideas were always beyond your means: let's make it twopence halfpenny." Unluckily the Government of National Defence began with the fivepenny tariff, and have in less than a fortnight had to come down to the twopenny halfpenny arrangement. I fear that the effect will be very discouraging.

All prices are rising. Coals now cost 3*l*. 2*s*. 6*d*. a ton. Horse is ninepence a pound. There was no "donkey" in the market yesterday (one of our party had been everywhere to look for it); but there is a luxury "very like hare," and commands a higher price. The cheek of a mule is a treat reserved for the army.

The "Bouillons Duval" now give one "plat de viande" only. This was their "carte du jour" to-day :—

Smoked horse sausage and vegetables.
Black pudding and vegetables.
Salt fish.   Eggs.
Fresh vegetables.

Well, it is a great blessing never to have had any appetite! I had no idea how handy it would come in; and then one can always "sup full" of the recollections of the dinners that have been given to us, and bored us. Large families are, however, in a different position, and shake their heads at higher prices and smaller rations.

The Prussians occupy Orleans!

The Provisional Government and the Corps Diplomatique are said to have left Tours (very naturally, as it is close to Orleans). No signs of the great rescuing army "cast their shadows before," and, indeed, as poor Mrs. M—— said of "Anonyma" in the park, we are "as bad as we can be to be alive."

As I fancied would happen—the Government dared not get a judgment either against Sapia or Flourens, so henceforth mutiny is the order of the day in the republican army. Flourens does not the least "give himself for beaten"—on the contrary.

It seems very unlikely that Mr. Corbin will be able to leave Paris. He has Bismarck's permission, but not that of Trochu, and has just written to me to say that he sees no hope of getting off. I am sorry, as he is really going to America on "urgent private affairs." Bismarck's "lasci-passare" is sufficiently strong :—

"I have the honour to inform you that I authorize Vicomte de Lancastre, chargé d'affaires of Portugal, to leave Paris through the Prussian lines.

"The same permission is given to Messrs. Azenas and Bustamente, with six of their countrymen; and to Mr. Martin, chargé d'affaires of the kingdom of Hawaii.

" They must be furnished with a certificate signed by Mr. Washburne, the Minister of the United States, proving their nationality and identity.

" You will kindly inform them that packets, letters, and any other writings they may carry, should be handed open to the advanced guard, failing which they will expose themselves to the severity of military law.

(Signed)   " BISMARCK."

We went down to Auteuil by train to-day, and then walked through the Bois to Boulogne. What another scene of destruction ! The whole wood is destroyed on the left, and a great deal of it on the right hand. Between the station of Auteuil and the gates leading to St.-Cloud, instead of that wild part of the wood it is now a large plain of jagged stumps, with a few fires burning, and a few artillery horses shivering. The place is so altered that it is difficult to find your way.

Outside the gate, where the " respectable " people used to wait to see the disreputable world return from Sunday steeplechasing, the scene changes, and you are in a camp of " Liners." Every hundred yards is mined. There are nine soldiers to one civilian, and the whole of the shops are shut. When we got up to the wide space before what used to be the bridge, we found every corner occupied by people, who sought to be (without danger) " spectators of the fight "—like Eliza on the wood-crowned heights of Minden. Without thinking what we were doing, we advanced towards the barricade which protects the bridge. "Get out of that," said a chorus of sentries, soldiers, officers, and of course civilians; and on looking up I found our old friend " The Black Man's Head," a Prussian outpost.

We went on down the Rue de Boulogne, trying to see the ruins of St.-Cloud. When we got to the end of the street we found another barricade, and quickly warned as we were, drew upon ourselves two needle-guns. The officer on duty said, "If you want to see St.-Cloud you must walk into this garden." It was the very last outpost, a charming villa, with stables, hot-houses, gardens, &c. We went to the end of the garden, and found a sentry, to whom a friend was talking. "You can see the ruins from there," said he on duty, " but I must not permit you to pass." " But là bas, monsieur can see them quite well," said Off-duty. We therefore got on a heap of earth, and saw below us the shining river, a narrow road, the Prussian outpost, and the walls—black and broken—of what was once the Palace of St.-Cloud. It is only one more added to the list of ruinous and wretched spectacles to which our eyes are getting daily more and more accustomed.

Just then Off-duty said to On-duty, " Look out, sentry, to the left;" and we all peered through the loop-holes. " Six hundred metres," said On-duty, taking out his cartridge,—for they do not load the chassepot till they want to fire. " Try four hundred," suggested Jules, and the sight was set, and the poor sentry, whose blue and yellow uniform was standing out in dangerous relief, was aimed at deliberately, but missed, mercifully.

" Let me try," said Jules; and he tried at five hundred. The only effect was to get us a rattler on the walls: but nobody was hurt; and I am almost ashamed to say that one of our party went on picking a bouquet, which is now on my table. I should tell you that this was no solitary " potting of sentries;" it was a little rifle fight extending for several miles up the Seine.

At half-past five Mont Valérien opened a very heavy fire; St.-Ouen following suit, and distant batteries answering. We had to make a rush " to save gates," and were lighted home by a glorious aurora borealis. It is a curious mixture, this life of camp and city, this fusion of soldier and civilian; but if any one of my acquaintances had a plethora of health and spirits, I should advise him to come here and be cured amidst these scenes of ravage, destruction, demolition, devastation, and general ruin. Here Trochu and the republicans "make a solitude and call it"—war! They have made the solitude, and are striving to make the war.

But what do we hear to-night? Just that which I have written. "Never was so reckless a reconnaissance as that of Friday. The generals knew beforehand that they sacrificed their men to explore—

"*Quos Deus vult perdere prius dementat!*"

Tuesday, October 25th.—A wet day, and no news. Before I was up, had a letter from the Embassy to say that there would be a British exodus on Thursday. I do not think they will get leave. Everything, however, points to some great event within a fortnight. The *canard* has been flitting about for the last ten days. I hope it is not to be a modern Moscow. Your own "fireside" is all very well, but fire advancing in columns is a little too hot.

If we are bombarded, the person best off will be Mrs. B——, Rue de Berlin, who is so frightened at lightning that she has fitted up her cellar as a boudoir, and retires there at the first flash. She can sit there in safety, and send to the next room for some of the B—— port, which, judging from its pedigree, should be good.

The plot thickens, and Paris thins.

It is Earl Granville who has ordered off the Embassy at very short notice. It will be very droll if Wodehouse and his " young friends " are all obliged to " se replier en bon ordre," as has happened to others. But I suppose there are changes in Paris and Prussian views, for Mr. Corbin and Chevalier Wikoff got off, out of Paris at least, to-day. When one has lived in a place eight years, one can hardly leave it in twenty-four hours—there is no time to pack up the *penates*. But English diplomacy should be Irish, it is so addicted to blunders. Moreover, having seen the first two or three " beats " of the " battue," one would not like to miss the bouquet.

I was much amused to-day, and so will be Mr. James Weatherby if he sees this. I went to get my " meat ticket," and who do you think gave it to me ? A serious official (who smiled curiously as I went in) in undress National Guard uniform :—" Name ?" " *N.* or *M.*, as the case may be." " How many people ?" " Three." " Good ! Call to-morrow ! And now, how are you ?" It was Mr. Grandhomme, secretary of the Jockey Club. I have received many tickets from him ere now, but one for beef—never! I asked him if he was now secretary to the Hippic Society for the Consumption of Horse.

Eh, bien! I prefer a "good thing" with a horse at Longchamps to a good thing, even if "regularly cooked up, across the flat" of a dining-table. The serious question is, that the allowance of meat is reduced fifty per cent. already, and even that will not continue long. Donkey is ten shillings per pound this very day, owing to the run on Lyons sausages. Fancy the "poor little foal of an oppressed race" having so jumped up in the market.

It seems that the exodus of to-morrow is led by Henry Wodehouse, but the genesis is due to Washburne. I do not envy *pro-tem.* ambassadors. We dare not say chargé d'affaires, for who charged him, and by, with, what, and to whom is he charged? But everybody wants something of him, and nobody says " Thank you " for any favour.

We have no government. Certain people dropped the reins of government, and quick enough the others picked them up. But what are they when I want anything? Several lawyers commanded by several regiments of men who carry about groceries, and who are commanded by those who sell them, and

from whom the *ucquit* is taken.   Only, will that make
France a great nation ?

The "colonel" to whom I have just paid forty
francs for some Marsala (and very dear under a regular
dynasty too), seems as if he would like to eat up
alive all the existing men in power—or rather I
should say in office.   Well, there was more tint at
Flodden field.   Get new and better, or we shall
not have a new France.

Wednesday, October 26th.—Another soaking wet
day—pouring from 4 A.M. to midday.   In my opinion
this is very serious, as I confess to thinking that the
volunteer military spirit will not bear dilution.

My news, which nobody else hears, or rather hears
without listening to, marking, or digesting, is decidedly
bad.   In the first place, there is a great feeling of discontent in the lower orders, who swear that they do
not get everything to eat as usual.   This does not
appear to be true, though it is a fact that with money
you still can get an extravagant dinner at a restau·
rant.   Then the allowance of meat has been reduced
one half, and the regulations for distributing it are so
bad that a poor woman just told me she waited from
5 to 10 A.M. in a pouring rain, and then got not quite
a pound of mutton, with much bone, for two people

for three days. Somebody complained, and the National Guard on duty said—"Very soon you will not get any." The general answer to which was—"So much the better; that which we get is not worth the trouble we undergo to obtain it."

Exeunt omnes, wet, weary, hungry, and discontented.

But the cause of this reduction of rations is more serious than the reduction itself, and excuses the Government for having started too liberally. Disease has appeared among the cattle! We were warned of this, but, as usual here, nobody heeded it, and the motto—"Sufficient for the day is the evil thereof," was carried on, from the rulers who dropped the reins to the misrulers who seized them as they fell, and burnt their own hands in consequence. Finally, I hear that the English exodus has a very bad effect on the people of Paris.

The Government does not publish, as it professes, every detail of the siege. No word is yet said of the heavy firing at 5 P.M. on Monday. It was heavy enough to make an old soldier who had been in nineteen actions exclaim—"There's the beginning of a big battle."

The "Figaro," without being reactionary, is writing very sensibly about the nuisance of the iconoclasts, and the assumed "republican virtue" of men who were, and are, "just like any other fellow." You may change the names of streets, and even palaces, yet Napoleon III. and Haussmann did find Paris brick, and leave it marble. Well, it does not matter—What does? In a few years our grandsons will perhaps be betting on races at Longchamps, or dancing at Mabille after a "Grand Prix d'Orléans."

I have seen a good many people, French and English, to-day, and all confirm the idea that "affairs march badly." A soldier from the front came into Mr. Jones's just before I was there, and said he had received as "rations" one ounce of meat and a little broth in thirty-six hours. Another complains that at the attack of Malmaison on Friday, the officers took their men into action, and left them to get out as best they might.

There has been great difficulty in the way of the English exodus—which is not only English, but American and Russian, Belgian, Swiss, and Chinese—but Mr. Wallace has again come to the rescue, and has given a fair sum. Great praise is due to Mr. Alan Herbert for all he has done in these troubled times. Colonel Claremont too should be thanked by every Englishman who wanted to know anything "officiellement" or "officieusement," and his position with an unrecognized government in arms was most exceptional and most puzzling. Yet he has been polite and pleasing to all.

I am bound to say that the scene at the Embassy to-night was very strange. Where all the people came from, and who they are, would puzzle an experienced Parisian to say—yet there they are. I never was so much astonished as I was at the quantity and quality. How are the people all going to escape, for to go to Versailles viâ Charenton means miles! They applied to John Hawes—Count F. de La Grange's old coachman and faithful servant, and he said, "I would much rather have let you the horses, but I have just sold thirty to a butcher." Bless me, I have ridden them all.

I saw a dreadful sight to-day—a fact to record and to be read, but not believed. Two Mobiles carrying to the spit a very fat poodle, which, let us hope, had died a natural death! What is the "natural death" of "Chou-chou?" There he was, dead, however, and is by this time eaten.

I heard a curious fact to-day about our fight on Friday. A shell was thrown among a lot of Moblots under Gennevilliers, and they ran away like boys. An old soldier in command shot three of the foremost bolters with his revolver; the rest came "right to their front," and stood like men.

The name for horse-flesh now is "Siege venison."

There is a deal of illness: three hundred and sixty deaths in a week from small-pox, and I am told on very good authority that typhus must succeed to a diminution of wholesome food, especially as the people of Paris are not cleanly or fresh-airy.

Thursday, October 27th.—As a punishment for past sins I arose this morning and was in my tub before it was daylight. Now there are phases of life more pleasant than a cold bath and a candle. My object was to see the English off. Unluckily, that which I foretold occurred. Count von Bismarck refused permission, and as he is now Emperor of Europe, Europe must obey. So the English stopped in Paris, and I had to go back to bed, a second sleep, and another cold bath. It is all very well. I was not going away, but hundreds were, and really our Embassy seems to know less about the affair than any one else. Why, at 6·30, when I was at the Embassy, declare that the people were going in the morning, when they knew that they had no permission?

I was asked to go to the Prussian lines, which I should have done with great pleasure, without really caring twopence what became of the exodus. But in the mean time we are laughed at by every other Embassy. That's a pretty machine, said a minister to me at the British Embassy last evening.

We suffer enormously from marauders. One was found dead in the cellar of a house at Gennevilliers. He had "looted" a bottle of turpentine, and died drinking it.

There was again very heavy firing during the afternoon and night.

For the first time I saw *mule*. It was procured by a small restaurant keeper in the Rue Neuve-St.-Augustin for an American dinner.

Friday, October 28th.—More rain, and very strong wind—altogether a dull day, and the English "revenants" perfectly furious. Nobody can say when they will get leave to go. M. Mégy, who murdered the Sergent de Ville who went to arrest him, has now struck his superior officer on parade. He is to be tried by court-martial, and will probably get a pension for life.

It is said that the Czar has asked the King of Prussia to beg of Bismarck to permit Thiers to come back to Paris. Is this the "nouvelle route à Orléans" which we hear is about to be opened?

Nobody seems to know what has happened at the front, and as it chanced I could not go out. But I saw a real live Prussian in "grande tenue," even to his brass helmet. He was brought in as a prisoner of war by three National Guards in a cab.

We went round the Palais Royal, where two-thirds of the shops are closed. The Rue de Rivoli, with its stalls of vegetables, indecent prints, and vile caricatures, is very like Shoreditch.

The newspapers have now killed Napoleon III., Prince Napoleon Jerome, and the ex-Queen of Spain —that is the news of to-day.

We saw a leg and a shoulder of lamb, each cost twelve and sixpence, and a head which cost one and eightpence! Eggs are threepence halfpenny each. But you need not starve even now, nor even "mount," *i.e.*, eat horse.

To-day's bill of fare of the "Cercle des Frondeurs":—

Anchovies with butter.

Spiced beef.

Salad à la Révolution.

Jumbled eggs au Chester.

Heard of a man who has seen a ham. So we starve by degrees.

To see Potel's shop, with two ounces of butter in the window, was droll !

We are kept from soup and sausages by equine antipathy, but I hear that the sausages are chiefly compounded of donkey. It is amusing to see the crowd round any shop which contains food, and to hear the remarks !

Saturday, October 29th.—We had another soaking wet night, and I fear the soldiers must have suffered considerably. There is no doubt the Prussians were driven back towards the Forest of Bondy by a night surprise; but, except in prestige, we are little gainers. The enemy, too, is said to have got a long train of guns into Versailles under cover of the action. Opinions differ to-day more than ever. I believe the weather affects the spirits. One says it must be over in a fortnight, and that meat will not even last till then. The next man gives two months, and twenty thousand oxen (this would last six weeks) on their way to our relief, or rather restoration. Baron Ferdinand de Lesseps is very sanguine, and says that if the French will make no terms they must win in the end.

M. Thiers is expected back. As he has quite failed,

Bismarck will let him pass : he never allows any one to pass with good news.

There is another quarrel among the advanced politicians. M. Félix Pyat, in "Le Combat," declared that Bazaine had proposed the capitulation of Metz, and to treat for peace with Bismarck, in the name of the Emperor Napoleon. This declaration created a wonderful sensation. Some National Guards went at once to M. Rochefort and M. Ferry, who instantly denied that there was any truth in the statement; and M. Rochefort said that M. Félix Pyat was a coward, who hid himself at Victor Noir's funeral, and had always got out of the way when his friends were in any trouble. M. Rochefort added, that he was determined to go out with his men to the very first battle, and challenge M. Pyat to go out with him. In the mean time, M. Pyat says that the news is authentic, and was told to him by M. Gustave Flourens, who had it directly from M. Rochefort. And so the matter stands; a very pretty quarrel.

Now we have as it were under trial, Rochefort, Flourens, Pyat, Sapia, and Mégy, each of whom tells his own story about his own little urgent private affair. What is truth?

Earl Grey once went to see George the Fourth on a question of the utmost importance, when the King said he had not written a certain letter. Sheridan, whom Lord Grey met in the ante-chamber, said that the King had written it, and he had read it. Earl Grey said—"They were both such confounded liars that I did not know which to believe." I leave the application to you.

We have a corps here, called the "Friends of France," who are just going to get their baptism of fire under General Ducrot. This legion consists of ninety-five Belgians, forty-seven Swiss, twenty-nine Italians, twenty-eight English, twenty-one Dutch, sixteen Luxembourg, fourteen Americans, twelve Swedes, ten Austrians, ten Spaniards, seven Poles, three Russians, two Greeks, one Turk, and one Dane. They are a remarkably neat-looking corps, and will, I believe, do good service.

The value of the Crown jewels, now in the Bank of France, has just been ascertained. It amounts to 1,198,000*l.*

I have just seen my allowance of meat for three persons for three days. It is one mutton chop, about half as big again as those which Mr. Green gives to his "dear boy" at Evans's.

The latest novelty in eating is the donkey butcher's shop in the Quartier Latin, which is kept by the man who used to let out the donkeys at Robinson's, so " ces petites dames " who used to gallop them to death now cook them and eat them.

Sunday, October 30*th.*—Again very heavy rain. Indeed, I begin to see two elements of peace in the far distance—bad weather and want of food. I do not think the Moblots can stand the one, and I am sure that the National Guards will not like the other. The Prussians, too, have at last mounted strong batteries at Meudon. There was heavy firing at midnight.

M. Félix Pyat says that M. Flourens received the Bazaine news from M. de Rochefort, and to-day M. Flourens says that he *did* tell M. Pyat, but that it was not M. Rochefort, but another person connected with the Government who told him. Again I ask, where is truth? One " on dit " is, that Pyat is a Government spy.

The following is a true story :—The general in command of Paris the day of Châtillon, when the French ran away, wrote an article for a Paris paper, saying that Paris was quite undefended, and that (as was true that day) the enemy could walk in when they please. The article was published, and created great confusion both in and out of the Government ; then the general repudiated his article, and the editor was prosecuted; since then he has been arrested by express desire of the same general, and his motto now is, " Put not your faith in patrons."

If Diogenes, with his best lantern, was here to-day, he could not find a " man." That is the want of Paris—a " man" and *organizer.* The National Defence Committee is chiefly occupied in making decrees which they have no power to enact, squabbling among themselves, changing the names of streets, and while I write the guns of Prussia are within range of the Faubourg St.-Germain! Can folly go farther ? The " circumstance" has come, but about that " man," who ever comes with it ? " Le Figaro " says that the self-made Government of the 4th of September has no power to do away with the civil order of the " Légion d'Honneur." They might suspend it till the end of the siege, but with the triumph or fall of Paris their power ceases. Indeed, all France seems to forget that Napoleon III. is still Emperor, though a prisoner of war, and the Empress still Regent.

I wonder what has happened in Europe! This makes forty-two days since I have seen an English letter or paper.

I have just been informed, on the best possible authority, that the Garde Nationale and the Mobiles obtain and consume one-fifth part of all the meat killed in Paris, while no provision of meat is made for the wounded.   This is a fact, and the gentleman who told me spoke his mind to a semi-French, semi-English committee of which he (an Englishman) is a member, and said, that in such days as these the wounded should be cared for before any one.

Our allowance of mutton was ten ounces for three people for three days, price tenpence.   "Ass meat" at eleven and eightpence per pound, and Liebig are in great demand.

A friend of ours yesterday dined, or tried to dine, off a bullock's nose and ears; but it was a failure, so they had bread and marmalade!

"Very light food," said Mrs. X.; "what with potted meats, feet, and ears, mixed with jam, I am going all askew."   Excuse these dining details.   Food is now with us the real "question du jour."   I prefer a "carte du jour" on the same subject—but let that pass.

It is a fact that cats will not eat horse : I mean cooked horse.

Monday, October 31*st.*—Though it is eight pounds a ton, go and fetch a bit of coal to mark this last day of October, 1870, which is indeed—

"Dies carbone notandus."

The "Electeur Libre" publishes (in large type), and dare not do so if it was not true, the fall of Metz through famine, and the capitulation of the whole garrison. So much for all the French reports of "successful sorties," "communications of good news," and "plenty of provisions." Metz has been said all along to be the key of the Paris question. I fear it is so— that the key is found, and will open the gates to Bismarck, William, Moltke, Fritz, and Co.

Not only does this last disaster destroy a general and an army which might have come to our aid, but frees the army which was keeping Bazaine in check, and which is ere now *en route* to assist in assaulting us. The "Official Journal" says not a word of this! The imbecility of the ostrich when he puts his head in a hole is strong-mindedness in comparison with the acts of the Government of National Defence! Their official days are numbered, I should say.

But I have not nearly finished my evil tidings. The Prussians yesterday re-took all the ground which the French forced from them on Friday. Bourget was retaken in one hour! As usual, General Trochu tried to keep a place with a few infantry and fewer artillery, and, as usual, the Prussians sent out four times as many men, and four times as many guns. The place was as nearly as possible surrounded, but one of the forts just saved it.   As it is though, there is a heavy loss and many prisoners.   The " Official Journal," which made so much of the capture, now says that the loss is of no consequence.   The worst system in the world.   The press and public begin to call for the fall of the " Rein Seizers," but who after them? That is the question.

We know that " parmi les aveugles un borgne est roi," but we have no *borgne* even.   I say to the doomed city, Put ashes on your head, chains round your neck, and crawl to Versailles and pray for peace, since you cannot produce even

> " A one-eyed monarch of the blind."

Thiers is back.   I said he would be let in if he was bearer of bad news.   The Prussians have now open communication from Berlin to St.-Cloud, and from St.-Cloud to Orleans.

De Fonvielle, the Maire, did not lose a day yesterday.   No!   He pulled down the statue of Prince Eugène, who I always in my ignorance considered as rather a good French citizen ; ordered it to be cast into the burning fiery furnace and coined into cannons, and then set up the image of Voltaire in its place. Now Voltaire, though a Frenchman, was a thorough Prussian.   "Fous est braiment bon Prussien," said

Frederick the King. But instead of "Deo erexit Voltaire," we say to-day, "Voltairio erexit Fonvillius."

Never mind! I dare say a statue of Fieschi will depose Voltaire in a few days.

Famine details! We just met a coachman leading a bay brougham horse, rising seven—grand action, warranted sound and quiet in harness, "an aizy goer"—coupled to an ass of mildest mien. Happening to know the coachman, we inquired where was his master?

"Master's hoff," was the reply, "and has there his no post, we as no letters. I have no fodder and no money, so I am taking these two to the knackers." I should say that last year at this season the horse would have been worth four thousand francs (160*l*). (John Hawes would have asked six thousand, and said he was "own brother to Gladiateur.") I don't know the value of donkeys, but say seventy-five francs (3*l*. can't hurt you). Our citizen friend expected to get ten pounds for the "stepper," and five pounds for the patient one—donkey being more valuable "pour la cuisine" than the nobler animal.

A lamb to-day, killed and prepared for the butchers, cost to the trade two pounds fifteen shillings and tenpence.

Just as I had written the above lines a rather stronger

storm of drums and trumpets set in than even we have been accustomed to during the last six weeks, and as we have drums in our ears and trumpets on the brain, of course we took glass and went to the balcony to inspect. Thousands of National Guards were marching in every direction, and as they were not, as a rule, in heavy marching order, were too clean to be coming from, and too late to be going to, the forts or fortifications, it struck us that something was in the air.

Parenthesis.—My dear friend, were you ever in a besieged city for six weeks, hearing drums and trumpets, and seeing nothing but soldiers from the "réveil" to "lights out"? If so, you will understand the morbid state of military music into which we have fallen. A beat of drums draws us to the window; the call of a trumpet tears us from our bed. During the writing of the last forty lines, I have three times put on my hat, and clutched up my field-glass, and seen—a regiment at drill!

But to return "à nos moutons"—Ah, if we could! We turned out as soon as we had time to make a toilette sufficiently "canaille" for the Communists, and wended our way towards the Place Vendôme, the head-quarters of the National Guard. There we found some thousands of the citizen army ready to march. "And the affair of the hour?" we asked of a fat and friendly corporal. "The Hôtel de Ville is attacked," was the reply, which, I confess, did not astonish me after Bourget, where it seems the action began with 4000 French and four guns, against 13,000 Prussians with many batteries. Later the French advanced a reserve of 15,000 (no guns —they were forgotten, and only got up when the action was over), which the enemy met with 25,000 men and several mitrailleuses (the cartridges of the French mitrailleuse got so damp that the gun could not be fired). Total—19,000 French and no guns, *versus* 38,000 Prussians with many guns. Add to this the fall of Metz, and I repeat that I was not at all astonished to hear of an assault on the Government of Defence, and an attack on the seat of their (want of) judgment.

THE DAY OF THE TWO REVOLUTIONS.

I marched off at once to the Hôtel de Ville. As I passed along the Rue de Rivoli, I saw on every side the signs of a brewing storm. All the concierges were outside their gates, and their wives, who should have been "doing the first floor," were talking to other conciergeresses, who should have been "doing" the "entresol" and the "second." Men in trousers with red stripes were carefully putting up their shutters, and the farther I advanced the more developed was that " early closing movement." At every corner there was a group of politicians or patriots—usually the nucleus was formed by a man in the wrong and a passion, and another in the right with a newspaper, which he kept striking with his right hand and saying (appealing to the gallery), "If the citizen would read." The gallery was filled by blouses, Mobiles, and that deaf old man with a cough, snuff-box, and spectacles, who is always at the corner of every street in this city.

" Bang the field-piece, twang the lyre" (as Mr. Jingle said on the same occasion), here come three different divisions of National Guards debouching from three different points. Two very bad quarters own them too—Belleville and Villette—and on they stream towards the Hôtel de Ville. The street is one mass of *soi-disant* soldiery. They march at ease, with arms reversed, arms slung over their shoulders, trailed or given to little boys to carry for them, which is rather like riding out on a hack to meet your enemy. Those who are not "intriguing" the returning battalions are singing either Offenbach's or patriotic airs. The officers, as a rule, seem ignored, and only leave the pavement when it is time to order the men to " form four-deep," which they do when marching in quarter distance column. They are opposed by the American Versailles Railway omnibus, a vast vehicle like Noah's Ark, filled though by singular instead of dual animals, which still runs on rails to the very verge of Prussia—that is, somewhere about the Seine.

The further we advanced towards the Hôtel de Ville, the more evident was that state of affairs so dear to demagogues—so dreaded by decent people. Some of the regiments had the "Red Flag." At that sign I saw shop doors snap to with double springs. Curious remarks were made by the people —that lounging, cigar-smoking, blouse lot, which nothing but the *levée en masse* seems able to touch (they will shirk that by showing their shoulders and the brand on them)—and their female friends.

A lady with a child four years old was calmly going down to assist at the Hospital of the Luxembourg—in the cause of which she had spent more health there than, and all the money she can, afford— when a *tricoteuse*, whose grandmother no doubt "took her knitting" to the guillotine as an "outing," growled out, "To perdition with the little animals of that race."

Drums and clarions—another division. They are Mobiles, and take possession of the steps of the Hôtel de Ville. They do it firmly. "Is the House of Justice of the metropolis to be invaded by Moblots?" is the cry; and row—I can use no more illustrative word—row No. 1 is very nearly coming off. The Mobiles and the Belleville-Flourens Nationals actually come to "charge bayonets;" but then the God of Battles cried "ground arms." Yet it was touch and go.

Close to me stood a lady and gentleman—the latter a Frenchman, who had been on duty for thirty-six hours. He is one of the few Parisians who are really as much at home in an unstuffed saddle at Melton as in the "Bi-bi" of a boudoir in the Faubourg St.-Germain, to which he belongs. He had put on "mufti" after hours of uniform, and had a cane in his hand. "Bah!" said a blouse, "now at least we shall sweep away those nothings with the cane in their hands." The sinner is a clever diplomatist, whose gains from the Government have never been seventy pounds a year, and whose property employs hundreds of Parisians.

Just as I reached the front of the Hôtel de Ville a great battalion of National Guards arrived. The doors were closed—they were strong—and the vast building was black save in a series of windows from which ladies and gentlemen, and I might add cooks (for your republican in the matter of cooks is as strong as he is in "Guards"), looked down on the curious, and rather dangerous scene. It was a sufficiently imposing spectacle, and was the second act of a drama, the curtain of which might easily fall on a tragedy. Thanks to a cobbler and a commissionnaire (both in uniform) whom I had known at home, I got a good place in a gutter, and was just in time to see the battalion march before the Hôtel de Ville.

It is a pity that I am recording facts, not telling stories; but they are facts, and it was wet, damp, and disagreeable, all elements to compel truth-telling. Just as I had taken up my position there came four or five (I heard four) reports from heavy guns, literally not many yards out of range. And what did our battalion do? The supreme of coolness in action—it halted under the windows of the Hôtel de Ville and ———, a very good-looking young fellow, evidently "primo tenore" at a good theatre, gave his musket to a comrade and—

Sang a Song!

He sang it very well, and the chorus was effective; but that forty thousand men should get wet in their uniforms, which they must dry for next day's parade, to hear a second-rate tenor in the open air, seems to me to be more injurious to health than useful to the Fatherland.

But all this time such serious affairs were being accomplished as history as not registered since 1792. As soon as the loss of Bourget—a deeper grief to the people than Metz, on the same principle that you feel the death of your aunt in Belgravia more than you do that of your uncle at the Land's End—was known, the reaction against republicanism was sitting in conclave exactly in the quarters where Republicanism sat in judgment (illustrated by bombs) on Imperialism. The judgment of Belleville (though since for a time reversed) was soon carried out. Flourens and his party marched on the Hôtel de Ville, and after being repulsed two or three times, Flourens, *ipse* Flourens, forced his way up the Grand Staircase, through the Audience Hall, into the Council Chamber, and with a select body of friends broke into the Privy Council; and if he did not absolutely make prisoners of Trochu, Jules Favre, and the rest of the Government of Defence, yet he had them watched for hours, while Flourens and Co. reseized the reins which Jules Favre and Co. had seized, each having with them equal right.

Does any one remember Dr. Johnson's remark about two most unpleasant insects? I see that to-day Paris politically holds the unpleasant Sage's matured opinion. The Sage too must have seen something of fleas : I have been in his chambers.

So it is evident that even-handed Justice does some-times compel the poisoned chalice to the right lips. If Trochu is betrayed, he may perhaps recall a 1st of September when Rouher and De Grammont heard certain words as " false as dicers' oaths ;" and as for Ducrot, who just then cantered up to offer his ser-vices, he should be presented with an " A B C," or railway time-table.

But every minute the plot thickened. " Very fishy," whispered to me an Anglo-Parisian, " and I can read the signs." For my own part, having some experience in mobs, I confess not to have been alarmed, thinking that there was probably much swagger and little real work : they do talk so much. I spoke to men of all classes, was followed as a spy by a man whom I caused to be followed in his turn, was asked if I was English or American, and saw that I should have been a deal more popular if I had said the latter. Advice to English—" Stop at home."

Windows opened about this time, and the air was thickened with bits of paper which reminded one of Chalvey Ditch and a paper hunt. It was nothing so good.   The fact was, the Revolution of the 4th of September, having been found Imperial, Legitimist, Orleanist, mild, inconsequent, milk and water, tory— was supplanted by another lot of self-made ministers, who took the reins from Jules Favre, and got on his side of the box just as easy as B. used to say to B. A. —" Let me take them this stage," and so they crossed from off to near.   Only I fear these fellows will upset the coach.

The crowd in the mean time hooted and shouted, and held private parliaments under lamp-posts, in which the opposition was always in a majority, the ministry retiring in a cloud of snuff and a bandana— a fearful snuffy flag.   "But, Sir, if you ——" "But, Citizen, I won't——"   "Yet the Citizen will allow ——"   "Citizen, I shall admit nothing!" "But the *commune!*"   "Here's a nice commune, a pretty little *commune*, here's a little commune, but· who knows what it means?" sang perhaps the smallest *gamin* for his age—he looked ninety, so wicked and worn was he—that I have ever seen.   It is an old song of '92.

Trumpets and drums! somebody else comes.   The unarmed division : they took their non-armament out in singing.   But all attention is fixed on the new anti-Republican Republicanissime Opposition ; any extreme measures advanced, and an allowance made for a quantity of real red-republican resolutions. They have come—called from Belleville, Villette, and Leicester Square—to govern France.

"At last he came, the great man in a great position, sent for from Rome to govern England," we read of Sir Robert Peel. We might paraphrase it, and say that, criminal prosecutions having lapsed, Flourens has sent himself from his hiding-place to annoy Paris. He proposed last night to govern us with the assistance of Dorian—ironmaster, rich, respectable, but who declines to "join the ministry;" Ledru Rollin—the less said the better; Victor Hugo—mad as a hatter and a poet; Félix Pyat (same category as Rollin) red as beetroot; Mottu—no religion, no education, will order donkeys to be killed because of the cross they bear; Delescluze—writes well, and conspires worse; Louis Blanc—opposed to Napoleon, but his grand-aunt was a Pozzo di Borgo (Pozza di Borgo would be purer Corsican): from this lineage he will inherit the républican tenure of Albert Gate; but I hear that he too cries off; and so, to use the words of a French friend, "the only elements of respectability are eliminated from the programme of the Insurrectional Government." Bonvallet—a very good minister of the interior. I have dined with him often : he is good in a plain citizen-style, but dear.   They should put him either to the " interior," or to " finance."   He had a *chef de cabinet*, no *cuisine*, whom you could not equal at " anguilles (slippery things) à la financière."   He might try his hand at the national " additions."   Martin Bernard —deputy in 1848 ; hates Napoleon III., and is a journalist.   Greppo—an apothecary by trade, I believe to this day in the Rue de la Paix ; but that is only retail murder with a licence.   His wholesale trade is assassination.   He did business with both Louis-Philippe and Louis Napoleon, but failed. Blanqui—conspirator born ; ætat, sixty-five ; a prisoner forty-five years.   If he had been one of the giants who conspired (instead of a provincial law student), and they had carried the gates of Heaven, he would have at once made explosive shells and got up a plot against Satan.

Such was the Committee of Public Safety announced to me by a National Guard, and afterwards printed.

All this time legion after legion of National Guards were pouring into the Place de l'Hôtel de Ville, their " crosses in the air," *i.e.*, the stocks of their muskets up and the muzzle down ; and inside, the Government elected by Belleville on the 4th of September was sitting at a long, green baize-covered table, staring vacantly at the wall where we used to see "S. M. l'Empereur" and "S. M. l'Impératrice" by Winterhalter. They were supposed to be deliberating, and were "watched" by, that is, they were prisoners in, the hands of Belleville.

One little episode that occurred I will mention. Flourens and another presented their revolvers at the heads of Trochu and Jules Favre, and said, "If you call your National Guards, or if they advance, you are dead men." Jules Ferry heard this, and got out of the room. He rushed up to the commander of the National Guards, and said, "Don't move a man; if you do they will shoot Jules Favre and Trochu." "No, they won't," said the Colonel, who knew his business and his men. "Go and tell them that if they shoot those two—and they must of course take the chances of the hour—I have eighty of their Nationals here in my power, and I will shoot them on the spot." The lawyer minister and the soldier governor are still alive. It is quite a treat to hear of one man with a grain of energy.

"Now I shall go to dinner," said an Anglo-Parisian. "Nothing ever happens in Paris between 6 and 8 o'clock P.M.,—Il faut dîner." So it is; *ruat cælum* the Parisian must go to dinner, and if the sky should fall he would order "mauviettes sauce d'enfer," and he would be right.   You take an Indian pickle, a tomato —but that has nothing to do with this diary of famine.

I too went to dinner.   It was so abnormal a day, and so curious a dinner, that I shall be personal about it.   We dined with Madame C——, and the party consisted of Count Viel-castel, Baron de Billing (both just off duty, having carried despatches to the outposts for thirty-six hours), M. Treitt, ourselves, and just as dinner was announced came Dr. Gordon, Inspector General of Hospitals, with the latest list of the "Government of Public Safety," which he had just received from a friend.

Sir William Temple's "thunderbolt in summer sky" was nothing to the little scrawl which I have now before me.   They were silent, and their hair stood on end!   At last some one said, "It means the Commune."   "Yes," said another, "it is '92!"   I have never seen a greater or more justified panic— justified, and for this reason: the hostess is as much French as English, and her grandfather was playing his part—a losing game—against the Commune of '92.   The grandfather of one of the party was be- headed in the Reign of Terror; and the grandfather of another deprived of all his property.   The very ser- vant who waited, who had been a drummer in the

Grande Armée, trembled at the announcement, which recalled his youthful memories, "We shall soon have a second reign of terror!"

When we sat down to dinner, the First Revolution of the 31st of October was as much an accomplished fact, and quite as legally installed, as was the Legal-Military Imbecility of the 4th of September, on the morning of the 5th. It was dog eat dog! Another revolution had been eaten up by its own offspring—a pretty litter.

Nobody got through dinner with much appetite, and digestion had evidently gone out on duty, and so waited on nobody. Dry moselle is not a bad remedy for low spirits, and our hostess prescribed a large glass each, in which we drank "Confound the Commune." Just at that moment the gentleman who sat next to me—a very old commander of National Guards—whispered, "There goes the *rappel.*"

We sat talking more lively from the effects of the ebbing of the "blue moselle"—and more clearly discussed the real effects of this dreaded Commune. This is the idea of pure French people whose families have for ages struggled through the stormy history of France: the "Commune" means the government of Paris by a set of men for whom only the extreme reds will vote. They will all vote, while the moderates will abstain ; and when in power, the Committee of Execution, elected out of the body of Maires, is absolute. They will do away with all worship, though they hardly now dare come to a Goddess of Reason ; appropriate all the Church property, decree equality of expense, and equal distribution of the residue of personal income ; stop all the theatres ; gag the Press ; dismiss the army ; repudiate all engagements entered into by previous governments ; and, in a word, do everything to prove once more to the civilized world that there is no such tyranny as *absolute* liberty, the motto of which is, "If you do not do as you like, I'll make you."

A very good fellow walking from Doncaster to the grand stand, to see "t'Leger" some years ago, found written up every five yards, "The way to H——." He wrote to me, "Comforted by this assurance, I walked on, and backed the winner." "Comforted" by the above lively historic recollections and predictions, we got on to our "café." Just as Michel was handing it round, came a noise, down went the tray with an exclamation, "Mais, bon Dieu, c'est la générale !"

"It's all over," said M. Treitt. "La générale" is the "tocsin," and it called all Paris to arms. A great street fight is, we will say, exciting, but it should not be taken immediately after dinner.

We marched off at once. It was a curious scene. Trumpets sounding every five hundred yards, doors opening in every house, and the half-dressed citizen soldiers rushing from their beds. Three columns were advancing from Batignolles, and at the "double" were making for the Hôtel de Ville. The Place Vendôme was so fully occupied by troops that you could scarcely pass—after midnight you were not allowed—all the men having ten rounds. The Mobiles kept out of sight, held all the outlets of the great thoroughfares; the line of rails of the Tuileries Gardens concealed in its shade some two battalions; the entrance to the now Ambulance was defended, and a perfect garrison was ranged before the door of Trochu. That gallant general was now at liberty, as were all except Jules Favre and General Tamisier; they had been rescued by Ernest Picard, who alone does not seem to have lost his head. Jules Favre held on till 3 A.M., when it was found that Republic No. 1 had been too strong for Republic No. 2. The "générale" we heard was the reaction of reaction.

It is useless to record all that happened between "la générale" and 4 A.M. on Tuesday, when the usurpers of the 4th of September, having quite out-numbered the usurpers of the 31st of October, General Trochu reviewed the National Guards, and sent them shivering to their beds, and so ended the second Revolution of Monday—for a time.

All is well that ends well. Paris was as it should be, too strong for Belleville and the parts about Villette; but France has had a narrow escape, and Paris for once was ashamed, and on Tuesday—

> " Come quei, che con lena affanata,
>   Uscito fuor del pelago alla riva,
>   Si volge all' acqua perigliosa e guata."

Paris looked back and shivered. I cannot forget that Prussian guns were thundering all the time, and trust that nobody will ever again say to me that France is a great nation.

Tuesday, 1*st*.—All Saints Day. What a beautiful satire it would have been if Mottu—" Mottu proprio" (to quote "Figaro")—had been gazetted "Minister of No-Worship" to-day! It nearly came off. He believes in neither God nor devil, and has not much faith in himself; as much as other people though, but let that pass.

There is proclamation out that the elections actually proclaimed and placarded by the Flourens Government for to-day at twelve o'clock were illegal. A patched-up affair! The Favre failure has ordained an election on Thursday, to see if it is necessary to have a new government or not. Then there is to be another plebiscite on Saturday, to elect maires. Two days of disturbance, and the Prussians are thundering at the gates of Paris ! A vote of confidence in a non-existing government, and two days of National Guards' service lost !

There are some six hundred mad people still at Charenton, and the Director finds it difficult to feed them. "Let them out," said a friend. "Good God, no !" said M. X——, "they will get into the Government."

Wednesday, November 2nd.—The talk is all of armistice.   He will be a bold minister who proposes it here !   The idea is execrated even by the mildest men in Paris.   "Why three weeks ?" they say.   "We may as well beat or be beaten now."   If Bismarck grants a truce, and allows Paris to revictual herself, then I say there is another added to the list of lunatics, whose waistcoats must be cut strait on account of this miserable war.

All the advisers of the Emperor were mad when they advised war.   His Majesty must have been a lunatic when he commenced it without shoes or soldiers, bread or generals ; Palikao was raving when he left Paris ; and the poor Empress was driven mad by the perfidy of her " faithful friends."   The King of Prussia is " touched," or in these republican times he would not be so far from home, and if Bismarck signs this armistice, he should at once, in the straitest of waistcoats and trousers, be sent to make No. 631 in the starving contingent of Charenton.

Halte-là !   Here's another lunatic ; get him a " chemise (rouge) de force."   General Garibaldi has accepted a commission in the army of France !   If this does not mean the restoration of Nice and Savoy, he is madder than Bedlam. "You have made me an exile in my own country, and sold my birthplace to France." Indeed it is a "mad world, my masters."

Wittgenstein, the Russian attaché, came back last night. He brings news that the Prussians are tremendously strong at Versailles, and have three hundred guns in position. They are all very sick of the war, but have not the slightest idea of retiring. They laugh at the French fighting, but admit that the artillery is very good, and so well served that they lose on an average twenty men a day. A shot from Mont Valérien last week killed two officers who were looking out of window at Meudon, and then passed through the house, killing a lot of men on parade.

There was a sort of row to-day at La Villette, where one Vallès seized the reins of mayoralty which M. Richard had let drop. He was in power two hours, and asked for six hundred pounds for expenses for the day. Rentes, 3 per cent., rose two francs, and closed 52,90.

Thursday, November 3rd.—Fine, but cold.

Universal suffrage appealed to by the Government of the 4th of September for a vote of confidence— "Oui" or "Non." Rochefort has left them, which, in spite of all they say, is a blow, and if he and his vote "Non," the end of my account of to-day may be bad for Favre and Co.

It seems that during the brief period when the Government of Public Security were in office—the first revolution of Monday—they and their followers not only ate all the food, drank all the wine (piles of dead men were found all over the house), but also smashed up all the furniture. There is no doubt that at one time some of the Favre Government did say they would grant the Commune.

Flourens and the colonels of the Commune National Guard are dismissed—a mighty mild punishment for open mutiny before the enemy, and Flourens cannot even plead "first offence;" his men, too, actually fired three or four shots. Among other acts committed by them was that of stealing a lot of the stamped voting-tickets and some officially stamped paper, which last has enabled some evil-doers to hoax all the papers with a forged despatch of a victory in the Vosges, which has done great harm. If found out, the forger will not be punished: the existing men dare not take extreme measures.

On Monday, two men presented a cheque at the Treasury for 240,000*l.*, signed "Blanqui." They were invited into the "Bank Parlour;" then Picard locked the door, and told them they were prisoners. The absurd points of this revolutionette are now coming to light. When the National Guards were advancing to rescue Trochu, Blanqui got very much alarmed, and, leaving his catspaw, Tibaldi, to draw out of the fire any chestnuts he might find, made for the door. It so chanced that General Tamisier, whom Blanqui knew to be very near-sighted, passed at the same time. Blanqui slipped his arm through that of the General, who mistook him for M. Dorian, and so the two got safe out of the mess together.

The temporary Government had ordered a great supper, and just as it was being served, the 106th battalion suddenly appeared from the basement— they having entered the Hôtel de Ville by the underground passage, of which their colonel had cunningly secreted the key—and drove them all out. The 106th, which is the crack Faubourg St.-Germain regiment, then sat down with the Mobiles to the supper ordered by Floureus. "Sic vos non vobis."

Gems from the clubs:—"M. Thiers is the Wandering Jew of baseness." "Thank God!" exclaimed an atheist at another meeting, "I am no Christian."

M. de Fonvielle, who erected the statue to the Good Prussian Voltaire, is already out of office.

Official life under a republic seems brief. " In the midst of office we are out."

We have another new street—the Boulevard Victor Hugo! It is part of the Boulevard Haussmann. The effect of these absurd changes is to puzzle postmen, and drive letter-writers and answer-receivers mad.

We walked up to the Buttes de Chaumont. It is the finest view out of Paris. It was as clear a day as ever was seen, and we had good glasses; but in the whole circle which we could command, we could not see (outside the walls of Paris) a living soul—not one; also, " Not a gun was heard." Going and returning we passed by the quarters of Villette, Belleville, and St.-Denis, and went by several voting-places; but all was as calm as a county town. There was ten times the crowd at the butchers' shops that there was at any Mairie.

Poor Ernest Baroche was killed in action last week.

We met one of General Berthout's staff, who told us that his chief is changed from Courbevoie to St.-Denis, vice General de Bellemare, removed on account of the blunder of Bourget, where the French lost twelve hundred prisoners. They have not yet published this fact, nor the list of killed and wounded.

This week revolution has swallowed up war, and the Prussians are as much forgotten as if they were under the lime trees at Berlin. General Trochu does not blame General de Bellemare, but being a republican general, he does not act as would an English or Austrian superior officer. The National Guards by their own inspiration went to St.-Denis to arrest De Bellemare, whom they would probably have shot, and so General Trochu "is very grieved, but must yield to popular opinion." But if General de Bellemare was not to blame, his sacrifice will scarcely "encourage the others."

Good inscription for a Moblots' wineshop close to the market in the Rue Puebla—"Au Secours contre la soif."

Pitch and toss is rather, I think, going out in the army, and tip-cat is coming in, to the danger of our eyes. What said " Punch " years ago ?

> " A quiet party, he was walking by,
> Up jumped a tip cat, and knocked out his eye !"

Friday, November 4th.—Two months this day since the collapse of the Empire, and the forty-seventh day of the strict siege. We have gained nothing except having rendered Paris really strong ; but then the enemy has gained little ; and we have had in the whole sixty-one days only one counter-revolution and a few street rows at Belleville.

Trochu, Favre, and the rest of the men of the 4th of September had a great triumph over the Commune yesterday.   Final result of the universal vote—

Yes . . . 557,996
No . . . 62,638

So the Flourens party are out of the hunt altogether; but as is always the case here, the existing Government, like each one before it, will succeed to the perilous inheritance of the ever-increasing discontent of Belleville, Villette, &c., where even now there are sixty thousand men as opposed to Trochu as to Napoleon.

Of course there was a semi-official announcement of the ministerial majority last night, and at midnight poor General Trochu, worn off his legs, and being in bed, ten thousand National Guards insisted on defiling past his house, and he had to get up and make speeches.   They were all at the same work at eleven this morning.   After this election I should suggest more fighting, and less talking and singing.

Yesterday at a concert for the wounded, a priest of the Madeleine, the Abbé Deguerry—who was as Imperial as Cambacérès on the 1st of September—insisted on making a speech, in which he abused the war and him who caused it, and the last words were—" city of pleasure and foul voluptuousness;" but he was especially hard on "Sovereigns who, hardly arrived in Paris, hastened off to hear the 'Grande Duchesse'!" How the ears of all the Sovereigns in Europe must have tingled beneath their crowns !

We hear most contradictory reports, all more or less from reliable sources—or what would be so in times of peace. We shall have an armistice for twenty-five days, and permission to get in a daily supply of food. Yes, objects the next comer, but there are two points against it. Where are we to get daily supplies ? and if we get them in daily, or in the lump, who is to estimate the requirements of twenty-four hours ? You say the population of Paris is two millions : say it *was*, but yesterday's voting clearly proves to the Prussians that there are only 475,395 votes in Paris, for they will naturally ignore your plan of concealing the number of military votes, and you will be rationed in proportion to your own published polling list. And, adds a third, Bismarck has said that unless some definite allusion to Alsace and Lorraine is made in the terms requesting the armistice, he will not be a consenting party. Opinions differ, you see, but there is no doubt that M. Thiers has acquired a new title, which will last him his life—"la vieille entremetteuse."

The King of Prussia is raving over this delay, and said in the hearing of several persons that he would take Paris, and if he could find no established government there, he would take all France, and re-create the Great German Empire.

The batteries at Versailles are built in tiers, as at Cronstadt, and the casemates get so hot that it is almost impossible to stay in them.

It is reported here (on the authority of Thiers) that Bismarck has tried to treat with the Empress Eugénie, about whom to-day this pretty pamphlet is being sold in the moral streets—"La Femme Bonaparte: ses Amants et ses Orgies." Truly Piétri would have prevented the hawking of such thrash even attacking the wife of the worst enemy to the Emperor.

I was amused at a trick played on a friend of ours at the election yesterday. He went very early to vote, being on duty, and got there just as the council of four was elected, and they were quarrelling as to whom they should select for their chairman and scrutineer. Now C——, the horsedealer, was there, and he had lately been cast in a horse case, having sold

my friend a lame horse. As soon as M. C——
saw this gentleman, he said, " Here is your man;
one of the notables of the quarter;" so he was
elected by acclamation, and kept in the chair from
eight o'clock till six.

We have just come from the Bois by the Avenue
de l'Impératrice. The destruction is heart-rending.
The Avenue ex-Empress is now very strongly barricaded indeed, and the " ride " on one side, and the
footpath on the other are both dug full of round holes,
six inches from one another and about a foot deep, each
having three strong pointed stakes firmly stuck into
the ground. I never saw such a " stopper " for horse
or foot before, and as a satire they have left up two
of Haussmann's notices—"Reserved for Equestrians!"
at the entrance to one, and at the other entrance,
" Reserved for Pedestrians—Forbidden to walk on the
Grass." The last regulation will not be violated.

The American ambulance is now in full vigour.
Tested by wet and cold it is found that their tents
and their system of warming are admirable. They
have made quite a show place of it too, without any
nonsense. Out of fifty-seven patients (and many
amputations) they have lost but two in six weeks.
Air, light, warmth, good food, cheerful situation, and
kindness are the American remedies.

Three per cent. of the army voted " non ;" that is, certainly not peace or armistice, nor the " men of September ;" and most, if not all, wish for a socialistic republic.

There are left in Vinoy's army about forty to fifty men to demoralize the others.   C'est assez !

Saturday, November 5th.—Weather fine, though it has turned very cold, but I hear that the Prussians look forward to the mild winter of Paris with great calmness, and almost pleasure. I am assured also that they can stand bad weather very well. The French troops will not, if better arrangements for feeding them are not made at once. Some days ago I wrote, that the Mobiles and Regulars had no meat, and to-day I read that the men who were defeated at Bourget had had no food for forty-eight hours; and that at the affair of Bagneux, where the Côtes d'Or Mobiles fought so well, they had had nothing for thirty-six hours, and this close to the forts, and all the roads to Paris open. It will kill boys, and such are most of the Moblots.

In spite of the reported armistice, the forts of Montrouge and Bicêtre were playing a lively duet all yesterday evening. No actual news of the armistice, and it seems doubtful if communications will be kept open. To remedy this, the "Figaro" to-day tells us (seriously) that experiments are being tried to get "return balloons" by steering those hitherto stubborn globes, and forcing them to sail in the teeth of the wind! M. P——, a pupil of the Ecole Polytechnique, declares that with four large birds he could take a balloon anywhere, and back again! The experiment was in a measure tested on Thursday, in the presence of M. Rampont, Director-General of the Post, and MM. Chassinet and Mattel, both connected with the postal service. Four eagles, taken from the Jardin des Plantes, were harnessed to a truck weighing four tons and a half, and they moved it easily. It is the steering which delights me! M. P—— is to sit in the car with a long pole, at the end of which is a lump of raw meat, on to which the eagles endeavour to pounce, and which the holder keeps pointing in the direction of the course he desires to keep. This is not written to be laughed at, but seriously; and after all, any one who has ever seen a Whitechapel costermonger urging on his tired "moke" by a deceptive carrot tied just out of reach to a stick stuck in the bridle, will at once appreciate the directing medium. I see difficulties though. Just to begin with, where are we to find all the eagles? But the Imperial bird may still save France.

The English seem to have given up all idea of getting away! There is grievous grumbling, and the "revenants" complain that Russians, Americans, and Italians are sent *full* away, while they are kept *empty* here. *A propos* of English :—A man named Drake died from his wounds here in an ambulance Rue Saint-Dominique, and was buried to-day in Père la Chaise. I only know he was English, and in "Les armeés de la France." Another Englishman named Childers has been gazetted for bravery and coolness before the enemy, being one of the last three to retire from a position.

The food is getting scarce, as you will see from these quotations :—horse (three weeks ago fourpence) one shilling and twopence per pound, venison eight shillings a pound (very scarce), a fowl twenty shillings, a leg of lamb (as big as a Norfolk turkey's leg) twelve and sixpence, veal twelve and sixpence, and calf's liver six and eightpence a pound. Beef and mutton keep regulation prices—tenpence halfpenny and ninepence per pound ; but then there is none of either left. I saw a *three* days' ration for *three* people issued by Duval yesterday. It consisted of three cutlets of the size known as "Epigrammes," and would give a very small mouthful of food per diem to each person. It is no wonder then to see a dog ready for the spit hanging outside a shop, on the front of which was displayed this placard :—

"Grande Boucherie Hippophagique.
Canine et Féline.
Vente au comptant."

It was close to the Mobile Barracks, on the Boulevard Rochechouart.

I have just been to look at the Grandes Halles, but did not find them better than the markets St.-Honoré and de la Madeleine, but I lunched full of such horrors that I shall require no meat to-day. Horse is bad enough, but the sight of stall after stall decorated (!) with the heads of horse, mule, and ass is perfectly awful, and the —— "Thank you, the eau de Cologne."

I never felt less like breaking the Tenth commandment, and indeed I do not think I shall ever eat beef again. It is positively touching to see the live fowls in cages, the geese in covered baskets, with holes for their heads, and the rabbits and guinea-pigs in boxes, basking in the herbs and vegetables, with which they will be eaten to-morrow. I saw an old buck rabbit gazing on some onions, "unconscious of his doom," and thought there was quite a moral to be deduced from that rabbit-hutch. Poor old bunny, I wonder if he had a smothering feeling.

The Government has been aroused into a little life by the affair of Monday: has appointed General Clément Thomas—a veteran republican who commanded the same corps in 1848 (ah ! that age, how bad it is for generals on active service !)—Commander-in-Chief of the National Guards, in the place of General Tamisier, who was not sufficiently energetic. They have also, it is said, arrested Félix Pyat, Maurice Joly, Tridon, Vésinier, Pillot, Cyrille, Ranvier, Ducoudray, and Goupy. Flourens and Blanqui have contrived to conceal themselves. They say they will all be tried by court-martial, but it is too late now ; besides, we know that " they say" is a common liar.

Speaking of Blanqui, Victor Hugo said, "He is a celebrated unknown." Flourens is nicknamed the " Cretan Hero"—yet I should not be astonished if the " Hero" and the " Unknown" did not contrive to get up an ugly row on the day when the armistice is proclaimed. There will be people of their opinion, and the Government will be terribly unpopular during the first twenty-four hours. The Government of

National Defence is thus analyzed:—Trochu—a soldier who dips his sword in ink and sheaths his pen; Favre—pompous and hesitating; the façade of the Pantheon painted by Sechan on calico at a penny a yard; Jules Simon—soured and sentimental, distilling vitriol; Pelletan—a bomb, the fusee damped on the 4th of September; Glais-Bizoin—Sancho-Panza on leave; Crémieux—a great politician of St.-Pèlerine; Rochefort—a companion you prefer to see in another man's house; Gambetta—prudently bold and boldly prudent, stands half way between the advanced and moderate parties, so as to get the voices of both; Ferry—a petty mediocrity and a petty audacity; Garnier-Pagès—too wise to save the capital; Ernest Picard—a clever man, much bored with his present " friends."

Two National Guards meeting in the street to-day, one in full uniform—the other in " mufti." " What," said the former, " have you got on your armistice clothes already?"

Nothing perhaps brings home to one the effect of a " levée en masse" so much as some scenes we witnessed to-day in the Rue de Rivoli. The pavement is lined with little peddlers' stores of every small kind, and nearly every man selling them was more or less in uniform; as were also the citizen boot-cleaners, who were operating on the feet of their comrades.

"Figaro" never misses a chance of a *bon mot*—"c'est son métier," but I think this might have been spared :—"At last Bazaine has effected his junction with the army of MacMahon."

Although this is only the 5th of November, it is our 9th, or rather, it is twenty Lord Mayors' days condensed into one. We have just been to the Hôtel de Ville to see the "show." We passed through some election districts, but if the Parisians had been ordering twenty dinners, they would have been much louder and more demonstrative than they were while electing twenty Maires. Yet it is very important, as the Communists are at work.

A speech of a Moblot from the Indre, heard at the Hôtel de Ville on Monday :—"What is it! This large town got no common! Why, our village at home has a little one."

Another speech of a National Guard, in very fullest uniform :—Friend coming into the café sees him, and says—"Why! you've got your uniform at last, now they talk of an armistice. What will you do if they hint at peace?" "If any one talks to me seriously of peace, I'll go at once and get my musket." Funds to-day were—3 per cents., 54,50.

Sunday, November 6th.—" Restrain your appetites, and you've conquered human nature," says the great Squeers, and I presume that Count von Bismarck is a disciple of the same school, for there is to be no armistice because the Prussian minister " expressly repelled the question of revictualling." How any one in his sound senses could for one moment imagine that Bismarck would allow Paris not only to revictual, but to take the votes of Alsace and Lorraine, which France has as much lost as the Austrians have lost Venice, is beyond my comprehension. Many clever men, however, did think so, and the people were as much excited as they are to-day depressed. In one way I think this refusal may benefit France. In twenty-five days of idleness chiefly spent inside the walls, I think that the discipline both of the Mobiles and the Urbane Guard would have gone back three months.

This is a translation of the official notice of the failure of the Thiers-Bismarck negotiations, published in the " Journal Officiel " to-day :—

Paris, November 5th, 1870.

" The four great neutral Powers—England, Russia, Austria, and Italy, took the initiative in a proposal for an armistice having for its object the election of a National Assembly.

"The Government of National Defence laid down its conditions, which were : the revictualling of Paris, and the election of the National Assembly by the whole of France.

"Prussia has expressly rejected the revictualling; besides which she has not admitted among the reservations the votes of Alsace and Lorraine.

"The Government of National Defence has unanimously decided that the armistice thus restricted should be rejected."

So much for the public opinion of Europe, and especially of England, which I was assured Bismarck dared not resist. Probably the Count cares very little for the rest of Europe, and as for "the right little, tight little island," considers its opinion very much as he would that of the Republic of San Marino. A man who has triumphed over half Europe cares naturally very little for Mrs. Grundy. This has brought things to a crisis, and I am not sure that it is not best so.

If, as I hear, fresh meat will only hold out a fortnight, and the dry supplies are not very great (there is plenty of bread-stuff and wine), we must make peace or fight an awful battle before Christmas ; and indeed, as the troops would on lower rations be getting weaker every day, I should think Trochu would attack (if not attacked) at once. On the other hand, if Prussia is boldly come to take Paris by storm, and not to sneak in disgracefully under cover of famine, why does she not attack ? Every day makes Paris materially stronger, and I am firmly persuaded that as long as the National Army keeps in forts and behind walls, they cannot only resist, but (if not starved themselves) wear out their enemy. If they will and are driven to attack, I fear they will be beaten in every sortie. This will be an important week, and perhaps that " beginning of the end," of which we have heard several times already.

It is said that the gilded dome of the Invalides is to be covered. It would certainly be a satisfactory target for Prussian artillerymen ; but then it is unlucky to touch that cupola, and especially to gild it. *Ecce signum :* Louis XIV. had it reburnished, and in two years began the series of reverses which ended in the Treaty of Utrecht ; Napoleon I. again brightened it up in 1813, and fell in 1814 ; and Napoleon III. regilded it in 1869, and was a prisoner in 1870 !

Another preparation for the siege, and very practical. Our " femme de ménage " says she has been for two days in a quite grand apartment, helping to pack jewels, lace, china, and linen worth two thousand pounds, which are put into cases and bricked up in a hollow place in the cellar wall.

Only thirteen out of the twenty Maires were elected yesterday ; the other seven not obtaining the requisite majority are destined to another scrutiny to-day. Among the thirteen chosen were three of the " Flourentins" of last Monday—Bonvalet, Mottu, and Clémenceau ; Delescluze will be elected to-day, so the Government may well beware of scotched snakes. That they are alarmed by the Communists is evident from the resolute way in which they are arresting them. It seems they held a sitting in a church on the 1st of November, and declared they would upset Favre and his friends, and assassinate Trochu.

In addition to the list I named yesterday, they have made further capture, and to-day the following persons are under arrest :—MM. Félix Pyat, Maurice Joly, Tridon, Mottu, Lefrançais, Millière, Jaclard, Vésinier, Pillot, Cyrille, Ranvier, Ducoudray, Goupy, Vermorel, Razoua, Tibaldi.

Possibly you think I exaggerate the dangers of the Commune. To prove that I do not, I give you a faithful copy of the programme of " Blanqui the Bolter " (a free translation of his last nickname) :—

" All churches to be closed to public worship, and used as granaries, or clubs, or for some other revolutionary purpose.

" Every ambulance to be purged of its priests, who must be arrested, armed, sent under fire, placed in front of the Patriots (by-the-way, this is quite the Mazzini-Blanqui theory), and exposed to the utmost danger. They shall be martyrs. To go to Heaven will be their reward. We, who do not believe in Heaven, desire that they die first. Let them be the cuirasses of fathers of families, and for once in their lives they will have been of some use.

" The first object of our care must be the barricades. There exists for them a credit of two thousand four hundred pounds, a Committee, and a President; but we cannot find them, and the Prussians constantly advance.

" No citizen must go out unarmed. Let him take any weapon, revolver, dagger, bayonet, anything, and arrest the agents of Bonaparte still in Paris.

" The Journal, the Club, and the Commune must demand the concentration of all means of subsistence, and an equal ration for all.

" Any individual who is cognizant of the concealment of money, gold, silver, jewels, or other valuables, to declare the same to his Maire.

z 2

"A list of inhabitants, their name, age, and profession, and the name and address of the proprietor, to be placarded on every house. The concierge to be answerable.

" By these measures we alone can be saved.

" BLANQUI."

It seems that Captain Baroche, who had been cruelly taunted with treason and Bonapartism by Flourens, Blanqui, and their organs, died the death of a hero. When his regiment retired, he took off his hat to his men, and walked straight into the enemy's line, fired five shots from his revolver, "à bout portant," and then fell, literally riddled with balls.

M. de Fonvielle has made a mistake: he erected Voltaire, and did not scratch out the inscriptions of the deposed Prince, so the astonished passer-by reads that Voltaire was "present at Suez, Marengo, and Wagram!"

It is reported that the dwellers on the Quai Voltaire are going to pray that it shall in future be called the "Quai Prince Eugène."

Purity of election :—

X——. "Of course you are going to vote 'Yes,' like a true Republican as you are?"

Y——. " No! I have always voted ' No ' at all elections, and I am too old to change."

Two female celebrities, who made a good deal of noise in the demi-monde of Paris, when that semi-hemisphere existed, died here last week—Madame de Narbonne, who was accused of poisoning the Duc de Bauffremont, and Mdlle. Markowich, who was called " Box-on-the-ears," from the number of those insults, always ending in duels, which she used to occasion. Both, I believe, died of small-pox, which is raging in some parts of Paris.

The weather is brilliant.

" 17 *Brumaire, an* 79," which, being interpreted, means *Monday, November 7th*, 1870.—The elections of the Maires are not considered very satisfactory even by the revolutionary optimists. I confess to thinking them very bad. I begin, however, by saying that Mottu, the Nothingarian, elected a Maire, has not been arrested. He deserved arrest, but apparently could not command it. Perhaps it " requires interest," as Sydney Smith said about being hanged. Mottu then is a Maire, and Bonvalet, Clémenceau, Delescluze, and Ranvier, all "men of the 31st of October," are also elected—a quarter of the twenty. Flourens and others made an unpleasantly good score, while Favre made speeches and Trochu bows !

Are we to pray for the advent of the Prussians? We need not go far to find them; they are to-day at Montretout, within shelling range (by the admission of the French) of the Elysée, with some three hundred guns and two hundred and sixty thousand men at Versailles alone.

The report to-day is that Ducrot is going to make a rush on the lines of the enemy with all Vinoy's corps and one hundred thousand Mobiles, leaving the National Guards and the sailors to defend Paris and the forts; that would relieve Paris of nearly two hundred thousand mouths requiring beef, wine, and tobacco; but they cannot go out without a great fight, and then ! Their aim would be to join Bourbaki, if they could, and then marched on the rear of the invading army, there might still be hope. As it is, I have read mentally when re-entering any of the gates of this beleaguered city, the fatal motto :—" Voi chi entrate, lasciate ogni speranza."

The game is played out; and in the mean time the Government of National Defence has *not* arrested Mottu, Blanqui, or Flourens, which they were bound to do; and have created fifty-five Chevaliers de la Légion d'Honneur, which they had no more right to decree than I have to knight the commissioner-citizen who condescends to clean my boots. How long will it be before they learn that they are only a species of vestry tolerated for a purpose, and can no more make a binding law than they could make a treaty which would be diplomatically recognized, or a loan which would be financially accepted by the great European houses? Their business is the defence of this unhappy city.

Mr. Wodehouse and his British flock leave to-morrow. Colonel Claremont, purely out of kindness, for I happen to know that he has his "permission," or even "order," to leave, remains here, thinking he may help the yet remaining English. Baron de Beyens (Belgian) and Count de Moltke (Danish), Ministers, remain, and Prince de Sayn-Wittgenstein, with M. Obreskoff, are still at the Russian Embassy. The Prince has just returned from Tours, Florence, Strasbourg, Lyons, London, and Versailles, and reports that France has hundreds of thousands of armed men in the provinces, but no officers, and no organization—"Vieille histoire, mon cher!"

During the Indian mutiny a captured rebel general was asked how many *men* he had under his command. His answer was brief: "Thirty thousand Sepoys, not one *man*." And then they shot him, and served him right.

At dinner to-night at Madame ——'s the talk was all of war, famine, and supplies. I do not think I can better describe it than by asking you to suppose yourself present at a party exactly half French and half English; but as it is the fiftieth day of the siege, perhaps you would like to see the

"MENU DU JOUR—17 *Brumaire, an* 79.

Potage à la bien bonne femme.
Choux à la réaction.
Yac de Tibet.
Salade à la Montrond.
'34 Claret and '20 Port.
Huit mendiants."

I must say a word about this "menu." "Yac" is, as you already, I am sure, know, the "Poëphagus grunniens" of Linnæus. If you do not, you ought. It is also "an ox found in Thibet. The bushy white tail is much prized in the East, where it is used to brush away flies : it is also an emblem of authority." Here it is a sign of soup, and the "ox" itself is rather like venison. This one was bought from the Jardin des Plantes (which paid four hundred pounds for its passage over), and the filet cost one pound four shillings and twopence !

And the "Salade à la Montrond"—do you know it? It is the great breakfast dish before shooting here, and is admirably adapted for a siege, as it is "werry filling at the price." However, this one took a distinguished diplomatist two hours to compose :—Boiled beef, tomatoes, Indian pickles, watercresses, anchovies, Worcester sauce, potatoes, sardines, Chili vinegar, onions, cayenne, beetroot, truffles, beans, peas, cabbage, olives, oil, vinegar, pepper, and salt. That was the farrago of the salad of Count de Montrond, the pupil in gastronomy of that illustrious *gourmet* Talleyrand, and in taste only second to the Gamaliel at whose iron feet he sat. Go thou and do likewise ; stir it well, and ice it in summer.

But to return. This was the conversation :—"I suppose, monsieur, they must attack now?" "Well, I suppose so; but they are in no hurry. They have an election or two to get through, and the lawyer must draw up the plan of the campaign while the general reads his brief before addressing the soldiers."

"Know poor Baroche ! Of course I did. Plucky fellow ! Was turned out of the Board of Trade for accepting three thousand pounds from Mirès to get one of his measures hurried on : started making sugar, and made a lot of money at Creil. You remember, Count, he fought Rochefort in Belgium."

"Yes, monsieur, the armament goes on capitally! A hundred at least came to me to-day asking for arms, but I could not give them any." "Pardon, M. le Baron, but what did they do?" "Do! why, went home perfectly happy."·

"But surely all your absent French do not pay the tax of absence?" "Non, monsieur, pas tous; but they try it on. The Government of National Defence issued an order that all 'useless mouths' should be filled out of Paris, and now wishes to tax the absentees in proportion to their rent. I resisted for a widow of thirty and her son of seven, and I triumphed."

"Yes; she's dead. Caused nine duels in three weeks." "Tell me, X——, is that Duc de Rochefoucauld who was killed at Châteaudun, the Duc to whose ball you got me invited?" "Ah, you remember that fancy-dress ball—the best thing of the Faubourg that year. Ah! your lovely compatriote, 'Queen Mab,' I see her now" (here he kisses the tips of his fingers). "Yes, it is the same Rochefoucauld-Doudeauville; young, one of the richest men in France, with 'Gaudinière,' and the best house in the

Faubourg—all to make life worth living for. He took his volunteers (uncalled for) from his park into action, and fell fighting."

"And so, T——, you believe in reaction?" "Yes; it set in last night at the club-meeting at the Alcazar, where they shouted 'Bah! assez de votre Commune,' and voted a sword of honour to Colonel Ibos, whose Mobiles turned the Flourentines out of the Hôtel de Ville."

"What sort of man is Flourens?" "Oh! he's not a man; he's a monkey in boots."

"Do you know Blanqui?" "Merci! non, mon ami. I know of him! I was talking a few days ago to two of the reddest of the Red, and one of them said, 'Blanqui! Ah, yes, Blanqui! I know for certain that he has been a police spy for twenty years.'"

"Henri, is it true that the little Fitz-James has escaped from the Prussians?" "They believe so at the club. He has been trying his hand as a navvy. Poor Duke! he'd be a long while making a railway!"

"And so, mon Colonel, you believed it was serious on the 31st?" "So serious that I thought the first act of the drama was over."

"Where was the weak point?" "Weak point! One on each side. Flourens and Blanqui had not the pluck to shoot Trochu and Favre, as they should have done, to act logically up to the theories of their school; and if they had done so they would have been rulers of France; and Trochu and Favre dared not fire the volley down the streets last Monday which they must 'command' within a few weeks. One volley would have been a dose on the 31st of October; God knows how many it will require later."

Then some one asked this simple question, which cannot be translated without loss (not being like a bishop):—"Pourquoi donc appelle-t-on les guerriers du Major Flourens des 'tirailleurs'?" "Dame, parce qu'on ne les a jamais vus tirer 'quelque part.'"

Suddenly it appeared that half the party had forgotten they were on duty.—Coffee, Benedictine, and a rush for cabs. Boom! goes Mont Valérien, and we are back in the siege.

Three per cents. fell 1,50, and closed at 53.

Tuesday, November 8th.—The morning papers are extra dull to-day.

Jules Favre has drawn up another legal document, I beg his pardon, has written another State paper to the representatives of France at foreign Courts, setting forth Bismarck's refusal, and the reasons of it. It is a lachrymose document, and written as by one who has *pitié de soi-même!* Imagine Bismarck, Moltke, Fritz, and the King concerning themselves about the opinion of Europe, much less about the feeble moanings and appeals for "out-door relief" of this "Bar," for, excepting the military element, such is the Defence Government. Favre, Crémieux, Picard, Arago, Ferry, Gambetta, and others, all belong to the "Devil's Own." And as for the Mairies of Paris, they are infested by advocates. Imagine a great nation ruled by barristers and editors—Inner Temple and Fleet Street—and the Chinese in force on Primrose Hill, and you will have some idea of Paris on this fifty-first day of siege and first of starvation.

I hear that a sword of honour is to be offered to General Trochu. Had they not better wait a little?

The editor in chief of the "Messager de Paris" (organ of the Banque de la France) has just been to see me. He says the state paper of Jules Favre has not given any satisfaction, and that the attempt to get an armistice was known beforehand to be au effort to "make a hole in the water."

We took a wonderful walk to-day with Dr. Gordon. Starting from St.-Lazare, we went to the entrance of the Bois, and then made the circuit. First we went to the Lake of the Ladies! The whole wood is destroyed on the left hand down to the Cedar Tree Hill at Mortemart, at the end of the Boulogne Road. The Cedar Tree is represented by an empty battery and rifle-pits. On the right the Bois is clear to the Porte Maillot, and half way down to the lake. The cafés and the shelters for men and horsewomen stand up stark like ghosts of dead buildings, and not a pane of glass, a marble chimney-piece, a bit of furniture, or a scrap of paper has escaped these wanton destructives. The wreck of the wood is alive with charcoal burners and old women, " looting" fire-wood. The lakes are dirty and stagnant; the Island, where brides were as plentiful as the ducks they fed, was as desolate as Juan Fernandez.

What has become of the brides, and their grooms? There is no marrying or giving in marriage in a besieged city, and I fear many of the " chers époux " have been rowed over the Styx. Perhaps the Lake boatmen too have gone to assist Charon. And the ducks and the swans, where are they?—killed, roasted, eaten, and let us hope digested.

The Bois is in all the glory of autumn's tints, and nothing could be prettier than the walk from the gate of Boulogne to the race-course. Whichever way you looked some great military work met the eye. The 125th of the Line was bivouacking in a series of most cleverly-contrived huts, made of underwood and thatched with pine; dinners were cooking: drums were beating, and orderlies rushing in every direction.

On the race-course there were some thousands of men at drill so temptingly near to the railway station battery at St.-Cloud, that every moment we expected to be disturbed at our botanical studies by a shell "plumping" into squares of infantry. Mont Valérien had his eye on the enemy, and every now and then sent a shell whistling through the air "à son adresse."

Our friends will be pleased to hear that the "Tribunes" are untouched, but what Mr. McKenzie Greives would say to the condition of his favourite turf I cannot imagine. The windmill and the old tower of the Monastery of Longchamps have been respected, so has the Villa Haussmann, but it is "Officers' Quarters."

Friend of my youth, do you remember where, "in early days and happier hours," we used to breakfast before the races, at the Cascade within hearing of rippling water? There it stands to-day, surrounded by soldiers' huts, and is itself the head-quarters of a battalion. The roads and paths are all fortified to an extent which has made it one of the strongest positions round Paris. The Avenue des Acacias has not been touched, but that too is intercepted by frequent barricades.

But perhaps the most curious transformation scene is that of Mr. Wallace's (late Lord Hertford's) villa of Bagatelle, which has been appropriated by the Defence Government. It is a long line of buildings, stables, conservatories, faced by a wall which extends some hundred yards, and ending at the great gates of the entrance yard; then the villa and the terrace gardens extend another hundred yards. Every yard of this wall, all the buildings, even the lodges, are pierced for rifles, and a strong battery has been erected on the terrace before the drawing-room windows. If stones could really preach sermons (I have heard several sticks do so), those of Bagatelle would be at no loss for texts. It has itself been Legitimist, Orleanist, National Property (it was awfully knocked about in '48), then "the elegant retreat of a distinguished English nobleman," and now is again the property of the People. If the dead can turn in their graves, I am sure poor Lord Hertford will do so if he feels that "cette canaille" has got his house, for he hated a revolution as much as his grandfather, who, thinking the Reform Bill would destroy England, invested enough money to have a "clean shirt and a valet" in any capital of Europe, and sent large sums to America, losing by his caution five hundred thousand pounds.

The late Lord Hertford was an odd character. Within a year or two of his death he bought a *life interest* with a hundred thousand pounds which had just fallen in. Not long before, I met —— at the races, and he said, "By Jove! old fellow, I have lunched at Bagatelle!" "Nonsense!" "True. Three years ago my lord promised me a mutton chop. I was determined to have it, and so I went there to-day and I got—" "A capital déjeûner, of course," some one interrupted. "Oh, no! the mutton chop!"

But to return to the position. It commands a very undefended part of the Seine, but if the Prussians cross there now, they must traverse the Pelouse de St.-Jacques, under the fire of big guns and chassepots at point-blank distance; and, indeed, if MM. les Prussiens think it is now as pleasant and easy to walk about the Bois de Boulogne as it was when their spies first came over to see the Exhibition in 1867, they will break their shins, lose their way, be hoisted by mines of petroleum, perceive that for the purposes of a quiet walk the Bois is entirely alteied, and return to their quarters (always provided they are not killed, which is " force majeure") owning that they have lost a day.

The Cercle des Patineurs is denuded of its railings, but there were no soldiers, Mobiles, or otherwise in the Club; only one man paddling somebody else's canoe over the waters where we have so often missed our pigeons and found the ice too slippery. From there to the " Gilded Gates," which are pulled down, and are now placed as a trap for cavalry in the " Allée réservée aux piétons—Défense de marcher sur le gazon," there is a continued line of defence ; and so we get back to the place from which we came, and, looking round, ask, " Is it possible that this can be the spot where we have often waited half an hour to cross, and is this the road down which really splendid 'turns-out' reached four deep for a mile ?"

And all the change occurred in " la vie d'une rose, l'espace d'un matin," on the 4th of September, and the First day of the Year One of the Republic of 1870.

Mr. Wodehouse with his Britishers left to-day.

Wednesday, November 9th.—The birthday of the Prince of Wales, Lord Mayor's Day, and the fifty-second day of siege.

At last a sign of energy. A hundred thousand

National Guards are to be Mobilized within forty-eight hours. They are to be armed with chassepots, and put in everything on a level with the Line. I fancy that the chassepot will puzzle them at first. The general belief is, that as soon as this corps is ready, there will be a great attack. I wish I could think that the result was not a foregone conclusion.

A Prussian officer said to a French gentleman at Creteil, "We shall take two of your forts directly. Attack us! You will never be so mad. Why, we shall eat you alive." Count von Bismarck, more modest, told M. Thiers that he should take one in a day or two.

In the mean time, one division of National Guards borrowed to-day a band (probably some of the orchestra of the Concerts des Champs-Elysées, which is now an artillery camp), enticed a general, and had a nice little inspection; and I hear that we are to have a great blessing of banners, when new colours are to be given *aux épiciers.* It may perhaps be asked if a day's drill would not be more useful, but "que voulez-vous?" the National Guard, no more than Apollo, is always with his bow bent.

Truly, the Government has no easy task here! Several days this week they have had to garrison the Hôtel de Ville against an expected sortie from the enemy at Belleville, and troops were under arms or confined to barracks all round the Prison Mazas, in which is confined, for mutiny and treason, Ranvier, who has not only been imprisoned this week, but has been also elected Maire of the 20th Arrondissement, and it was fully expected that his constituents would attack the prison and rescue him.

A French gentleman who has just left here, and who is very favourable to Favre and his friend, said, "It is no use. They are no use; they have once or twice given way to the boulevards, and now they are their slaves. It is a civil application of the military error of officers elected by their men. Power must come from above."

The difficulties of General Trochu and M. Favre are very serious questions for those in Paris. It is not that they are very energetic or efficient, but if anything happens to them, what would come after? The very idea of the next step downwards in democracy makes the staunchest French heart fail.

Once upon a time there lived an old woman called Respublica, an Italian by birth, but a naturalized Frenchwoman. She was a cantankerous old party, with peculiar ideas about other people's property. Her theory was, "What's mine is my own, and what you have got we'll share," and she carried her theory into practice, and so was ever at war with her neighbours. She had been several times tried, and always condemned. Now this old woman had two sons—Cain and Unable. They were quite unlike—the elder was Red, and the younger often looked blue. They were always quarrelling about the stewardship of a great property, into which the family contrived to thrust itself when the tenants quarrelled with the landlord, which happened at the expiration of every lease— leases never ran more than eighteen years. Cain upset the whole business, and appropriated all the property, tithes and taxes, and frequently suddenly prevented the owner taking a life interest in his own estate. This last Cain did by advice, and through an instrument drawn up by Dr. Guillotin, D.C.L. However, the career of Cain was very short, and he was exiled to a square, in the midst of which may still be traced the ruins of another "world." Then Unable got into office, and blundered about, agreeing with everyone, and also offending them. At last Cain, who had returned in the disguise of a patriot of the period, got quite furious, contrived to lead his brother on to the edge of a "Common," and there smote him and slayed him! But the wicked triumph of the first political murderer did not last long. General Reaction arose in great force, took him, and gave him Cayenne (that is " pepper "), and then with a loud voice cried out, " There is but one system of management, and Fitz-roi is his prophet—Allah il Allah ! Bismalah !" Marsh-mallow ! and lo ! they took the foreigner (by education) and appointed him steward, giving him a crown as a " denier à Dieu." So he accepted the office, and kept it till the proprietors, who are very fickle, wanted a change.

Mr. Wodehouse contrived to get away yesterday viâ Creteil, with about seventy-five compatriots. They had to be at the Palais de l'Industrie at 5·45 A.M., and they did not get through the Prussian lines till 2 P.M., having travelled about thirty miles. It was bitterly cold, and the Prussians took them in three divisions, as there were three nationalities—Swiss, Austrian, and English. It is needless to say that our great popularity on both sides got us off last ! Wodehouse has had a hard task. I don't think Paris will see him again.

There was a great discussion among some French and English in the evening about the " exodus," and the cause of it. How did they go ? and why did they go ? Did they ride, or walk ? was it fear or food which set the English off on what I fancy is likely to be a chase worthy of the very wildest goose ? The answer lies in a nutshell : They were drawn out by horses, and driven out by horse.

Mr. Washburne acted for Bismarck, and every letter, paper, and certificate was examined in a wet fog and a north-east wind.

The last Mobilism is to wash your dirty linen in the private apartments of the Tuileries, and then hang it out on the gilded balconies over the Quai and the Gardens. " Le Figaro" thus describes this transaction :—" Une guirlande molticore de gilets et caleçons de flannelle, dont l'effet ne manque pas de pittoresque!" Now I know. I have no bump of admiration, but I really cannot conceive even the greatest gusher finding anything picturesque in a private soldier's flannel shirt! But *de gustibus!*

They have now written and chalked (it is a " chalk" government, you see) " Liberté, Fraternité, and Egalité" in every possible place. Luckily chalk rubs out easily, and I dare say the incoming dynasty will pay for a little paint.

END OF VOL. I.

LONDON:
SAVILL, EDWARDS AND CO., PRINTERS, CHANDOS STREET,
COVENT GARDEN.